# 100 GREAT
# GAA
## MOMENTS

# 100 GREAT
# GAA
# MOMENTS

# JOHN SCALLY

BLACK & WHITE PUBLISHING

*To the Memory of Julia Devine*

*Don't cry if you love me*
*If you knew the gift of God and what Heaven is.*
*If you could hear the angels singing and see me among them.*
*If, only for an instant, you could contemplate, just like me, the*
*Beauty before which all beauties turn pale.*

**SAINT AUGUSTINE**

*There is no moment to surpass the magic of a great GAA moment.*

**DERMOT EARLEY**


*What a gift we had from the gods.*

**ANTHONY DALY**

(After the Clare vs Galway 2018
All-Ireland hurling semi-final)


*I love this game. I just love this game.*

**JOHN MULLANE**

(After the Cork vs Limerick 2018
All-Ireland hurling semi-final)

First published in 2018
This edition first published 2019
by Black & White Publishing Ltd
Nautical House, 104 Commercial Street
Edinburgh EH6 6NF

1 3 5 7 9 10 8 6 4 2    19 20 21 22

ISBN: 978 1 78530 244 2

A CIP catalogue record for this book is available from the
British Library.

Typeset by Iolaire, Newtonmore
Printed and bound by CPI Group (UK) Ltd, Croydon, CR0 4YY

# CONTENTS

## PART III - MAGIC MOMENTS

# FOREWORD

Winning the 2017 All-Ireland was a big thing for the Galway team. You're always going to feel pressure when you're going into an All-Ireland but the big thing for this group of players was that a lot of the guys were on the team in 2012 and 2015. We didn't want to lose three on the bounce. We didn't want to be on another losing team. It had been twenty-nine years since Galway last won it – in our own minds enough was enough.

It was also a big deal for my family. My brother Ollie played for Galway for almost fifteen years and never won it; he was unlucky not to win it. It was a sense for him that we have it in the family now. I could've been taken off ten times in that game and my dad wouldn't have minded. He was more overjoyed than anything.

It's great for the next generation, for the kids. For twenty-nine years they've never witnessed the All-Ireland hurling championship in Galway. If we can inspire the next generation of Galway hurlers, then that's the main thing.

It's brilliant because Galway isn't a traditional county for winning All-Irelands, when compared to the likes of Kilkenny, Cork and Tipperary. It's only our fifth ever All-Ireland. For us to win our fifth All-Ireland is pretty special; we have to embrace and celebrate it, as they don't come round very often.

For Galway hurling fans it was a great GAA moment.

This book is a celebration of a hundred of those great GAA moments. I hope you enjoy them all.

**JOE CANNING**
*September 2018*

# INTRODUCTION

To this day I still don't know why Joe and Jim were called 'the terrible twins'. Okay, they really were twins but that still does not explain the terrible.

What really puzzles me is the genetic aberration that could have produced two people who were so totally unalike in every conceivable way as brothers, let alone twins. Jim was a young version of Robert Redford. Joe looked like he was born to play the baddie in a James Bond movie. Jim was outgoing, gregarious and carefree. Joe was reserved and had a vulnerability about him and a sadness that clung to him. He left a sense that his mind often travelled in a land uninhabited by the rest of us. During term time, Jim seemed to live outside the gates of the local convent school but Joe would not be caught dead there.

The contrast between the two brothers was most evident on the football field. From the ages of twelve to fourteen Jim was spoken of as the most promising player seen in Roscommon since Dermot Earley. In full flight he was a sight to put a permanent tingle in the blood, with his swashbuckling solo runs which cut through opposing defences like a knife through butter. His exceptional ability was matched only by his complete lack of dedication.

Judged on natural ability alone Joe would have earned the ultimate put-down: 'He couldn't kick snow off a rope.' But as a tough as teak corner-back Joe's ferocious commitment meant that he was not only chosen on the team, he was always captain. His speeches were short affairs. The most memorable came on the day I won my first medal in the first year school league final. Its contents in full were:

*If not us – who?*

*If not now – when?*

But it was the passion that was stamped all over his face and especially the way he smashed his fist off the bench that really inspired us. As he whipped us up to a frenzy Jim was hiding in the dressing-room toilet smoking his customary two fags at a time.

Joe's normal gentle nature off the field was put aside on it – when he was meaner than a gunshot grizzly bear. Everybody dreaded marking him because he tackled with the intensity of a medieval martyr.

After a big game Jim treated us to a lengthy exposé of how he won it for us as Joe invariably silently limped away.

My abiding memory of the two brothers goes back to our first training session for the under-16 championship. The sound of thunder cracked the air and rain spilled down on to the stand roof, rattling like applause on metal slats. It was the kind of wind that seemed to peel the flesh off your bones and then come back for the marrow.

Our coach, Br Seán, was a traditionalist. His idea of training was to get us to run around multiple laps of the pitch. After the first five he introduced an innovation.

He told us that if every time he blew his whistle we were to jump high in the air and imagine we were catching the decisive ball in an All-Ireland final. As the rest of us silently cursed Joe was way ahead, running like a cheetah and soaring like an eagle to catch imaginary balls.

The drill went on until we got level with the dressing room for the third time. Then Jim, way behind the pack, started to zoom towards the dressing room. Br Seán, his face purple with a mixture of cold and annoyance barked at him, 'Where are you going lazy-bones?'

To which Jim coolly replied, 'I'm just going in to get my gloves. That ball you want us to catch is shockin' slippy!'

The GAA has given me many great moments. Sadly I never actually created any. Why? My doctor told me that I had a body of a thirty-year-old. The only problem was that was when I was eighteen.

I played a bit of hurling. I gave it up when one of my teachers was watching me playing a game with not great success and he said to me, 'Cut five inches off your hurley.'

'Do you think my hurley is too big for me?' I asked.

He just turned away and said, 'No, but it will fit into the bin much easier.'

So I decided to write about sport instead. My local priest expressed his concern about me working with the media, in case my morals would be contaminated. He quoted Leo Tolstoy at me, 'All newspaper and journalistic activity is an intellectual brothel from which there is no retreat.'

Bitter experience has taught me that if someone wants to find fault with you they will. It is a bit like the story of the Garda sergeant, a total so-and-so, who was on his last day in the town before he retired from the force. He was a mean and spiteful man and had 'caught' everyone in the town for some offence or other. The only person who had escaped was the parish priest. The Garda was determined to rectify that situation on his last day. He knew that the priest always cycled home after saying morning Mass so the Garda stood at the bottom of the hill. His plan had been to step out in front of the priest, forcing him to swerve and topple over and then he could 'do him' for dangerous driving. He carried out his plan, but although the priest swerved he kept control of his bike. The priest stopped to wish the Garda well on his retirement. The cop said, 'Jesus, you were fierce lucky not to fall then.'

The priest replied: 'Indeed I was lucky but then I had God with me.'

The Garda nearly danced for joy as he said, 'I'm doing you for having two on a bike.'

Notwithstanding the fact that everybody would go about the task differently, the pervasiveness and the power of the GAA in Irish life and the way it has indelibly inhabited our thinking process over the last 135 years demands serious examination.

Love it, hate it or try to be indifferent to it, Gaelic games subtly shape Irish social history and everyday life. As the 2018 season has illustrated so vividly with an epic Munster hurling championship culminating in Tipperary's 'phantom' goal against Waterford; Carlow's rising; Fermanagh's shock win over Monaghan; Seán Cavanagh's 'squabble' with Mickey Harte; 'It's Newbridge or Nowhere' and Kildare topple Mayo in a ground so packed you couldn't turn a sweet in your mouth; the King of Cool, Michael Bublé, ensures that the Leinster hurling final is won by a Connacht team in a Munster venue; Limerick end forty-five years of hurt against Kilkenny; a major controversy erupts about whether the testimonial soccer game for the late Liam Miller's young family should be hosted in Paírc Uí Chaoimh; Rena Buckley introduces Meghan Markle to camogie; Prince Harry describes Joe Canning as a 'bit of a god' and, of course, the new Super 8 structure, the GAA permeates the media, sets the mood of Monday's post-match workplace and dominates pub-talk. For many life and death still run second to major GAA events.

Gaelic games offer us a group identity, a spiritual home to belong, a sacred space where we can be among our people and therefore be ourselves. There is something innocent, something mysterious about Gaelic games' hold on our identity, which is completely impervious to analysis. This is its power. We all crave it, the sense of connection, the thought we can be better than we are, even if better only through someone else, our fifteen representatives.

In trying to select one hundred great GAA moments I did not want to just recycle match reports of a hundred great games; I wanted to document in some way the evolution of the GAA and to some extent the changing Ireland through the stories of some of its biggest games. I am taking a very liberal interpretation of 'moment' in the interests of giving as diverse a perspective as possible. To assist in that process I have picked not just matches, but some controversies, funny moments and the new leadership roles that prominent GAA personalities are increasingly playing in the wider Irish society. In this way I hope to hint at the magnificence and magic, the colour and the characters, and the skill and the style of the games I love so well.

# PART I
# Personal Favourites

We are all a product of our times. I grew up in an Ireland very different from that of today. It was a time when, like the famous D'Unbelievables sketch, you had to go to Mass early if you did not want to take a seat. A collection of memories like this is, inevitably, a personal one. Love of the GAA is at once a communal activity and a deeply personal one. I begin this collection with two very personal memories.

# 1

# THE WEST'S AWAKE

*Galway win the 1998 All-Ireland football final*

A litany of woes. Defeats snatched from the jaws of victory. Close calls. Demoralising trouncings. For thirty-two years that was the story of Connacht football. A procession of 'what-might-have-beens'. Galway in 1971 and '74: what would have happened if Liam Sammon scored that penalty? Roscommon in 1980: if only they could have scored their frees. Galway in 1983: fourteen players against Dublin's twelve and still a defeat. A match that years later can only be whispered about and the video is hidden away for ever. The definitive video nasty. A sucker goal given away to Barney Rock and a series of spectacular wides, when it always seemed much, much easier to score. A story burnished with repetition, no longer remembered as much as incanted like a prayer learned by heart. Mayo in 1989: if only Anthony Finnerty hadn't missed the second goal chance. The gods tended to write depressing scenarios for fans west of the Shannon. A history of disillusion shared by a whole generation. Each defeat remembered, running through the fingers like beads on a rosary.

This was a time when the most Connacht football could hope for was sympathy.

For thirty-two years it seemed that Gaelic football was hopelessly ill-equipped to carry the burden of emotional expression that those from Mayo, and all of us from the West of Ireland sought to unload upon it. What hurt for so long was that something we believed to be a metaphor for our pride was all along a metaphor for our desperation.

Connacht's reign of error reached its nadir in the 1993 All-Ireland semi-final as Mayo capitulated completely to Cork when they stopped playing, and Cork stuffed them by 5–15 to 0–10. We couldn't bear to watch. Yet we couldn't tear our eyes from it either, like watching a literal car crash, torn as we were between passionate partisanship and the knowledge that here was a lost cause – wondering if the inevitable beating would become a butchering. In the finite continuum of time along which all fans of Connacht football travel, this terrible moment is fixed, immovable, incapable of being blotted out, however fervently or passionately we later wished for its erasure. In a fog of self-disgust, a legion of Connacht fans had learned the hard way that to falter is to be swept aside. It was written into the nation's consciousness that Connacht football did not merit serious consideration.

*Alas and well may Erin weep*
*when Connacht lies in slumber deep.*

The appointment of John O'Mahony as Galway manager in October 1997 would change all that. He had qualities that were hard to define but easy to recognise. A man of self-reliance, of candour, he was not a prisoner of the uncertainties, nor the enforced servility of the previous decades. Yet

4

nobody predicted the benign revolution that was at hand. Our ideas about what is newsworthy dictates that David Beckham's sarong-wearing foray is more likely to grab the headlines than the plight of a generally mild-mannered schoolteacher on the Roscommon–Mayo border. O'Mahony had been great at making teams good, but would he be good enough to make this Galway team great?

Within twelve months he had taken his side to an All-Ireland final. Galway captain Ray Silke said in the dressing room before he led his team out, 'Right, lads. I'm going out to win an All-Ireland. Who's coming with me?'

In this patchwork quilt of a game that contained many bright colours things did not look promising for most of the first half. When Dermot Earley scored a goal for Kildare the Galway fans, drawn into the vortex of a furious expense of nervous energy, felt sick with contradictory, unarticulated emotion. They were beginning to feel an almost superstitious foreboding. These lost souls on the highway of life were driven downwards through failure after failure; fate was becoming real to them as a cold malignant force. This was a Connacht team that could win things: but would they let the title slip through their fingers yet again? Was it really true that you had to lose an All-Ireland before you could win one? One of John O'Mahony's favourite maxims was now to come into play: 'A winner never quits. A quitter never wins.'

Eugene McGee once incurred the wrath of Galway fans when he spoke of the 'fancy Dans' on O'Mahony's side but in the second-half display the Westerners produced a display of dazzling virtuosity with Ja Fallon masterfully orchestrating events. Heroes emerged all over the field, with Tomás Mannion, Seán Og de Paor, Kevin Walsh, Seán O Domhnaill particularly prominent. A bright new star was confirmed in the football constellation thanks to the stunning performance of Michael Donnellan, the boy genius evolving into the fully fledged legend, with his magnificent searing runs. Every team, to a greater or lesser extent, reflects the personality of its manager. It is no coincidence that O'Mahony's Galway represented a fascinating combination of wit and grit, of steel and style.

At first prisoners of hope, the fans from the west were both beguiled and sceptical, talking to each other to persuade themselves, listening to be persuaded that what lay before them was exhilarating – the combined intricate talents of the team fitting together in the second half like an expertly designed puzzle.

The real moment of catharsis came when Padraic Joyce smashed the ball into the net. The roar that followed was orchestral in its sound and feeling. After the goal Galway supporters inhaled the air, their thoughts sharpening with each breath as though they had been drugged for years and were only now, with a jolt, emerging from torpor. It wasn't just that Galway were winning. It was because they were playing the kind of slick, sweet, high-speed football that would win them new fans. A wave of euphoria washed over us and settled like a sea mist. To fans west of the Shannon, reared on a diet of disappointment, it seemed that everything around us was heightened, emboldened, made larger than in our dreams. Lives, which seemed complete enough only the night before, appeared to have gained an essential missing piece. For the previous thirty-two years we had known fleeting interludes of brilliance and gaiety, but had reason to fear the collapse that inevitably followed, which seemed to fit the proper order of the universe. We had a common currency of bad memories, events replayed at different points in the continuum of time, so that our personal memories were not our own at all, but merely repetitions of those of our fellows.

This day was different and we could feel the exhilaration swimming over our bodies like a spirit making its way through a room. Banners patterned in kinetic swirls of maroon and white were proudly displayed. We will now luxuriate in the memory of that day in September, and though these memories are but echoes of the actual, they are treasures we will not willingly part with. The image of that magic moment when the final whistle sounded is imprinted upon us, as light is upon photographic paper. A protracted communal intake of breath, then a brief tighter silence still, followed by a noisy guttural exhalation. Such a state of happiness is an occasional thing, like summer lightning. We know instinctively that no other sporting triumph shall ever be so dear. In an instant all the hard luck stories were washed away in the tides of history.

The 27 September 1998 was not just a victory for John O'Mahony and Galway. It was a victory for players like Mickey Kearins, Packy McGarty, Dermot Earley, Tony McManus, Harry Keegan, Johnny Hughes, Willie Joe Padden and T. J. Kilgallon, all of whom had soldiered so gallantly for so long but had missed out on the ultimate prize, and for a generation of Connacht football fans too, who had suffered and mourned in this valley of tears.

Turning points are generally the creations of novelists and dramatists, a necessary mechanism when a narrative is reduced to a plot and a moral is distilled from a sequence of actions, and the audience return home with something unforgettable to mark a character's growth. This was different, like a gift wrapped up in deliciously pretty paper, to be given, with discretion, to the right people. Galway's victory transcended football. It was about identity and how we felt about ourselves, as individuals and as a collective. This was a defining moment, an experience that redirected the revealed truth by whose light all previous conclusions must be re-thought. It was a story whose historical accuracy was of less significance than the function it served, a drama that seemed to be enacted just for us.

> *But – hark! – some voice like thunder spake*
> *The West's awake, the West's awake.*

It was Galway's glory. But their glory reflected instantly on all of us in the West of Ireland who had so often driven home from Croke Park, sick not just from losing but from underperforming, because each of the players were one of us out there and they had suddenly lifted the game to a higher plane. Sure, none of us were fit to lace Ja Fallon or Michael Donnellan's boots, but they carried us up there with them. Only five years earlier the theatre of dreams had been our torture chamber. Seventy minutes can miraculously heal a collective scar tissue.

In a perverse way it helped that we had experienced so much humiliation and disappointment in previous years. For supporters of Connacht football for most of the 1980s and 1990s agony was the only currency that could purchase ecstasy. If a sorcerer could magically turn pain into wealth, then all of us would have been as rich as Bill Gates. In 1998 we finally cashed in all our misery chips.

For many of us, who had missed out on the Galway three-in-a-row in the 1960s, the desire to see our team win the Sam Maguire was the only constant ambition we have ever held.

An All-Ireland victory was the fulfilment of the promise

of a life as it was meant to be lived for an entire province. The unthinkable had become the thinkable. The memory lingered long into the night only to be stopped gently by sleep, like a candle that has been pinched out. Yet a flame had been lit that day which would fuel an entire generation. The next morning we settled into the rhythms of a new life. The haunting echoes of failure were banished at last.

The win restored the hope that sport can still be the simple, challenging life enhancement it was first meant to be. The Galway team gave us football fans from the West of Ireland back our dream.

# 2

# HELLO DARKNESS MY OLD FRIEND

*Fans honour a fallen hero in 2010*

My second personal memory is bittersweet.

Happiness is not having what you want but wanting what you have. For sixty-one years of his life Dermot Earley was a happy man. When he died in June 2010 from a rapid degenerative condition, Creutzfeldt-Jakob disease, his death and funeral were lead items on the RTÉ news. Over five thousand people went on Facebook to comment on his passing. He was aged sixty-two. He had retired from the Defence Forces weeks before his death although he was not due to stand down until the following spring.

His son, Dermot, carries on his name.

'I was born in 1978, two days before Roscommon played Galway in the Connacht final in Pearse Stadium. Dad always said he got the family–football balance just right: 70 per cent football, 30 per cent family.

'At the time a member of the clergy threw in the ball. So when the midfielders gathered for the throw-in there waiting for them was Bishop Eamon Casey. He said: "Well lads, are ye nervous?"

'Thankfully Roscommon won. The next day the cup was smuggled out of Roscommon and brought up to my mother and me in Mount Carmel Hospital. I was placed in it. It was my first taste of inter-county football.'

Dermot Jnr began to notice problems with his father in 2009. He says:

'I suppose the first time we noticed something was wrong with Dad was that September. He had lost a bit of weight. Being in the job he was and being the healthy man he was who looked after his diet, we did not wonder about that too much.

'There were other things that drew our attention. He was having difficulty leaving the room or even finding the door or simple things like that. At the same time he was perfectly capable of having a strong conversation with you and from my point of view was still very able to tell me where I was going wrong in the football.

'Unfortunately from there the little things started to get bigger. January brought the diagnosis. He quickly went from being this larger-than-life individual who was so strong both physically and mentally to someone you could see actually getting worse and worse each week, to the point where he wasn't able to speak properly and get his words across.

'One of the complications was that a lot of people had many misunderstandings about his illness. Just two weeks ago somebody asked me: did he get it from eating something when he was on overseas duty? They did not understand that it was a degenerative brain condition and not something you get from eating contaminated food.

'The one thing Dad kept was his smile. I knew there were

times when he was aware he wasn't well and that it was tough for him, but the man he was always had the smile. A lot of people had come to the house in the last few months. On one occasion Mícheál Ó Muircheartaigh called when Dad wasn't really communicating at all but Mícheál sat down beside him and started talking. I was in the kitchen watching them and I saw Dad brightening up as he recognised the voice. It was a nice moment.'

Among the army personnel on duty outside the church on the day of the funeral, marshalling the huge crowd, was Sue Ramsbottom, the Laois star who is one of the greatest female footballers of all time. She and Dermot had formed an informal mutual admiration society.

The members of the 1980 Roscommon team were reunited to mourn a fallen comrade outside the church. In 1992 I had asked Dermot how he wanted to be remembered. He replied: 'As a good man.'

To which, Gay Sheeran remarked: 'It was one of those rare occasions when Dermot was wrong. He wasn't a good man. He was a great man.'

To misquote George Bernard Shaw, Gaelic football was not a brief candle to Dermot but a splendid torch which he had got hold of and wanted to make burn as brightly as possible before handing it on to future generations. On the day his father was buried, the family home was like a tomb with the stone rolled over the top, muted and enclosed in grief. Dermot Jnr faced a dilemma. Should he play for Kildare that evening in an important qualifier against Antrim?

'I suppose it's one of those things that maybe people might not understand or people might say you should have been at home with your family. Football in our house is a massive part of our lives. After all, it's the family that allows the person to go and make the commitment and go to all that training and miss out on all the other things they could be doing together. The love is there, the family want the player to succeed, and they allow them to do that stuff. All that week I knew the match was coming. My dad passed on Wednesday and I sat down and I talked to Mam and my brothers and sisters and I didn't want anything extra to change. There was enough already changing.

'At the same time I was conscious of the funeral and I felt that Dad would have wanted me to play. He knew how much it meant to me and he would have wanted me to go out there and give it my best. That's exactly what he said to me every time I played a match, go out and give it your best. It's the same thing I said going out to play against Antrim. But that night I went home, went up to my parents' house, my mam's house, and a lot of things go through your head. And I suppose for maybe that hour and a half of the game I was able to concentrate on that match and have that release. But again it's not something that requires any extra praise. Great loss happens to people every day.

'When it came to his removal there was a constant flow of people. It was something I will never forget to see the amount of people who wanted to say goodbye to him. We found it overwhelming. It seemed as if all of Roscommon had come to pay its respects at the funeral as well as representatives of the wider GAA family. Dad was given a military funeral, which is a fairly sombre event. As his coffin was laid in to the ground and after the last post was sounded and everyone was quiet I think it was Gay Sheeran who shouted out: "Up the Rossies." It brought a little smile to people at what was a very tough time.

'Dad would have had great anticipation before Roscommon's famous Connacht final win over Sligo shortly after his death. He would have kicked every ball during the game and, at the end, he would have had a big smile on his face. I think his spirit was all around Castlebar that day.'

As fate would have it the sporting gods decreed that Roscommon and Kildare both played their All-Ireland quarter-finals the same day in Croke Park. The rich wells of sentiment play a huge part in every corner of the GAA. Despite their tingles of anticipation, before the match fans recalled absent friends:

'I did not see it myself but I was told afterwards that during the first game, Roscommon's defeat to Cork, a huge banner in the crowd read "Earley – 8 – Legend, 1948–2010". Despite the rain many of the Rossies hung around to cheer me and Kildare on as a tribute to Dad. He would have meant so much to them and it was their way of paying their respects. It was a nice gesture and it meant a lot.'

# PART II
# Glory Days

In 1884 Michael Davitt wrote, 'Old men who have forgotten the miseries of the Famine had their youth renewed by the sight and sounds that were evoked by the thrilling music of the *camán*, the well-directed stroke of the *cul baire*, or the swift stride of the Gaelic forward in the pursuit of victory. Many dark days have dawned over our country. Sorrow and trouble have likewise made their way into the homes and hamlets of our people. It is certain that in some cases these clouds would have been darker and care would have eaten more deeply into the hearts of many had it not been for the pastime and pleasure created in the revival of Gaelic games by the Gaelic Athletic Association.'

The GAA has had, and continues to have, a massive cultural impact in Ireland. This section celebrates some of its most momentous moments.

# 3

# THE THUNDER AND LIGHTNING FINAL

*Cork vs Kilkenny 1939*

The founder of the GAA Michael Cusack said of hurling, 'When I reflect on the sublime simplicity of the game, the strength, the swiftness, of the players, their apparently angelic impetuosity, the apparent recklessness of life and limb, their magic skill, their marvellous escapes and the overwhelming pleasure they give their friends, I have no hesitation in saying that the game of hurling is in the front rank of the Fine Arts.'

Despite its vast history and our radically different web of cultural, social and economic contexts, hurling has in many ways changed very little – the changelessness is what it has been about since the beginning. Hurling takes us, at heart, into a mythic place, an ageless space alight with Celtic warriors – not men, but giants – who knows who they were, are and will be. It is not just part of who we are – it could be argued it *is* who we are.

When you ask someone who held the unique distinction of winning six senior All-Ireland medals in consecutive years (between 1941 and 1946) what his favourite personal sporting memory was, the last thing you expect to be told about is an All-Ireland final he lost! Yet such was the case with Jack Lynch: 'It may be paradoxical but the games of which I have the most vivid memories are of the ones we lost. Of these I remember best the first All-Ireland hurling final in which I played. It was Cork versus Kilkenny on 3 September 1939. I was captain of the team and hopeful of leading Cork out of a comparatively long barren spell. Cork had not won a final since 1931 when they beat Kilkenny in the second replay of the final.

'The match I refer to has since been known as the "Thunder and Lightning Final". We had all kinds of weather including sunshine and hailstones. It was played on the day that the Second World War commenced. I missed at least two scorable chances – of a goal and a point. I was marking one of the greatest half-backs of all time, Paddy Phelan, and we were beaten by a point scored literally with the last puck of the game. I can remember more facets of that game than almost any other in which I played.

'Although I was lucky enough to play in many All-Ireland finals, all the Munster finals were special. It was always about more than sport. It was a social occasion where men drank in manly moderation, but probably more than any other moment in the calendar it defined our identity. Looking back there was a lot of hardships in those days with rationing and so on. To take one example, both Tipperary and Kilkenny were excluded from the 1941 hurling championship because of an outbreak of foot-and-mouth disease. Yet, no matter how bad things were, like Christmas, the Munster final was always guaranteed to put a smile on people's faces.'

# 4

# CAVAN'S FAIRYTALE OF NEW YORK

*The Polo Grounds final 1947*

To shamelessly steal from Paul Simon, the nation turned its lonely eyes to New York in 1947 for the Polo Grounds final. The match was held in New York as a goodwill gesture by the GAA to the Irish diaspora in America. Once it was announced, it aroused great interest in every county. To get there was a great prize in itself. The teams left Cobh together for a six-day trip on the SS *Mauritania* to New York, after getting their vaccinations against smallpox, which were compulsory at the time. The fact that it was the first final played abroad gave it a much more exotic quality so it really grabbed the public imagination.

But what kind of machinations were going on behind the scenes in New York to make this event possible on the ground? A breathtaking series of discussions behind closed doors involving moral blackmail, bribery of a kind, intimidation and the blatant telling of lies allowed this event to happen. Locating the 1947 All-Ireland final in the Big Apple was one of the great achievements of Canon Michael Hamilton's career. Initially, almost everyone seemed implacably opposed to the project.

Machiavelli himself would have admired the 'promptings' behind the scenes that finally persuaded a controversial Central Council meeting at Barry's Hotel that it was worth carrying through. Folklore abounds of how Bob Fitzpatrick, of Miltown Malbay, delivered a passionate speech to congress, complemented by the prop of a tear-stained handkerchief, which swung the vote as he read from a bogus 'emigrant's letter'.

Many years ago, Kerry's Joe Keohane gave me the Kerry perspective: 'Before the final, Kerry, Cavan, Galway, Laois and Mayo had toured in New York. Mayo in particular could have clocked-up frequent-flyer credits, thanks to the clout and cash of a judge from Bohola, Bill O'Dwyer. After he was elected Mayor of New York in 1946, the GAA had the cachet and the connections to locate its premier event in the world's most famous city.

'The decision gave new oxygen to the championship that year as every team in the country dreamed of a trip to New York. This was most apparent in the Munster final that year when we defeated Cork on their own turf at the Cork Athletic Grounds. With the clock ticking, Cork were awarded a penalty.

'I argued with the referee for two minutes, and helpfully stood on the ball and almost sunk it into the mud. When Jim Aherne struck the ball it dribbled weakly along the pitch. All the time I was arguing I could see the skyline of New York getting clearer and clearer!'

For Cavan, the trip to New York was particularly welcome because in previous years they had experienced many bitter disappointments. As one of their biggest stars from that era,

Mick Higgins, explained: 'Initially, most of our team would taste the bitter pill of defeat in three All-Ireland finals before getting their hands on the ultimate prize. We lost to Kerry in 1937, Roscommon in 1943 (after a replay) and Cork in 1945.'

The late Mick Dunne is one of the unsung heroes of the GAA, having served twenty-one years as the GAA anchorman with the *Irish Press* and an equal number of years as Gaelic games correspondent with RTÉ. Mick was *the* expert on perhaps the most famous game in GAA history.

'Three thousand came in on an excursion train from Boston, and large contingents from Detroit, Pittsburgh and Chicago. There were specials from Hartford, Springfield and Newark. Lonely strangers were asking, anyone here from my county? This was much more than a football game. It was a rally of the scattered Irish, seeking friendship, warmth and renewal of the spirit. In a big way it was Galway races, Punchestown, Puck Fair.

'The Monday before the game, the players took the energy-sapping twenty-nine hour flight from Rineanna to New York via Santa Maria in the Azores, Gander and Boston. To compound the problems, the take-off was delayed by twenty-four hours, which led Kerry's Eddie Dowling to claim that he had thirty glasses of beer before boarding. Twenty-five officials and subs had already travelled by ocean liner, the *Mauritania*.

'A cavalcade of thirty cars, eighteen motorcycle cops escorting them with sirens screaming, drove the awestruck footballers through the famous avenues and streets. The Mayor hosted a lavish reception at City Hall where no fewer than five thousand people attended. On the morning of the match the Cardinal, his name was Spellman I believe, welcomed the team from the pulpit in St Patrick's Cathedral and was photographed with the team captains on the cathedral steps afterwards.'

This game was to become the stuff of myth. The New York Police Band played no less than three anthems, 'Amhrán na bhFiann', 'Faith of Our Fathers' and 'The Star-Spangled Banner'.

Joe Keohane was a little underwhelmed by the attendance: 'Despite the hype at home, the game was in fact poorly publicised and advertised in New York, and this was reflected in the fact that only 34,491 people attended. The pitch was too small and rock hard. In fact, the surface had a crucial bearing on the outcome because Eddie Dowling was on fire that day and scored one of the goals that put Kerry in the lead and seemingly on course for victory, but he was knocked out cold when he fell on the ground and had to be carried off. This was the turning point of the game.'

By coincidence one of the biggest stars of the Cavan team, Mick Higgins, who scored a goal and two points in that match, was born in New York. His memories were much more upbeat: 'The pitch was used for baseball and was much smaller than the usual Gaelic pitch. The grass was scorched and even bald in a few places and there was a mound in the playing area. The ground was rock hard and the weather was scorching hot. Kerry got off to a great start but Peter Donohoe was on fire for us that day. The American press described him as "the Babe Ruth" of Gaelic football after the greatest star in baseball of the era. We had a great leader and one of the all-time greats in Gaelic football in John Joe O'Reilly – the young army officer who died so tragically after a short illness in 1952 at the tender age of thirty-four. We won by 2-11 to 2-7.'

Famously, Micheál O'Hehir had the surreal experience of appealing over the airwaves to the New York telecommunications people not to cut off the commentary, a move which caused mild panic at home in Ireland as people listening on RTÉ radio thought they were going to miss the climax of the game.

# 5

# THE RING OF FIRE

*The golden era of Christy Ring*

Nobody did more to transform our national game into our national soap opera than Christy Ring. Such was his legend that it was said he could shoot the eye out of your head from two fields away.

When asked his opinion of himself as a hurler, Jack Lynch was understandably reticent: 'I would prefer to leave this assessment to people I played with, or against, or who saw me play.'

However, he was much more forthcoming about his opinion of other great players. Inevitably the analysis began with Christy Ring: 'Christy Ring was the greatest hurler that I knew. I know there are some who will contend that others were better – Mick Mackey, for example. I think Mick Mackey was the most effective hurler that I played against. Mackey was great but in my opinion Ring's hurling repertoire was greater. He was totally committed to hurling, perhaps more so than any player I have ever met. He analysed games in prospect and in retrospect. In essence he thought and lived hurling.

'I note the observation that Christy Ring made in his article "The Spirit of the Glen", which depicts the hurling club Glen Rovers (1916–73): "My hurling days are over – let no one say the best hurlers belong to the past. They are with us now and better yet to come." Typical of Ring's brilliant mind.'

Clare legend Jimmy Smyth came up against Ring often: 'Nicky Rackard was the third best hurler of all time behind Mick Mackey, but the greatest of all was Christy Ring. Forward play has deteriorated since my time but back play has come on a lot. They mark forwards so tightly now you can hardly do anything. I just wonder how Ring would cope now. He would still get a lot of scores but I think he wouldn't have got quite so many.

'Ring was like Muhammad Ali. He once said, "modesty is knowing where you stand". He always knew. If he thought he had played below his own high standards he would be the first to say so. He was well aware of his own ability and didn't believe in concealing the fact that he knew. I remember we were playing in a Railway Cup match once and he said to me, "When I get the ball, you run in for the pass. And remember. I don't miss."'

Jack Lynch was amused by one aspect of Ring's impact on Cork hurling after his retirement: 'A few days before the 1972 Munster final between Cork and Clare, Cork dual-star Denis Coughlan pulled in for petrol, and who drove in beside him but Christy Ring. Christy started to talk to him about the match and asked Denis to show him his hurley. Christy decided to take a few swings with it but somehow broke it. The blood drained from Christy's face but when he recovered his composure he told Coughlan not to worry. He pulled out a hurley from the boot of the car. It was the one he used in three of his greatest All-Ireland triumphs. It was too heavy for Denis though, so Christy called back to him a few hours later with a hurley that was a ringer for the one that he broke. "That will bring you luck", said Christy. With Cork leading comfortably in that match though, Denis was sent off for the only time in his career!'

Mícheál Ó Muircheartaigh provides the definitive epithet for Christy Ring: 'Hurling is a game for the gods and the gods play it. When they wanted someone to teach them the game they turned to one man: Christy Ring.'

# 6

# BAREFOOT IN THE PARK

*Tipperary win the 1971 All-Ireland*

The GAA is part of Michael 'Babs' Keating's DNA: 'Coming from where I was in rural Tipperary, we all had the dream of wearing the jersey, of walking behind the Artane Boys Band and playing in Croke Park. The one thing we had was the confidence that if we got to an All-Ireland we would win it because of the power of the Tipp jersey. Football was in my blood. My granduncle, Tommy Ryan, won two All-Irelands with Tipperary. He was playing in Croke Park on Bloody Sunday and helped remove Michael Hogan from the pitch after he had been shot by the Black and Tans. I played football for ten consecutive years with Munster. The fact that I came from a football area meant it came easier to me. I could play football just by togging out because I was brought up with a football, whereas with hurling I had to work a bit harder.'

Babs did not taste immediate success: 'I had huge disappointment at under-age level, losing four All-Ireland finals at minor and intermediate level. Then, having won an intermediate All-Ireland in 1963, three of us arrived on the Tipp senior team for the first league game against Galway. We played in the most games in the league, but of the three new boys, I was the most vulnerable because the Tipp forwards were so strong.

'A highlight for me was playing in my first All-Ireland against Kilkenny in 1964. Seamus Cleere was the hurler of the year in 1963 and he was an outstanding wing-back. The one thing about that Tipp team was that they had the forwards thinking like backs, and the backs like forwards. Cleere had scored a couple of points from the half-back line in the final the previous year. When you have a half-back scoring like this, he's a seventh forward. My role was to stop Seamus. Luckily enough the first ball that ran on between us I got and scored a tricky point. I made a goal for Donie Nealon as well as doing my own job, so I ended up as Sports Star of the Week and on a high. The hype at home then was as big as it is now. The only thing was that the media coverage wasn't anything like as intense as today. I was back at work on the Tuesday morning. There was no such thing as banquets here, there and everywhere. Having said that, there was a better atmosphere in Croke Park then because you were closer to the ground.'

For Babs the 1971 All-Ireland final has special significance.

'Long before players were handed out gear for free we were very conscious of the importance of equipment. I had the very best pair of football boots, but the night before the final my bag was stolen with the boots in them. I got a spare pair but they didn't suit the conditions so I took them off. Micheál O'Hehir famously described me in his commentary as, "Barefoot in the Park". I was marking Fan Larkin, and guys like Fan and Ted Carroll were not the sort of fellas to be walking around without some sort of protection. Fan never stood on my feet. He tried it a few times but I was gone before he could make contact!'

# 7

# HEFFO'S ARMY

*Dublin bestride the GAA world like a Colossus in the 1970s*

There are three kinds of people in this world: those who can count and those who can't. In my time there have been two constants. If you are a GAA fan it is a fact of life that you will spend a lot of time talking about referees. Referees are intrinsically involved in the sweat and the rancour of the game. Sometimes they do the job well, but often they don't. The second constant is that fans, especially of losing teams, will spend more time talking about managers than players.

Times change and we change with them. One of the biggest changes in the world of the GAA over the last forty years has been the prominence of the manager. It began in the 1970s with Kevin Heffernan and Mick O'Dwyer. Without Heffernan and O'Dwyer, who knows what Gaelic football management might have been, and without the rivalry between their two counties that ignited the GAA in the 1970s, it is doubtful if Gaelic games would enjoy the same profile as they do today.

Heffernan initially came to prominence as one of the finest players in the history of the game. As a consequence he was selected at left full-forward on the Team of the Century in 1984 and the Team of the Millennium in 1999. The tactical acumen he would later showcase as a Dublin manager was already evident in his playing days when he pioneered the role of the roving full-forward. The high point of his playing career came when he captained Dublin to a 2-12 to 1-9 victory over Derry in the 1958 All-Ireland final. He also won three league medals and seven Railway Cups. He scored no less than fifty-two goals and 172 points in his career with the Dubs. Heffo was central to St Vincent's dominance of club football in Dublin when they won an astonishing thirteen consecutive senior championships from 1949 to 1962.

Those of us who watched Dublin's unconvincing win over Wexford in the opening round of the Leinster Championship in 1974 could not have dreamed that we were watching the future All-Ireland champions. Heffo's transformation of Dublin was Gaelic football's equivalent of the Eliza Doolittle story in *My Fair Lady*.

The ingredients of his success were simple. What he set out to do was to try to get a team that could win. They had a poor record in the preceding years, and morale was at a very low ebb. What they wanted to do was simply start winning games again. To begin with, Heffo got a fairly large group of players together, many of whom he knew from earlier days and many of whom were recognised as good footballers, but had no success at county level. It was critical for the success of the project to get a reliable free taker, so Heffo persuaded Jimmy Keaveney to come out of retirement. Jimmy always had the skill, but getting him fit was a little more difficult. However, he really put in the work and without him the Dubs would not have won those three All-Irelands in 1974, '76 and '77.

Credit is also due to Heffernan because of his ability to adapt to changing circumstances. Tactics did not come into it in 1974. The only instruction the backs were given was to win the ball and get it quickly to the forwards, whose instruction was simply to win the ball. After losing to Kerry in 1975, tactics came in the following year and a more professional approach, including watching videos of their opponents. Heffo watched a video of Kerry beating Cork in the Munster final and picked up one of Kerry's key tactics. The Kingdom tried to pull out the opposing full-back line and pump the ball over their heads to get their forwards to turn around and run in. Heffo countered that by keeping either Robbie Kelleher or Gay O'Driscoll back to act as a kind of sweeper.

Heffo's protégé, Pat Gilroy, kept Kevin's flame burning when he won the All-Ireland with Dublin in 2011.

The GAA owes Heffo a lot. Gaelic football was not fashionable before his Dubs came on the scene, but they did a massive PR job for the game, as was seen in the number of Dublin jerseys being worn at the time, which later spread to jerseys in the other counties, generally when they had a taste of success. Heffo's Dublin team made Gaelic football sexy because of the hype they generated.

# 8

# THE GREATEST MATCH OF ALL TIME?

*Dublin vs Kerry 1977*

Johnny Giles once said, 'The team with the least ifs, buts and ands, always wins the championship.' There is a lesson for everyone there, and it's one that Kevin Heffernan learned very early on. For over twenty years he drank from a glass that continuously refilled itself: the last, long, cool swallow as necessary as the first, his thirst unquenchable.

The 1977 All-Ireland semi-final is often spoken of as the greatest game of all time, as two great teams went toe-to-toe, with Dublin eventually coming through ahead of Kerry.

In conversation, Jimmy Deenihan offered an anatomy of the most successful trainer in history, Mick O'Dwyer, who had his nadir in that semi-final.

'He was very discerning. He could look at a player and know if he was drinking. He was a great judge of a player's condition. He could smell the drink on an individual. If he thought people weren't serious he would crucify them in training and give extra to anyone not toeing the line. He had a good understanding of people. Some would call it cunning. He was quick to make up his mind about someone, and if you entered into O'Dwyer's confidence you had a supporter for life. He could read your mind and he could detect when someone was not sincere. He punished mediocrity.

'He nearly lost his job after we lost that semi-final. In Kerry there is very little tolerance for failure, and we had lost to the Dubs two years in a row. Micko was wounded by the criticism and it hurt him deeply, but he was not going to tolerate a third year of failure. He showed the next year that he had learned a lot of lessons from that defeat. People speak of it as a great match, but for me it was a seminal moment in the development of that Kerry team. We were going to put things right after it and O'Dwyer had us primed to crush the Dubs. It was real rivalry and both teams pushed each other to get the best out of themselves. Dublin won that battle but, in the long term, we won the war.'

Pat Spillane is not convinced that the Dublin–Kerry rivalry was a completely positive thing for the GAA.

'Everyone thought Kerry and Dublin won in the 1970s and 1980s because of frightening physical regimes. This was actually incorrect, but it was a good rumour to throw out at the time. Everyone aped us. What is even worse is that fellas with no knowledge of football earned a great living by training teams at inter-county level, and even more alarmingly at club level, and driving players into the ground through running. When people heard about these tough regimes they said knowingly, "Isn't he a mighty man."

'Two things happened as a consequence. The standard of football dropped alarmingly because we were producing athletes and runners rather than footballers, and the second thing is that these men are responsible for the huge number of injured ex-players who are the result of that intensive training from these years.

'Too many teams are like sheep. They follow the crowd. If one team does a hundred laps a night, the next one has to do 120 laps. If one crowd trained up a one-hundred metre hill, the next found a two-hundred metre hill, and then the next had to climb a mountain. When one crowd goes for a swim, the next has to swim in a lake and the next go swimming in the sea.'

# 9

# PEOPLE OF GALWAY, WE LOVE YOU

*Galway show the West's awake in 1980*

The 1980 All-Ireland hurling final generated the most famous speech in the history of the GAA when Galway's captain, Joe Connolly, paraphrased the words of Pope John Paul II at Galway Racecourse the previous September, 'People of Galway, we love you.'

For star forward Noel Lane, it was a proud day: 'We won that day because our leaders, especially Joe Connolly, stood up and were counted. We were a powerful team and that side should have won more than one All-Ireland. It suited us that day that we were playing Limerick rather than Cork or Kilkenny, and that gave us confidence. It felt like it was for us that day, though Limerick could have considered themselves unlucky.'

Lane gives a lot of the credit for the victory to one man: 'Cyril Farrell was a brilliant manager. His talent was shown especially in the way he managed players who were that bit more difficult to manage, like Tony Keady and Brendan Lynskey. Cyril had a different strategy for each player.

'In 1988 I was back starting on the team, but after scoring 1-5 in the All-Ireland semi-final to my amazement and disgust I was dropped for the final on the Tuesday night before the game. I hadn't seen it coming. I let Cyril know my feelings on the subject in no uncertain terms and in choice language. I left Ballinasloe in a hurry and went home feeling sorry for myself and believing an injustice had been done to me. I proceeded to Loughrea and drank twelve pints of beer. On the Thursday night, realising that I was lucky to be there at all, I went up to Cyril and said, "You heard what I did on Loughrea and you heard what I said to you on Tuesday night, but if you want me Sunday I'll be there."

'I came on after half-time. It was one of the great All-Irelands. There was great rivalry and great duels. One of the decisive factors was that our full-back, Conor Hayes, had Nicky English in his grip. If they had moved English we would have been in trouble. I think the captaincy played on Nicky. I got in around the square and scored a goal that was instrumental in us getting the result.'

For Lane, one incident illustrates Farrell's genius: 'The week before an All-Ireland final the team was training in Ballinasloe on the night the team was due to be announced for the final. There was a terrible storm that evening with thunder, lightning and incredible rain. Lynskey and Keady did not travel down from Dublin. Farrell felt like shooting the two miscreants but knew he could not win the final without them. Things were tense for a while, especially as he never picked a team until the squad were there to hear it first. He arranged a training session for the next evening and this time the two stars were back and victory was secured.

'Cyril always preached we were better than everybody else. He had great passion and would get us to see the opposition in terms of what they didn't have, more than what they did have. He inherited Babs Keating's team in 1979 but really showed his skills with his "second team", from 1985 to 1990. He would have worked with most of that team at minor and under-21 levels. He knew everything about them: what they ate and drank, who they slept with, and their strengths and weaknesses.'

Sylvie Linnane lined out at right half-back on the Galway team that won the breakthrough All-Ireland in 1980 and at right full-back when Galway won All-Irelands in 1987 and '88. Sylvie gives a nuanced reply when asked about the team's coach Cyril Farrell.

'Cyril was great to motivate a team before a big match. In 1987, in the All-Ireland semi-final, we were up against Tipperary. When they won the Munster final their captain, Richie Stakelum, said, "The famine is over." That was the motivation he used to beat them. We had lost All-Ireland finals in '85 and '86, and there was no way we were going to lose three in a row, although Kilkenny really put it up to us in a tough match. The problem with Cyril was that he wasn't quick enough to make changes on the sideline when we were losing in Croke Park, especially in All-Ireland finals.'

Sylvie retains great memories of his first All-Ireland win: 'I remember the incredible reception we got when we won the All-Ireland in 1980. It was clear how much it meant to people. The great thing was they were all there again when we lost the next year.'

Unfortunately, injury prevented Iggy Clarke from lining out in Galway's historic All-Ireland triumph over Limerick. However, his presence was publicly acknowledged following Joe Connolly's tour de force in his acceptance speech.

'In the All-Ireland semi-final against Offaly I was flying

it. A high ball came in, falling between the half-back and full-back line, which I retreated to gather. I gained possession from Mark Corrigan and dodged his tackle. Out of the corner of my eye I saw Pádraig Horan coming to tackle me and I avoided him, but I failed to see Johnny Flaherty, whose tackle from behind drove up my shoulder blade and broke the clavicle. As I went down I could feel the heat of the rush of blood. I knew I was in trouble. I waited for the free that never came. Seán Silke was behind me saying, "Iggy let go of the ball." I opened my hand and he cleared it down the field. I was removed on a stretcher and faintly heard the applause of the crowd in my ears but in my mind I clearly saw my prospects of playing in the All-Ireland disappearing fast.

'The pain was unreal. I was placed against the X-ray machine in the Mater Hospital and was afraid I was going to faint. A nurse tried to take off my jersey but it was agony so I told her, "For God's sake cut it off." I suppose I kept half-hoping for a while that I might be back for the final, but it was not realistic.

'During the second half [of the final] I came out from the dugout and went up to the Hogan Stand. I had to mind my shoulder and didn't want to be crushed by people at the presentation. I had an inner feeling, you might say a premonition, that the lads were going to win even though the game wasn't over. On the way, people kept asking me if we were going to win and if I was praying. After his wonderful speech, Joe Connolly handed me the cup which enabled me to feel part of the whole victory. It was such a beautiful moment to hold it up in front of the crowd. We all felt that we were part of a turning point, a special moment in hurling history when Galway would take its rightful place at hurling's top table.'

# 10

# SÉAMUS DARBY ENDS KERRY'S DRIVE FOR FIVE

*Offaly vs Kerry 1982*

Offaly manager Eugene McGee must take a lot of the credit for Kerry's failure to win the five-in-a-row in 1982. His Offaly team asked a lot of questions of Kerry in the All-Ireland semi-final in 1980 and the final in '81. Of course, McGee's decision to send on Séamus Darby with just a few minutes to go seems the greatest substitution in the history of the GAA as he sensationally got the winning goal. Nobody in Kerry will ever forget it!

As a manager, McGee first came to prominence in club management in the 1970s with University College Dublin. But it is that 1982 All-Ireland win that has immortalised him. The first half was open and it was a very good game of football. In the second half it started raining fairly heavily and the game deteriorated a fair amount. Kerry dominated for a long time and Offaly were lucky enough to stay with them. Martin Furlong's penalty save from the normally lethal Mike Sheehy was very important. If Kerry had scored that,

Offaly may not have come back. The rest is history. They were four points down and got two frees to put them two points behind. Then a long ball came to Séamus Darby and he banged it into the net. All Croke Park went wild, but there was still a minute and a half left in the game and they had to hold on with all their might.

Eugene McGee's reaction to the win was to say, 'The magnificent players on that team personified not only their own accomplishments but the sacrifices of generations of Offaly people who made that moment possible. I am very conscious of all the people who organised games and travelling arrangements down through the years, regardless of personal inconvenience or harsh weather. Without those people, the sequence which led to Offaly's historic success would not have started. The fact that the years of disappointment have been wiped out with that win gives me a certain amount of pleasure.'

Pat Spillane remembers the game with less exuberant memories: 'In 1982, Kerry had planned a trip to holiday in Bali in the Far East, to celebrate what we had expected to be our five-in-a-row. After sensationally losing the final to Offaly one of the lads said that the only Bali we would be going to was Ballybunion! Another said, "It won't even be the Canaries this year. All we'll get is the Seagulls."

'It has been said that we didn't underestimate Offaly in 1982 – they were just better than we thought!'

# 11

# THE EXCELLENT EIGHT

*Mick O'Dwyer leads Kerry to eight All-Irelands*

I love the story that when someone handed Mick O'Dwyer an orange, a scarce commodity in wartime Waterville, the youngster thought it was a football and gave it a kick down the road.

A neighbour once asked him if he had ever been to Lourdes? O'Dwyer responded: 'Did Kerry ever play there?'

Micko's great Kerry team were the prototype of the successful team. They had the four obvious things: they were fit, they trained hard, were talented and gave 100 per cent. They had six other ingredients though that made them so successful. Firstly, they never depended on one or two individuals to produce the goods. If Mike Sheehy and Eoin 'the Bomber' Liston were having an off day, the likes of John Egan and Ger Power produced big performances. Secondly, they were very much a team. Mick O'Dwyer did not want to see anyone come off the field happy after a defeat. There was no point in saying, 'I played well but the others let me down.' O'Dwyer always drilled into them that they won as a team and they lost as a team. Thirdly, they were able to handle success – not after 1975, but after the defeats of 1976 and 1977 they were equipped to do so. They used this capacity to motivate themselves to achieve even more success. They enjoyed it when it came, but they also knew it was just a brief interlude unless they came back and won again the following year.

Fourthly, they had a positive attitude. Each of them always believed that they would beat their man even when they were marking a more skilful player and, collectively, as soon as they put on the Kerry jersey they believed no team would beat them. That is not arrogance, but positive thinking.

Fifthly, the Kerry players were very intelligent. It is vital to a team to have players who think about the game, especially about improving their own game, but in particular players who can read a match and when things are going badly never lose their composure but can turn things around. Sixthly, they had inspired leadership from Mick O'Dwyer. His man-management skills were excellent, he instilled belief and got them right physically and mentally for the big day. He also knew how to motivate them. When it comes to motivation it is different strokes for different folks. O'Dwyer knew what buttons to push to motivate them individually and collectively. He always provided the team with good feedback. It was always positive feedback, which was more effective than negative. Above all, he was a winner. Winners have critical skills; they do not leave winning to chance, leave no stone unturned and they make things happen.

Pat Spillane is ideally placed to analyse O'Dwyer's success. 'Nowadays players have diet plans and schedules for the gym. In our time, when we won the All-Ireland in September, we weren't seen again until March or April. Micko did have a problem with what were termed "the fatties" on the team who put on weight, like John Egan and the Bomber. He would bring them back earlier for extra training. He would always have a few rabbits or hares to set the pace for them. The interesting thing though was that there never was a complaint from Egan or Liston.

'O'Dwyer's final year with Kerry came in 1989 after three successive defeats to Cork in Munster finals. That year he thought he could get one last hurrah out of the team. It is probably the six-million-dollar question for a player or a manager coming to the end of their career: is there one last kick in the team? That year O'Dwyer felt the only way he could eke out one last title from us was if he had us all really, really fit. He had us training in a little all-weather track in the Kerins O'Rahilly pitch in Tralee. We ran and we ran and we ran. It is one of the rare mistakes he made. Unfortunately all of our energy was left on the training field and when it came to games we had nothing left in the tank.

'It was not that he was great on tactics. He wasn't, but like sex, the movements in Gaelic football are somewhat limited and predictable, and tactical genius isn't everything. His real talent was that he was a great man-manager.

'O'Dwyer's key to success was man-management. He made you feel that you were the greatest. The other secret was motivation. He realised early on that medals weren't the thing. He always dangled carrots. He started with holidays and then moved on to better holidays.

'He is a loveable man, driven by football. Football is in his blood. It is his fix. What people forget is that competition for places on that Kerry team was ferocious. You knew that if your standards dropped you would find yourself on the sub's bench. O'Dwyer was a great man for keeping you on your toes. From time to time that meant suggesting that particular subs might be moving up the pecking order. Of course if that was true someone on the first team would have to lose out and everybody was determined it wasn't going to be them so the pace of training was upped.

'Micko had a kind of aura about him that made players want to earn his favour, and a completely natural, straight-from-the-heart sense of how to inspire players. He was able to bring the best out of his gifted but sometimes difficult stars.

'O'Dwyer could be the archetypal "cute Kerry hoor". Whenever he thought anybody was watching us train who might be on a spying mission, he had us play soccer. However, in the interests of cultural purity it was never called that. He referred to it as "ground football".'

# 12

# AN END TO THE FAMINE

*Tipperary win the 1987 Munster final*

Michael Lowry has been one of the most controversial figures in recent Irish political life, but he was to play a significant role in the revival of Tipperary's hurling fortunes in 1986. His meeting with Babs Keating would change hurling history.

Keating recalls, 'When Michael became county chairman he asked to meet me. We met in a private house, the late Seamus Maher's home, because I wanted to meet in secret knowing the stories that would go around. To be fair to him, he could give me the power to pick my own selectors. I'll always remember he said, "You have the job but we have no money." The County Board was broke after hosting the Centenary All-Ireland in 1984 and the economic situation was very bleak. I got the idea to start the Supporters Club. Then I decided we would raffle a racehorse and Christy Roche bought an ideal horse for us. I got everyone I ever knew to buy a ticket, like Charlie Haughey and Jack Lynch. I remember being at home one morning and getting a call from Niall Quinn when he was at Arsenal. He told me he had sold seven tickets for me and listed a who's who of Arsenal greats who had bought one.

'My back-up team was Donie Nealon and Theo English. They had played for the county for about twelve years and I don't think Cork ever beat them. They couldn't understand why there was such fear of Cork and they transferred that attitude. Our captain, Richie Stakelum, would always say that at that stage Tipperary had such fear of Cork.

'People talk about the great team Tipperary had in the '84 Munster final, but that team brought Tipp into Division Two. We played our first league game away against Antrim and won it fairly impressively. The great thing that happened was that in our second league match we played Laois and they beat us by ten points in Thurles. We got rid of six or seven players and went in a different direction. If that defeat had come later in the campaign it would have been much harder to regroup. As with everything in life, you need a bit of luck. We got it with that game in Laois.

'One thing I did every January was to take out the two selectors and their wives for a meal, and told them to pick the team they would play in the All-Ireland that year. The three of us had thirteen identical choices that night in '87, so we only had to find two players.

'We had huge confidence going into the Munster final, even though Cork were 3–1 odds-on favourites. We had come from nowhere in Division Two and had twelve new personnel. We had money behind us. When we travelled away for big matches we stayed in five-star hotels. I will never forget the first game we played against Cork. Both teams got to the ground at the same time. Our bus was in the Tipperary colours, the Cork players were in their jeans and jumpers. Our lads looked like film stars in their blazers. Richie Stakelum said it was worth five points to us.'

Nicky English won six All-Stars in seven years and was hurler of the year in 1989. He is ideally placed to give an insider's guide to the game.

'When I came on the scene, Tipperary changed managers almost every year because we weren't winning Munster Championships. That means there is little or no continuity and a lot of good players are thrown out in the wash before they have the chance to develop. We came close to winning in a high-scoring Munster final (that we should have won) in 1984, when Seánie O'Leary scored a late goal to win for Cork.

'Things changed when Babs came on board. He did things differently. He raised a lot of money and arranged things in what was a radically different way back then, though county players take it for granted now. He got us blazers and we stayed in hotels before matches. Things were tight economically in the 1980s. There was no money around. The Tipperary County Board were putting all their money into upgrading Semple Stadium. All their financial focus was on infrastructure, not on looking after players. Up to then, we would drive through on match days and be stuck in traffic. Anything we needed in terms of gear or hurleys was got for us. Before that you got your own hurleys and handed in receipts, and often there was a long delay before you got your money back. Sometimes you wouldn't get your money back at all. It is hard to quantify how much all this helped us on the field of play, but it did make an impact. Babs blazed the trail and every football and hurling team followed to a greater or lesser extent. He brought a whole new attitude and confidence. Babs believed, and we believed because of him.

'Winning the 1987 Munster final was my greatest day

in hurling. The fact that we beat Cork after extra time in a replay added to it. Tipperary hadn't won a Munster final since 1971, so that's why Richie Stakelum's comment that the "famine days are over" struck such a chord. The emotion our victory unleashed was unreal. Nothing has ever matched that feeling.'

# 13

# A PARABLE OF THE GAA

*Meath vs Dublin 1988*

Meath legend Bernard Flynn offers a fable of the power of GAA friendships.

'Dublin's Davy Synnott and I worked together for Tennents. The week before the 1988 Leinster final, Davy and I were in the papers every day because we were going to be marking each other in the game. The hype was incredible, and Tennents milked it for all it was worth and had arranged a reception for sixty publicans after the match. On the match day my wife, Madeline, was in the stand with Davy's wife, Marie. Davy was a clean player, and had burst onto the scene in the previous few years like a breath of fresh air.

'I got the first few balls and then he hit me. Then I got a score and he did it again. I said, "Davy, cop yourself f\*\*king on. You hit me twice, and if you do it again I will bust you." The ball came out towards the middle of the field and I caught him with my elbow as far as I could and burst his nose. The referee didn't see my elbow but did see Davy turning around and giving me a box. The game stopped. The crowd were going crazy. Davy was sent off. As he walked off he started to pump blood and the referee couldn't understand why. I remember him pleading with the referee that I hit him first.

'I was lying on the ground and thinking of my job, the first decent job I had in my life, and my new Opel Ascona that made me feel like I was Don Johnson. I thought of my boss who was watching me playing and I was worried that I would lose my job and my car. I thought of the publicans who were going to be at our reception. I thought of Marie and Madeline together in the stand. All of these thoughts went through my head in seconds.

'There was a huge euphoria after we beat Dublin in the Leinster final, but then I met Madeline, and Marie was with her and she was inconsolable. She had a bit of a go at me. Then Davy didn't show up at the gig. Although it was one of Seán Boylan's big things that the team went together, after the match I got the word back to him that I had to find Davy. I went back to the gig. Hours went by and still no Davy, and Marie was very worried. My boss decided to have a party in his house in Swords, and Davy arrived. After an hour of drinking and thrashing it out, we made up.

'I crashed my lovely car late that night. I had to do a promotion in Gibney's in Malahide the next day. I was in a state. Who was the guy who put his arm around me and got me through it? Davy Synnott. What did he do? The next day was a bank-holiday Monday. Great man that he was, Davy drove me to the event, and got all the stuff I needed and helped me with my promotion in the pub. That's what the GAA is all about. I'll never forget him for that.'

# 14

# O HAPPY DAY

*Leitrim win the 1994 Connacht final*

Gaelic football needs every nostalgic prop it can muster, and when many of the controversies of today are forgotten, the powerful grip Leitrim's Connacht-final triumph exerted on the popular imagination will never vanish. In his radio commentary, Mícheál Ó Muircheartaigh said it was easy to imagine the Leitrim fans who had gone on to their eternal reward, leaning over the bannisters in heaven watching the drama unfold. The images leaned against their thoughts until they could no longer resist giving themselves up to their embrace.

At the centre of that famous victory was Mickey Quinn who played underage football for Leitrim for five years, nineteen years for the senior team (1978–97) and nine years with the over-40s. He made his senior inter-county debut in 1978. Although he was under six feet tall he could hold his own with giants like Liam McHale, but his toughest battles were with Willie Joe Padden. Throughout the 1980s, Quinn experienced nothing but disappointment.

'In 1983, Galway beat us by a point in injury time. I was sick the night before the All-Ireland final when Galway were preparing to meet Dublin, knowing we could have, and should have, beaten them, but that we hadn't the confidence and lacked quality in the full-forward line.'

Things changed for the better for Quinn personally, and Leitrim generally, when P. J. Carroll became manager.

'We went on a run of fourteen or fifteen unbeaten games, which was very unusual for Leitrim, and won an All-Ireland B final in 1990. I won an All-Star that year and as it was the first one in Leitrim it caused a lot of excitement in the county, and gave me a new lease of life even though I had had two or three trips with them as replacements at that stage. It meant everything to me because it was always my burning ambition. Winning an All-Ireland with Leitrim was too much to hope for. We were playing Leinster in the 1984 Railway Cup in Ballinasloe when the journalist David Walsh told me that I had missed out on an All-Star the year before by just one vote.'

The most memorable year for Leitrim was to be 1994, but their nearest neighbours had to be dealt with first.

'Roscommon had been the biggest bogey team for us. We had great battles with them in previous years but no matter what we threw at them they always seemed to have the upper hand. That spring though, in Carrick-on-Shannon, we relegated Roscommon from our division in the National League. We knew then we could beat them and we did in the Connacht Championship. In previous years we should have beaten them, but that year they should have beaten us! We went on to take Mayo in the Connacht final. Although we made a dreadful start, we had great belief and that was in large measure due to our manager.'

A major catalyst for Leitrim's taste of glory was the management of John O'Mahony.

'He is a very tough trainer. He took everybody back because he drove us so hard. There were evenings that we would turn up for training in Kells that would be so wet you wouldn't let your dog out in it. We'd be wondering if he would send us out in the absolute deluge but he would be out just in a T-shirt and tracksuit setting up the bollards. We'd be thinking, "This guy is off his rocker," but he was setting us an example. Then he stood in the corner and blew the whistle and we came out. There was always method to his madness. He brought us to train on the biggest sand dunes in Sligo and often there would be no hot showers afterwards, but that toughened us up and then we were ready to move on to the next phase.

'What it took for us to win a Connacht Championship was massive. Winning an All-Ireland is nothing to Kerry because they are used to it, but winning a Connacht title was a huge burden for us mentally as we had never won one. John O'Mahony brought a psychologist on board, Frank Cogan. He started off by getting us to set goals. Then before our first game, in his distinctive Scottish accent, he asked what score we would concede. We said seven points. He asked, "Why not no goal and no point?" When we started to giggle he asked again, "Why not?" Each time we came up with a reason he came back and asked, "Why not?" Then when he asked us how much we would score we said, 2-10. He asked us, "Why not 7-24?" We all laughed and again he came back with, "Why not?" Then each time we offered a reason he again replied, "Why not?" Eventually we started to think why not? Then he split the defenders into one group, the forwards into another and got us to come up with our individual goals. The psychologist would then board the team bus about twenty minutes before we reached the ground on match days and that reinforced the messages he was putting across. That's the way John was. What he did for Leitrim was priceless.'

# 15

# FROM CLARE TO HERE

*The banner is raised in 1995*

In decades of watching supreme contests, in a wide range of arenas, there have been few matches that have unleashed a greater flood of excitement and pleasure than Clare's All-Ireland hurling victory in 1995. Across the nation enthralled listeners heard Mícheál Ó Muircheartaigh saying with breathless enthusiasm the magic words, 'We've gone forty-five seconds into injury time. It's all over and the men of Clare of '95 are All-Ireland champions.'

Clare's triumph was the hurling equivalent of the ugly duckling who was turned into a swan. Their manager, Ger Loughnane, is a man born under the sign of contradiction. He was always looking to get into his players' heads.

'In the run-up to the '95 All-Ireland semi-final I had emphasised over and over again the importance of not getting distracted by crowds or noise or by anything. On the morning of the final we trained in the Alsaa complex, near the airport. While we did our very light workout there were planes flying over us constantly getting ready to land.

At the end I called the players together around me. Just as I was about to start talking another plane came in and P. J. "Fingers" O'Connell looked up at it. I saw my chance so I let fly! I roared at him, "If you are distracted here, looking up at a plane, what will you be like in Croke Park with sixty thousand people roaring down at you? Are you going to look up at everyone of those?" I can tell you that when the next plane came in no one moved their eye upward! If I had planned it I couldn't have timed it better. It was a lesson in distraction not just for Fingers but for the whole team. In all the years after that nobody once looked up when a plane came in!'

There was one shocking moment for Loughnane in the build-up to the final.

'We were obviously going to be staying in a hotel in Dublin on the night of the All-Ireland. About a fortnight before the final I met two officers of the County Board, one being Pat Fitzgerald, the county secretary, to discuss the arrangements. We were standing on Abbey Street in Ennis, with people passing by. I said, "We're going up to the All-Ireland. The crucial thing at this stage is to book the hotel. The least thing every player should get is a room of his own." Pat was completely genuine and as all the players were bachelors he was concerned about the "extra-curricular activities" that might go on in these rooms, and of the Clare County Board being seen as condoning them. His attitude was on ethical grounds and I totally respected that.

'The other official said, "Oh, them c**ts will be riding like f**k all night."

'That was his attitude to Clare players going out to play in an All-Ireland final.'

Some officials on the Clare County Board never forgave Ger Loughnane for not living down to their expectations. Not surprisingly, Loughnane had an unorthodox way planned to mark the victory.

'We did something in Clare that was totally innovative. We had just won the All-Ireland for the first time in eighty-one years and something special had to be done to reward the players. We decided we would set up a Holiday Fund Committee that would be totally independent of the County Board. I went into the travel agent and was looking for something different, and I began to look at the East and stumbled on Thailand. Back in '95 everyone associated going to Thailand with Bangkok and sex! Here you have a team full of bachelors going to Bangkok! When the news broke all hell broke loose!'

Loughnane believed that it was vital for the team's legacy that they won the second All-Ireland. One of his most glorious triumphs was viewed from an unusual angle and achieved with a little help – albeit completely unintentional – from one of his friends.

'With about twenty minutes to go in the '97 All-Ireland final I went along the sideline and overheard Len Gaynor, who I knew for years, telling Michael Ryan to stay inside. I decided immediately to bring on David Forde. I went to the selectors and said, "We'll bring on Fordy, but we'll play him as an extra wing-forward." They looked at me but I told them to trust me. A comical situation then developed with Len telling Michael Ryan to stay inside and I was telling the man he was supposed to be marking to stay out! This meant that Forde was totally loose. He won that All-Ireland for us. He scored two points and set up another one by playing as an extra wing-forward.'

# 16

# DANCING AT THE CROSSROADS

*Wexford win the 1996 All-Ireland*

The joy in Clare in 1995 was replicated by Wexford fans in 1996. After he retired from playing, Martin Quigley immediately took charge of piloting Wexford's fortunes. His new role was no bed of roses.

'Managing is not nearly as enjoyable as playing. When you are playing you only have to worry about your own job, but when you're the manager you have to worry about everybody else. There are so many things outside your control as a manager, from players getting injured to bad referees' decisions which can cost you a game. Once I retired as a player I missed the buzz of it and I got involved in managing Wexford almost immediately. With the benefit of hindsight I should have taken a break from the game and turned to management later, but while hindsight is great it's not any good when you have to make a decision. I should have given myself a bit of distance from the switch to playing from managing. It's hard to have a clear perspective when emotionally you're too close to the centre of things.'

How would he assess his own term in charge of Wexford?

'I'm not the best person to judge. Ultimately a manager is judged by results. In my three years in charge we got to two league finals but we won nothing. I suppose though any manager is only as good as the players he has at his disposal.'

Quigley was replaced as Wexford manager by Christy Keogh. Among Keogh's innovations was to enlist the services of Cyril Farrell to assist the team in their preparations for the Leinster Championship, particularly the clash with old rivals Kilkenny. The move did not have the desired impact, as Kilkenny inflicted a heavy defeat on the Slaneysiders. How does Quigley react to the criticism that was aired at the time that instead of rallying Wexford, Farrell's mere presence inspired Kilkenny?

'I wouldn't pay any heed to that sort of talk. Anyone who thinks that Kilkenny need Cyril Farrell's involvement to be fully motivated to beat Wexford in the championship knows nothing about hurling, and Kilkenny hurling in particular. Kilkenny had a strong team and beat us badly. I don't think it would have made much difference who was managing us that particular year. The one thing that Cyril's involvement did achieve was to dramatically heighten the expectations within the county. Not for the first time though they were to be cruelly dashed.'

In 1996 Wexford became the home of the 'Riverdance of Sport', and the story of paradise regained. Why did they win the All-Ireland that year and not earlier?

'Expectations were low in 1996 because we had been beaten in the league semi-final. To me the key match in 1996 was not the All-Ireland final, but beating Offaly in the Leinster final. That really set them up as a team of winners. I think the supporters played a huge part in Wexford's win – almost as much as the team itself. It was fascinating to see the way the support snowballed in the county throughout the championship. It was said there were eight thousand Wexford fans at the Kilkenny match, but there were forty thousand there for the final.

'I think there were two crucial factors to explain why Wexford won that year. Firstly, there was Liam Griffin and the passion, motivation, organisation and leadership he gave to the team. Secondly, there was Damien Fitzhenry. I don't want to cast any aspersions on anybody but Wexford had been waiting for a long time for a goalie up to that standard. He was the best goalie in Ireland in my opinion. If I had to pinpoint one player on the pitch who meant the difference between victory and defeat in 1996 it would be him.'

# 17

## SPORTING ECUMENISM

*Ireland vs England at Croke Park in 2007*

In some parts of Ireland, if you praise the sunshine you'll be told, 'It'll never last.' Yet there is ample reason for optimism about the ongoing health of the GAA. As chief executive of the Irish Sports Council, John Treacy is ideally equipped to offer a dispassionate appraisal of the role of the GAA in Irish life.

'I think there's a danger that we take them for granted. A number of years ago we hosted a gathering for all the top sports officials in the EU. We showed them a hurling match and they were watching it with their mouths open. They couldn't believe that amateur players could produce a game of such skill and speed. All through the day they kept asking about it.

'For an amateur organisation it is a staggering achievement to have created an incredible stadium like Croke Park, especially in the middle of Dublin. They have shown incredible leadership. The GAA has adapted to the changing times. They are keenly aware of the need to bring modern marketing methods into Gaelic games. I think a critical step came in the

1990s with the decision to introduce live coverage of a large number of games on the TV. Young people get their heroes from television. If you go down to Kilkenny you will see almost every young boy with a hurley because they want to be like their heroes. In recent times you can see some young lads with hurleys walking on the streets of Dublin. You would hardly ever have seen that twenty years ago. That has not happened by accident, and shows the forward-thinking approach the GAA has taken.

'They have shown great creativity in the way they have managed to defy the tide and ensure that they continue to get so many people to volunteer. The Economic and Social Research Institute produced a report on the social capital aspect of sport, and it is basically ninety pages of glowing tribute to the GAA and the way they have harnessed the voluntary capacity. Instead of saying to people, as in the past, give us all your time – they now say give us two evenings and a Saturday morning to train a juvenile team or whatever. We can't put a price on the kind of social value the organisation brings.

'However, their finest hour for me was when they revoked Rule 42 and opened up Croke Park to Ireland's soccer and rugby games while the old Lansdowne Road stadium was being demolished and the Aviva was being built. Nobody will ever forget the extraordinarily unique atmosphere that day when Ireland played England in that momentous rugby match. The emotion that day was unreal; as evident in the sight of big John Hayes bawling his eyes out while the anthems were being played. You could hear a pin drop when they played *God Save the Queen*. The respect was phenomenal. It was a day when everybody was so proud to be Irish. A special day in the history of a very special sporting body, and one I take my hat off to.'

# 18

## NOTHING COMPARES TO YOU

*The Brian Cody era*

Brian Cody lost a senior All-Ireland title in 1999, when hot favourites Kilkenny lost to Cork. DJ Carey recalled the pain afterwards.

'We were kind of in shock. I remember walking out of Croke Park and there were still Kilkenny people around, coming over congratulating us, saying "Well done" and all that. It just rubbed it in more. To think you have to go home and face these people the following night. They come out clapping you, and you've just lost an All-Ireland. It's gut-wrenching. I took it badly. It upset me a lot.'

In 2000 Cody won his first All-Ireland as manager against Offaly. The next year, though, Cody was to experience the bitter taste of defeat again when Kilkenny were sensationally beaten by Galway in the All-Ireland semi-final.

'After winning the All-Ireland in 2000 there was great hype about us. We thought we were great lads and a small bit of that seeped through to our hurling. We definitely didn't put in the hard work. It was a turning point for some of us, that we had to cop on. It was a wake-up call and nobody does those better than Brian Cody.'

Carey's high opinion of Cody is shared by Nicky English: 'I don't believe in the cult of a manager. The way I see it, a bad manager will stop you from winning an All-Ireland, but a decent manager will win the All-Ireland for you if he has the players, and that's the key. It is players who win the All-Ireland, not managers. The one exception I would make is that I rate Brian Cody very highly. He has achieved so much over such a long period, but above all he changed the tradition of Kilkenny hurling. He has brought in a new system and a way of playing which has become part of the hurling culture now in Kilkenny.'

Nickey Brennan joins the chorus of approval for Cody: 'The whole science of training has developed a lot and managers today have much more support staff, from physios and dieticians to people who look after the stats. Kevin Fennelly succeeded me as Kilkenny boss, and he had a relatively short term, and then Brian Cody took over. The funny thing about Cody is that he didn't have a very impressive record in club management when he took the job, but the one thing he brought was a fierce passion for hurling and he was a great thinker of the game. It maybe took him a while to fully get his feet into the management game, which is understandable, but he's a quick learner. The style of Kilkenny play has definitely changed under his management. He is fortunate in that he inherits a great assembly line of talent, and for that great credit must be given to people down the line in Kilkenny, as I know Brian would be the first to acknowledge. While he has honed their skills, the Kilkenny player of today tends to be a strong, physical player, and even those who may be small of stature in a few cases they tend to be well able to handle themselves physically on the field. The type of play brings a strong physical dimension to the game, and it must be said that they have an exceptional level of skill; some teams have opted for a very physical approach in the past but they don't have the skill levels. Kilkenny bring both elements to the table. Brian also has a great capacity to get players to take personal responsibility for their part of the pitch, but equally to group together and to fight the cause as a team. If you're an attacker, you have to take on responsibility as a defender to stop your opponent from clearing the ball under the defensive system he has brought in and vice versa. He has made very good hurlers into extraordinary good hurlers. He's got people to believe in a system. They are single-minded when they play for Kilkenny. Nothing fazes them. Nothing gets in their way. They are not distracted by what they might gain out of the match. They are, of course, very well looked after by the Kilkenny County Board, but they are not allowed to have anything else interfere with their play. I think apart from the skills and the tactics, that attitude is as important to Cody's success. If any other football or hurling county was to take anything out of the Cody era, it would be to adhere to the coach's code without any question because that's why ultimately other counties fail. Okay, many of them may not have the same skill levels, but if you have the single-mindedness and camaraderie that Cody has instilled then you are on the road to success. That philosophy has given Kilkenny the success it has today.

'As a player, I was going for the three-in-a-row in 1984; as a selector, I was going for the three-in-a-row in 1994; but we failed both times. As president, I presented the cup in '06 and '07: you can imagine how nervous I was in '08 that I would put the hex on Kilkenny's three-in-a-row! Thankfully I didn't deprive Brian Cody of his glory!'

# 19

# THE HEARTBEAT OF THE GAA

*The pride of the parish*

Joe Brolly is the most strident critic of recent trends in relation to the GAA, particularly in areas like the growth of the Gaelic Players Association (GPA) and commercialisation, and in what he sees as 'elitism'.

'Don't get me started on the GPA! I find the corporate values that have infested the GAA, as evident in the Sky deal, very sad. Where I see the true ethos of the day is in the clubs. The club is the heartbeat and the soul of the GAA. When I go to somewhere like Crossmaglen and see the centrality of it to the life of the local community, I come away inspired and uplifted.'

Dermot Earley was perturbed by the future and about the impact of major sociological changes in Ireland on the structure of the club.

'In rural places especially I've seen big changes insofar as the traditional loyalty to the club is weakening. There's a lot more young fellas going into third-level education now, and they are emigrating for the summer and playing in America or somewhere and not in their local club. There's a lot more mobility now in the workplace and guys are moving around from place to place but are generally not willing to travel back to their parish for training every evening, so they are switching to clubs in Dublin or wherever. In the club versus county stakes, the county is winning. Each of these changes on their own are not that significant, but when you add them all together they become very significant and they are decimating some of the clubs, especially in the rural areas. I have to say I'm very worried the old-style club may be in danger. The GAA will succeed and progress as long as it has the support of the people; the club is the cell of growth and renewal.'

Joe Brolly's assessment of the future of the club is more upbeat: 'In the mid to late 1990s my concentration became focused on Dungiven. It is very hard when your dream in a county like Derry is to win an All-Ireland and you actually do. I don't subscribe to the view that you have to win two All-Irelands to be a great team. I didn't even know what that means. As you get older you start to appreciate the real power of the GAA: the sense of togetherness and community and the importance of the club.

'In 1997, Dungiven won the Derry Championship for the first time in six years, which was a long time for that team. We trounced Peter Canavan's Errigal Ciarán in the Ulster final – it was like waking from a dream and realising it was real. The down side was that I got injured late in the game and was not really fit for the All-Ireland semi-final. We had a man sent off early in the game which we lost by a point. It was a crushing disappointment.

'I gave up playing with Dungiven when I was thirty-six because it was a 130 mile round trip, and I transferred to St

Brigids in Belfast. I've got five kids, so that eats into your time. It has given me a new lease of life. The club is based on the Malone Road. Bob McCartney, the controversial Unionist politician, made a great comment on the changing demographic about the Malone Road – which used to be home to the Protestant aristocracy but now belongs to the Catholic nouveau riche. He said: "*Tiocfaidh ar lá* has given way to *Tiocfaidh our lá-di-da*!" I am heavily involved in under-age training in the club and you see all the Bentleys in the car park. It was hairy enough though when I started playing there, particularly as you get punched in the back of the head as you are hearing: "I'll give you a f\*\*king All-Star."'

Despite Damien Duff's criticism of GAA 'dinosaurs', the GAA is continually renewing itself and the club is at the heart of it. Jackie Tyrrell annoyed Galway fans and former player Damien Hayes before the 2018 All-Ireland semi-final by describing the side as resembling 'a rugby team'. However, nobody has better evoked the intimacy of the bonds of the club than he did in the acclaimed TV series *The Game*: 'The fellas from the club are the lads you invite to your wedding. They are the ones you turn to when you are in trouble. They are the ones that will carry your coffin.'

# PART III
# Magic Moments

The GAA is rightly proud of its traditions. However, if not renewed, traditions run the risk of ending up as museum pieces. This section documents some of the moments that contributed to the richness of the GAA's tradition, but also highlights the dynamic nature of the tradition as the people's movement grows and gains momentum in a unique journey of continuity and discontinuity. While it has been faithful to these traditions the GAA have equally been very imaginative and creative in adapting to changing social, economic and media landscapes.

# 20

# THE PRAIRIE FIRE

*The newly established GAA fuels the sense of Irishness*

From the outset, Gaelic games have been one of the most formidable imaginative batteries that allow Irish exiles in the four corners of the earth to feel they continue to belong to 'home'.

Michael Cusack claimed that the new organisation spread like a 'prairie fire'. However, women did not play a central role in the early years of the GAA. Although the tide of change was also impacting women, much of the establishment in Ireland continued to be male-dominated. It is instructive to consider the institutional Church's attitude to the newly established Ladies' Land League as an indication of its attitude to women at the time. The organisation was set up in January 1881, and by May had 321 branches. The women became responsible for a detailed register known as the 'Book of the Kells'. This was a record of every estate, the number of tenants, the rent paid, the official valuations, the name of the landlord of the agent, the number of evictions that had taken place and the number that were still pending.

The register was compiled from weekly reports sent in by the country branches. The Ladies' Land League was also active in relief work – when notice of a pending eviction was received, a member travelled to the area with money for assistance.

The League quickly fell foul of the institutional Church. This was not perhaps surprising given that involvement of women in such a political group was entirely new. Archbishop McCabe of Dublin denounced the organisation and, in the same breath, recalled the traditional modesty of Irish women and the splendid purity of St Brigid. He went on to state that the proper place for women was 'the seclusion of the home'. In a letter read at all Masses in the Archdiocese of Dublin in March 1881, he continued: 'But all this is to be laid aside and the daughters of our Catholic people are called forth, under the flimsy pretext of charity, to take their stand in the noisy arena of public life. They are asked to forget the modesty of their sex and the high dignity of their womanhood by leaders who seem utterly reckless of consequences.'

Thankfully the GAA have rightly dispatched those sexist attitudes to the dustbin of history as is evident in the fact that both ladies football and camogie are flourishing today.

One of Ireland's leading academics, Declan Kiberd, draws attention to the need to situate the founding of the GAA in a wider context where cultural nationalism was flourishing.

'At the start of the last century, our people experienced a national revival epitomised by the self-help philosophies of various movements from the Gaelic League to the Co-Ops, from the Abbey Theatre to Sinn Féin. In the previous two generations, the Irish had achieved such mastery of English as the *lingua franca* of the modern world that they went on to produce one of the great experimental literatures in that tongue. A few years later, the process of global decolonisation was headed by men like Collins and de Valera, who managed to dislodge the greatest empire which the world until then had known . . . The GAA played its major role in heightening the sense of the emerging national identity.'

# 21

# KEEPING IT CIVIL

*The GAA helps heal the wounds of the Civil War*

Although Limerick won the first All-Ireland in 1887, Gaelic football really came of age in 1903 when Kerry won their first All-Ireland. They beat Kildare in a three-game saga which grabbed the public imagination. Kerry won the first game but the match was replayed because Kerry had been awarded a controversial goal. So intense was the second game, which finished in a draw, that the referee collapsed at the end. On the third occasion Kerry were comprehensive winners by 0-8 to 0-2.

The following year saw the first taster of what would become one of the great rivalries in the GAA, when Kerry beat Dublin to claim their second All-Ireland. By now the first true star of Gaelic football, Dick Fitzgerald, had emerged. He won five All-Ireland medals, captaining the team to All-Irelands in 1913 and 1914. Like many men of the time, Fitzgerald was active in the IRA, as the movement for Irish independence gathered momentum. After the 1916 Rising he found himself interned with Michael Collins in Wales.

At the height of the War of Independence, on Sunday, 21 November 1920 – 'Bloody Sunday' – the political turmoil cast a deep shadow on the world of Gaelic games when the reviled Black and Tans shot dead thirteen people at a football match between Tipperary and Dublin in Croke Park. The Tipperary player Michael Hogan was killed, and the biggest stand in Croke Park was since named in his honour.

Gaelic football and hurling were always about more than sport in rural Ireland, and in Kerry in particular. Professor Liam Ryan pointed out that the GAA played a greater part in healing the many rifts which have threatened to rupture families and communities throughout Ireland in the last century than the Catholic Church.

'Neighbours, for example, who had shot at one another in the Civil War displayed a greater desire to forgive and forget when gathered around the goalposts, than when gathered around the altar. Nowhere was that more apparent than in Kerry.'

The late John B. Keane also saw at first hand the power of the GAA to heal the wounds of the past.

'Football has also been part of our identity here. In Kerry, football was called "*caid*" as it referred to the type of ball used. The ball was made from dried farm-animal skins with an inflated natural animal bladder inside. We take our football very seriously in Kerry but we also take politics very seriously. Sometimes our twin passions collide. This was probably most clearly illustrated in 1935, when Kerry refused to take part in the football championship because of the ongoing detention of prisoners in the Curragh.

'The Civil War not only cost a lot of lives; it split families down the middle and left intense bitterness. During one particularly bitter election campaign I decided to put up a mock candidate who went by the name of Tom Doodle. The plan was to inject laughter and reduce the bitterness. Doodle was the pseudonym given to a local labourer. My slogan depicted on posters all over the town was, "Vote the Noodle and Give the Whole Caboodle To Doodle". I organised a brass band and a large crowd to accompany the candidate to my election meeting. We travelled to the square standing on the back of a donkey-drawn cart. It was a tumultuous affair. In a speech that poked fun at the clientelist, promise-all politics of the time, Doodle declared his fundamental principle, "Every man should have more than the next."

'The one place in Kerry where the Civil War was put aside was on the GAA fields, and it did bring old enemies together.'

# 22

# SELDOM DID ONE MAN DO SO MUCH

*The central role of Micheál O'Hehir*

An elderly farmer in a remote part of Leitrim finally decided to buy a television. The shopkeeper assured him that he would install the antenna and TV the next day. The next evening, the farmer turned on his new TV and found only the pundits on *The Sunday Game* on every channel. The next morning, he turned the TV on and found only *The Sunday Game*, no matter what channel he put on. The next day, the same again so he called the shop to complain. The owner said it was impossible for every channel to have only the GAA pundits talking, but agreed to send the repairman to check the TV. When the repairman turned on the set, he was stunned to find the farmer was right. After looking on the set for a while he went outside to check the antenna. In a few minutes he returned and told the farmer he had found the problem. The antenna had been installed on top of the windmill and grounded to the manure spreader. The repairman sagely remarked, 'GAA pundits are like nappies. They need to be changed often and for the same reason.'

The media has played a huge role in driving the popularity of the GAA, but the relationship can be problematic. In 2012, after managing Donegal to only their second All-Ireland final win, Jim McGuinness would not agree to a press conference unless Declan Bogue, a journalist who had written a book that included co-operation from the former Donegal player Kevin Cassidy, left the room.

In the 1930s, the GAA entered a new era with the emergence of the greatest evangelist since St Paul. In 1938, Micheál O'Hehir made his first GAA commentary at the Galway–Monaghan All-Ireland football semi-final in Mullingar.

One of Gaelic football's great gentlemen and characters, Dermot O'Brien captained Louth to their third senior All-Ireland title in 1957. Of course he was equally famous for his powers on the accordion and his singing, and as one of Ireland's best loved show-business personalities he was responsible for hits like 'The Merry Ploughboy'. He had this to say about O'Hehir: 'Growing up there were few distractions apart from the wireless, with the wet batteries and dry batteries, and of course we listened to O'Hehir's commentaries religiously. Listening to the radio we never saw those great players, but Micheál, who really made the GAA, turned them into superheroes.

'Micheál O'Hehir was the man who brought Gaelic games in vivid form to the people of Ireland at a time when television was unknown and transistors unheard of. He showed that hurling and football, and games like that, are an art apart, their extent and depth perhaps not fully realised, rather merely accepted. He was a national institution. As we march, not always successfully, to the relentless demands of a faster, more superficial age, just to hear his voice was to know that all was well with the world. He painted pictures with words like a master craftsman. Young boys listening to him decided immediately they wanted to join the ranks of the football and hurling immortals. Irish sport is not the same without him. He was irreplaceable. Nobody ever did more for the GAA than him.'

# 23

# POETRY IN MOTION

*Monaghan's mighty mystic*

Monaghan currently have one of the greatest players of his generation in Clontibret's Conor McManus. However, they also produced perhaps the most famous man to play Gaelic games – and one of Ireland's greatest poets – Patrick Kavanagh.

An American film crew once went to make a documentary about Kavanagh in Inniskeen. When they visited the local pub they expected a great reception after they announced their mission, and went out of their way to state publicly, 'Patrick Kavanagh was a great poet.' The wind was taken out of their sails when one of the locals replied: 'Ah sure there's a man down the road, Peter Bunting, who could poetry the sh*te out of Kavanagh.'

Kavanagh was an abrasive character. He argued that all sporting subjects are 'superficial' and 'the emotion is a momentary puff of gas, not an experience'. The fact that Kavanagh's own sporting career was an unmitigated disaster may have fuelled his cynicism. Like Albert Camus, Pope John Paul II and Julio Iglesias, he was a goalkeeper. In the early 1930s he played for his local team, Inniskeen Grattans – succeeding Tom 'the Collier' Callan, who in the words of his brother Peter, was 'so stiff from farm work that he could only stop a ball that hit him'.

Kavanagh's most famous contribution was to wander off to buy either an ice cream or a drink, depending on whose version of events you listen to, while the opposition scored a goal between the deserted posts. The final ignominy came when he conceded the match-losing goal in the county final by letting the ball roll between his legs. His own supporters shouted, 'Go home and put an apron on you.'

His career as a sporting administrator fuelled even more venom. As club treasurer he kept club funds under his bed, which prompted some nasty rumours. Like Father Ted, who famously did not steal money but merely had it 'resting in his account', Kavanagh's own response to the innuendo was, 'It is possible that every so often I visited it for the price of a packet of cigarettes, but nothing serious.'

Kavanagh once took time off work on the 'stony, grey soil of Monaghan', to attend the county final. He was asked to predict the outcome of the match. After a dramatic pause, he responded, 'The first half will be even. The second half will be even worse.'

Once, having let in two soft goals, one of the fans shouted at him, 'Use your hands to stop the ball.'

The poet replied, 'That's what the f**king net is for.'

# 24

## COME ON THE ROSSIES

*Roscommon's golden era in the 1940s*

The 1940s saw the most glorious era in the history of Roscommon football, with the county's only All-Ireland successes in 1943 and 1944, both under the captaincy of Jimmy Murray.

Fifty years later, Murray told me: 'The first time I lined out in an All-Ireland final was in 1943, and an hour before we got to Dublin I was nearly standing up just to get my first glimpse of Croke Park. That was my dream come true.

'One of my most vivid memories of my playing career is of my brother, Phelim, telling me that the prince of midfielders, Paddy Kennedy, came over to him in the 1946 All-Ireland final and said, "Phelim, I think it's *your* All-Ireland." Phelim replied, "You never know, anything can happen, there's still over five minutes to go." Phelim's words were prophetic because Kerry got two goals in the dying minutes to draw the game, and went on to win the replay.'

Brendan Lynch was right half-back on that Roscommon team. He announced his arrival on the national stage in bold print in the All-Ireland semi-final against Louth.

'My lasting memory from the game was when the county secretary, John Joe Fahy, came running up to me at the end of the game and said, "Ye'll beat them in the second half if you play like that." I turned to him and said, "We have already." He looked shocked and said, "God did I miss it." He was so embroiled in the whole game, and the tension it created, that he had lost all track of time.'

It was not the medal that mattered to Lynch. 'The euphoria of winning was incredible. I felt like jumping out of my skin. I was on top of the world. I was twenty years of age and the world seemed my oyster. I've given away all my medals to my family. I read that Christy Ring had donated one of his All-Ireland medals to the foreign missions, and I did the same. It was the sense of achievement that mattered most to me.'

Roscommon had a slice of luck before claiming a second title in 1944: 'Sligo drew with us in the first round of the Connacht Championship in Boyle. They should have beaten us. We were lucky to survive. There were only two thousand people in attendance when we played Mayo in the Connacht final because of the transport problems during the War. We were worried by Cavan at half-time in the All-Ireland semi-final, but they collapsed completely in the second half and we had an easy win. The belief then was that you hadn't really won an All-Ireland until you beat Kerry in a final so we were all keen to do that. I was marking the famous Paddy Bawn Brosnan. He was a fisherman and fond of the women, fond of the porter, and fond of the rough and tumble!

'I made the most impact on their great midfielder Paddy Kennedy when I had a head collision with him and he had to be stretchered off. He asked me, "Jaysus what did you do to me?"'

Roscommon were not to recapture the same winning

feeling again. 'We were unlucky with illness. Phelim Murray got TB and spent twelve months in a sanatorium. I would consider Phelim to be Roscommon's best ever footballer. The nearest to him I have seen since was Dermot Earley, who was close to perfect. TB also finished Liam Gilmartin's career. We also lost John Joe Nerney, so we were never the same force again.

'Mayo beat us in the first round of the championship in 1945. We were suffering from burnout and they were hungry. It was a relief in a way because you had the chance to take holidays. I met Jimmy Murray that summer and he asked me how I was finding the summer without football. When I said I thought it was great, he told me he felt the same.'

Roscommon were to come within a whisker of taking another All-Ireland in 1946.

'It was a Mickey Mouse ruling in the GAA that cost us the title. We played Mayo in the Connacht final in Ballinasloe. They had a goal disallowed and then we got a goal that was going to be disallowed. Jimmy Murray grabbed the green flag and waved it and we were awarded the goal. After the game, Mayo lodged an objection. What should have happened was that the referee should have produced his report saying Roscommon won the match, and that would have been that. Instead we had to go into a replay and on top of the heavy collective training we were doing we didn't need another match. We lost Frank Kinlough with a leaky valve in his heart, and Doc Callaghan, our full-back, was injured. By the time we faced Kerry in the All-Ireland final replay they were getting stronger and we were getting weaker. I was never as happy as when the final whistle sounded in that game because the whole year, with the two replays and all the collective training, had been absolutely exhausting.

'It finished us as a team. We lost to Cavan in the All-Ireland semi-final in 1947, which meant they went on to play in the Polo Grounds instead of us. I didn't begrudge them. It was only right that players like John Joe O'Reilly finally won an All-Ireland.'

# 25

# HAT-TRICK HERO

*Kilkenny vs Tipperary 1954*

When he scored three goals in the 1954 National League final against Kilkenny, Tipperary's Billy Quinn, father of soccer star Niall, was propelled into national prominence. From an early age his career had promised much.

'When I was fourteen, in 1950, I was brought on as a sub in the All-Ireland final against Kilkenny. Tipperary had won all their matches up to then by a cricket score, so I never got a chance to come on and get used to the thing. It was crazy to bring me on for my first match in an All-Ireland final, because I had no idea where I was or what I was doing.

'I captained the minor team to an All-Ireland title in 1953. There was no real pressure on me. All I had to do was to call the toss and collect the cup! The only work I had to do was before the All-Ireland final, when our goalie got a panic attack on the way out onto the pitch. The lads called me back and I got him back up against the wall of Hill 16. He was more afraid of me than of the opposition, and he went out and played a blinder.

'We were so used to winning that I got the cup and threw it somewhere and we went home. There was no celebration as such. The big thing was to win the Munster final. There were massive crowds at the Munster finals then; when you came out of the ground your feet would hardly touch the road because there'd be so many people.

'The big thrill was to be changing with the senior team. The Munster final in Killarney was a classic match, though I'd an awful experience when a Cork man dropped dead beside me with the excitement of the game. The crowd invaded the pitch a few times and Christy Ring had to escort the referee off the pitch.

'This was not a new thing. A decade earlier, such was the intensity of one Cork–Tipperary match that a man had to be anointed on the ground. The entire crowd knelt down as a mark of respect.'

Quinn's inter-county career coincided with a barren spell in Tipperary's fortunes in the championship.

'We played Cork in 1956 and Séamus Bannon got the best goal I ever saw when he ran down the wing and lashed the ball into the net. But one of our lads threw his hurley twenty yards in celebration, the referee disallowed the goal, and Cork beat us. It was the greatest injustice I ever saw in hurling. We got dog's abuse listening in to the All-Ireland in Thurles because everyone was saying, "Ye should be there if ye were any good."

'I think the 1950s were a golden era for hurling, because you had a lot of great teams, like Cork, Tipperary and Wexford. Not only had you great players on all those teams, but go back and you'll find that each of those counties had five or six great players competing for each position. Christy Ring was the greatest player of the time, but Jimmy Doyle would run him a close second. He would get scores from left or right.'

In 1956 Quinn moved to Dublin for work reasons and although he played a few games for his adopted county, his commitment to their cause was not total, as there was always talk of a recall to the Tipp side. This indecision cost him the opportunity to play in an All-Ireland senior final.

'Dublin had a great team then, with exceptional players like Lar Foley, Des Foley and Des Ferguson. I thought I was going to go back playing for Tipperary, but I'm half sorry I didn't pursue the opportunity to play for Dublin more. They only lost the All-Ireland final to Tipperary by a point in 1961.'

# 26

## WEXFORD'S WONDER WIN

*Cork vs Wexford 1956*

Everyone has their favourite memory of Micheál O'Hehir. If he could only be remembered for one broadcast, I would like to suggest the 1956 final between Cork and Wexford, one of the greatest hurling finals of all time – which will be remembered, above all, for Art Foley's save from Christy Ring. Anyone who ever saw either Christy Ring or Art Foley play would, listening to O'Hehir, have a very clear mental picture of the handshake that passed between them after the save.

It was a match which captured the imagination like few others. Tradition favoured Cork. Going into the game they had won twenty-two titles against Wexford's two. Such was the interest in Wexford that two funerals scheduled for the day of the final had to be postponed until the following day because the hearses were needed to transport people to the match! Over eighty-three thousand people attended, but the match had to be delayed until 23 September because of a polio scare in Cork – the authorities didn't want a huge crowd assembling in any one place.

The crucial contest was that between Christy Ring, playing at left corner-forward and Bobby Rackard. Ring went into the match in search of a record nine All-Ireland senior medals, having won his first in 1941. Outside of Munster, Cork's greatest rivals were Wexford at the time. It was the Wexford man who would win out in every sense.

Wexford had the advantage of a whirlwind start with a goal from Padge Keogh after only three minutes. Two minutes later Ring registered Cork's first score with a point from a twenty-one-yard free. Wexford went on to win by 2-14 to 2-8.

Wexford had a special place in Ring's affections: 'We in Cork treated Tipperary as our greatest rivals, but I always loved our clashes with Wexford in Croke Park. It was a different climate in Croke Park because you didn't have the pressure of the Munster Championship on your back. It was the same for Wexford, they didn't have the pressure of beating Kilkenny on them. Both of us could relax a bit.'

Mick Dunne believes the credit for Wexford's triumph goes largely to one man. 'Nicky Rackard was one of the most colourful characters I ever met. He changed the whole sporting and social structure of Wexford. He went to St Kieran's College in Kilkenny, where he developed a love for hurling which he brought home to his brothers and to his club, Rathnure. Wexford had traditionally been a football power going back to their famous four-in-a-row side. But Nicky Rackard turned Wexford, almost overnight, into a recognised hurling bastion. He was crucial to Wexford's two All-Irelands in 1955 and 1956. It was a tragedy that he died so young. As people know, he had his problems with the drink, but I spoke to his brother, Bobby, at his funeral who told me it was a great shame he died because he had been doing great work for Alcoholics Anonymous at the time.'

# 27

# THE TERRIBLE TWINS

*Galway win the 1956 All-Ireland*

When I asked Mícheál Ó Muircheartaigh who was the greatest footballer of all time he gave me an interesting, albeit indirect, answer.

'That's too hard a question. I will say though that the best display I ever saw was by Galway's Seán Purcell. Most people remember him as a great Galway forward and for his association with Frankie Stockwell. Mayo had the best full-forward of the time, some would say of all time, Tom Langan, and Galway pulled off a shock move by bringing Seán back to mark him, and he gave the finest performance I ever saw. I saw him later that year in the All-Ireland semi-final against Kerry, and he was outstanding. Kerry were winning well and late in the game Galway moved him to midfield and he almost swung it for them. He had such skill and style that you could play him anywhere.'

The 1956 All-Ireland final, when Galway beat Cork by 2-13 to 3-7, was the apex of Purcell's achievement, as he recalled to me before his death in 2005: 'We had a great lead at half-time, and Cork came back to us in a big way. They really put it up to us and they got back within a point or so. We were lucky enough to get back one or two points at the end.

'We got a wonderful reception at home. I remember that quite well, coming from Dublin into Tuam. By present day standards the crowd was not huge but it was a great night. The match was broadcast around the town that day and there would have been a great spirit of victory around the place. When we arrived in Tuam I think the crowd met us and we were carried shoulder-high or on the lorry down to the town.'

That 1956 final turned Frank Stockwell into one of the GAA immortals. The late RTÉ Gaelic games correspondent Mick Dunne, coined the phrase 'the terrible twins', to describe Seán Purcell's unique partnership with Frank Stockwell. He explained the origin of the phrase to me: 'Galway's Seán Purcell was the best player I ever saw. It could be said that there were better players in different positions but as far as I'm concerned he was the best all-round footballer. I remember him at full-back in the Connacht semi-final in 1954 against Mayo. It was one of the finest individual displays I've ever seen. He played on the great Tom Langan, then Danny Neill and then John Nallen, but it was all the same, Purcell was superb. He was also a magnificent midfielder and he was the brains of the Galway team that won the All-Ireland in 1956 at centre-forward. He destroyed the Cork defence on his own. He had such a wonderful combination with the other Galway maestro, Frankie Stockwell, and they performed such a lethal duo that I described them as the terrible twins, and to my pleasant surprise the phrase entered the GAA vernacular about them.'

In conversation with me, Seán Purcell reserved special praise for Stockwell: 'We were known as the terrible twins because we had such a great understanding, and because we did a lot of damage to opposing defences. Frank was a fabulous footballer. It was just a matter of getting the ball in to him the best way we could. We tried all the old tricks we had worked on over the years. Things were much less scientific, I suppose, than they are now. We all contributed to each other, but we all knew Frank was the man to give the ball to and he'd do the rest. The fact that he scored 2-5 in the 1956 All-Ireland final speaks for itself. They were all off his foot, no frees. You have to remember, that was a sixty-minute final. I'm great friends with Jimmy Keaveney, but when he broke Frank's record by scoring 2-6 in the 1977 All-Ireland final, he had a seventy-minute game to do it in.'

# 28

## GALWAY GREATS

*Galway win three in a row in the 1960s*

Grace is but glory begun, and glory is grace perfected. The Galway team made each game they played in Croke Park a day of grace and glory. Their late captain, Enda Colleran, had furnished me with some revealing insights into Galway's three-in-a-row win. His first taste of All-Ireland success in 1964 was shrouded in sadness: 'After half-time, John Donnellan and I were walking out together. John was right half-back and I was right full. He turned to me and said, "I think there's a row in the stand." In one portion of the stand there was an awful lot of people moving around and I said to him, "There must be." We didn't take any more notice at all. We played the second half and we won. We were in such good form but I noticed our officials were very subdued when they came in.

'We went into the dressing room after all the presentations. John said, "I want to go out to show the cup to the old man." Up to that they couldn't get an opportunity to take him aside and tell him. At that stage they had to tell him, and then everybody changed. Actually, it wasn't a row at half-time but John's father had passed away in the stand. John's father had captained Galway and was a fantastic footballer. He died that day.

'It's amazing really, you think that an All-Ireland is the most important thing, but everything changed, the atmosphere was totally subdued, as you would expect. The next evening the Sam Maguire Cup was brought home in a funeral cortege rather than with a blaze of glory as is the norm. In fact, Mick Higgins, who played on the same team as him, was actually watching the game at home when he collapsed and died as well. According to rumour, when Mick Donnellan went to heaven and reached the gates, St Peter said to him, "Who won the All-Ireland?" And he said, "When I was leaving Galway were winning well, but Mick Higgins will be up soon and he'll have the final score."

'When we played Kerry in the All-Ireland final in 1965 they had a very physical side and hit us with everything. Mattie McDonagh was concussed during the game, but played on. That's the sort of man he was. He was going to put the team before his own health. He was a real father figure to that team. When I became captain I felt at first that he really should have been captain because he had won an All-Ireland medal eight years before the rest of us. Thinking he should have been captain raised my own performance because I knew if I didn't, I would feel terrible about it because I would have been letting Mattie down. Then I grew into the captain's role and became confident in it.'

A more tense occasion came when Galway were to face the favourites, Meath, in the All-Ireland. Colleran was due to mark sprint-champion Ollie Shanley, who had given a top-class performance in the semi-final.

'Everybody was saying to me, "You've an awful job in the final to mark him, you'll never mark him." Martin Newell and I went out to the Aran Islands for a few days, just before we started training for the All-Ireland final, and were sleeping in the one room; he was on one side and I on the other. He woke up at one stage of the night and I was standing over him. I was sleep walking! Martin told me the next day that I said, "By Jaysus, if I can keep up with Shanley, I'll mark him." It just shows you the pressure I was under.'

What was the secret of Galway's success?

'We had that vital ingredient you need if you are to win anything, that bit of luck. I think back especially to the Connacht Championship in 1965. Both Sligo and Mayo should have beaten us. It was there for them if they kept their heads. We were in terrible trouble against Sligo after they got two early goals but we just sneaked victory by three points. Against Mayo, we were losing by a point in the dying minutes, when they got a fifty-yard free. Three Mayo players were fighting over who should take it when one of them rushed up and kicked it straight to one of our half-backs. He then cleared it up the field in return, and we got the equalising point. And then we got the winning point almost immediately.'

Enda had no hesitation when I asked him his outstanding personal memory from the three-in-a-row triumph: 'It was the All-Ireland semi-final against Down in 1965, my best ever game. The ironic thing was that I had a terrible start to the match. I was marking Brian Johnson and he scored two points off me in the first few minutes. I felt that if I didn't get my act together he would end up as man of the match and decided to change my tactics. Down were storming our goal for most of the second half and I found that no matter where

I went, the ball seemed to land into my hands. I seemed to be in the right place all the time and made all the right decisions. Often I took terrible decisions, and went forward and left my man, and still the ball came to me. I was so thankful that a thing like that happened to me in an All-Ireland semi-final rather than in a challenge game with two men and a dog watching.

'At one stage Seán O'Neill had the ball around midfield and Paddy Doherty, completely unmarked, came at speed to the full-forward position. I had two options: one was to stay on my own man and the other was that Seán O'Neill would pass the ball to Paddy Doherty. I took the chance and ran for Paddy Doherty. O'Neill passed the ball to him, and I can actually remember coming behind Paddy, trying not to make any noise, so that he wouldn't hear me coming towards him, and at the last second I nipped in front of him and got possession. I felt he had a certain goal, only for that. It's amazing, with sixty thousand people present I still thought my approach had to be as quiet as possible.'

# 29

# DONKEYS DON'T WIN DERBIES

*The 1990 Munster final*

With typical reserve Nicky English makes no mention of an incident in the 1991 All-Ireland semi-final against Galway when he was struck a blow above the left eye, which might have caused him permanent eye injury, but which required nine stitches and caused a flow of blood which came with the intensity of the Niagara Falls. Despite repeated nudges, no comments on the incident are supplied.

'We won the All-Ireland again in '91, and it was important to us that we beat Kilkenny in the final since there were those who devalued our win in '89, because it was Antrim we beat and not one of the powers of hurling. Of course that's very unfair on Antrim, but we had to show to the hurling world that we were worthy of a place at hurling's top table. My hamstring went in that year and I came back too soon for the semi-final against Galway, and it went again. It went a third time because I didn't make it through the final. I think although we won the All-Ireland, the injuries were starting to catch up; and although we won the Munster title in '93 and a league in '94, we never could scale those heights again.

'I was also glad we won for Babs Keating's sake. He knew how to get the best out of us. There was the odd blip though. He once faced the problem of rallying us even though we were trailing Cork by eight points at half-time in a league match. After a number of inspirational words in an effort to instil confidence, Babs went around the team individually and asked each of them, "Can we do it?"

'To a man we replied, "We can. We can."

'He could feel the surge of belief invading the dressing room. Everything was going swimmingly until he turned to Joe Hayes and asked, "Joe, can we do it?"

'Joe took the wind out of his sails when he replied, "It's not looking good!"'

Nicky is keen to defend Babs from one long-running criticism. Keating's comments that, 'You can't win derbies with donkeys', before Tipperary played Cork in the 1990 Munster final, was seen as a spectacular own-goal when the Cork donkeys won.

'We did make mistakes in terms of selection for that match. I think after we won the All-Ireland in '89, our first in eighteen years, we coasted a bit and never had the same application as the previous year. We went to Toronto for a week in March to play the All-Stars, and that was another distraction. When Cork beat us, Babs was blamed for his remarks. People said that because it suited them. It might have been used as a motivational tool in Cork, but it was not the reason we lost. Cork were hungrier than us and that was the crucial difference.'

Babs addresses his controversial comments head on: 'It was a stupid remark and no more than that. It was used against us that year. We were decimated with injuries. It was a bluff game with us. We had no sub for the backline with injuries. We took a chance with Declan Ryan at full-forward, even though he was lifting bales with his father the day before and he just wasn't fit to hurl. Mark Foley got three goals that day and he never played liked that before or since.

'The next year both Mark Foley and the Cork full-back Richard Browne didn't perform well. Both of them are dentists. The boys in one of the pubs in Clonmel put up a sign, "Wanted for Cork: a centre-forward and full-back. Dentists need not apply."

'I knew we needed to win a second All-Ireland to be seen as a great team. We had one thing mitigating against us. I brought eleven subs with us on our trip to Florida and the Bahamas, but none of them really contributed to the team afterwards. We needed to find one or two new players to cover for injuries and we didn't. The underage teams weren't going as well as I would have liked and Nicky, basically, didn't play in '91 because of injuries.'

# 30

# MIGHTY MEATH

*Seán Boylan wins four All-Irelands*

Graeme Souness said, 'I have come to the conclusion that nice men do not make good managers.' Seán Boylan is the exception that proves the rule.

Yet he has an inner steel to him. In 1987 he sensationally resigned as Meath manager because he felt that the team needed to make a bigger effort in training. The players asked Joe Cassells to ring him and persuade him to return. The call was made and a change of heart ensued. At the first training session afterwards Boylan said, 'I believe I owe you ten pence for the phone call.'

To riotous laughter from the Meath squad Cassells replied, 'Nah, it's okay, I reversed the charges.'

Boylan's reign did not begin with titles. In 1983, the Royal County lost to the Dubs in the early rounds of the Leinster Championship. He laughs at the memory of one comic incident from that match.

'It was shortly after I became manager and Dublin were playing Meath in Croke Park. I wanted to make a positional change during the match and walked down along the side-line behind the goal in front of Hill 16 and all the Dublin fans were jeering me and slagging me. It was all in a good-natured way and there was no malice in it whatsoever. Because I was so new in the job and Meath weren't having huge success at the time this Garda came racing up to me and thought I was just a fan! I had a fierce problem convincing him that I was actually the Meath manager. After a lot of cajoling I eventually persuaded him of my identity and I said to him, "You do your job and look after the spectators, and let me do my job and look after these lads on the pitch." After we had finished our "chat" I walked back in front of the Hill again. This time the Dublin fans gave me a great ovation. They thought I was a hero because I had stood up to and had a big row with a guard!'

Meath seemed to have turned a corner when they won the Centenary Cup in 1984, to mark the GAA's 100th anniversary, by beating a strong Monaghan side in the final. Later that year they reached the Leinster final and ran Dublin to four points. But it was back to the bad old days in 1985 when they suffered a humiliating defeat at the hands of Laois in the Leinster Championship by 2-11 to 0-7 in Tullamore. Questions were asked about Boylan's stewardship, and he had to survive a vote at a County Board meeting to remain in office.

Although it was without doubt a low point for the Meath team it proved to be a blessing in disguise. Boylan found six new players who would play key roles in the coming years: Terry Ferguson, Kevin Foley, Liam Harnan, David Beggy, P. J. Gillic and Brian Stafford.

The tide finally turned when Meath beat Dublin in the 1986 Leinster final. Meath went on to win back-to-back

All-Irelands in 1987 and '88. They also won five out of six Leinster titles from 1986 to 1991 in the greatest run in the county's history, losing All-Ireland finals in 1990 and 1991 to Cork and Down respectively.

Dublin reigned supreme in Leinster from 1992–5. Boylan faced another apparent crisis in '95 when Meath lost the Leinster final to their great Dublin rivals by ten points. Boylan had to face another election. Again Seán reacted to major defeat by rebuilding the Meath team and was rewarded with another All-Ireland title in 1996. Not for the first time, Boylan's career served as a parable of the power of persistence. Three years later he took Meath to another All-Ireland title when they beat Cork in the final. After an incredible twenty-three years managing Meath, Boylan finally stepped down from this demanding job in 2005.

Pat Spillane offers an assessment of Boylan: 'I have no problem in saying that Seán is the second greatest manager I've ever came across in Gaelic football behind Mick O'Dwyer. He has had a remarkable career at the top level for over twenty years. He is an absolute gentleman.

'Where he differs from Dwyer is that he brought three different teams to All-Ireland glory: the '87 and '88 team, the '96 team, and the team he won the '99 title with, which featured some very average players. His greatest achievement was that he was able to take very ordinary club players and transform them into ferocious competitors who were willing to die for the Meath jersey.

'People often say Meath footballers are dogged, determined and stubborn – and that's only the nice things they say about them. A lot of players have the attitude of never going for a 50–50 ball unless they're 80–20 sure of winning it. Meath players never had that problem.

'The jury will always remain out about who, when Meath were regarded as "tough" and "hard", was responsible for their at times "over robust" tactics. Was it Boylan, or his senior players? It is something that I have never been able to get an answer to.'

The original 'Navan man', Tommy Tiernan, has offered a characteristically unique analysis of Boylan's team: 'They were what real men were supposed to be. They looked like they were dragged off the farm at dawn and were going back to work on the land after the match – apart from Liam Hayes, who was a bit of a god. He was almost good looking.'

# 31

# MORGAN'S MAESTROS

*Cork's double double 1990*


Teddy McCarthy had an unforgettable year in 1990 when he starred in Cork's double senior All-Ireland wins in both football and hurling. To add to his joy, the footballers were winning back-to-back All-Irelands. Behind every great player is a great manager.

In any conversation of the greatest Gaelic football team of all time, Billy Morgan is always a strong contender for goalkeeper. He was a great reader of the game, superb organiser of defenders, inspirational leader and had excellent reflexes, and he brought all of these qualities to the manager's job.

Much of Cork's success in the late 1980s and early 1990s can be attributed to Billy Morgan. He brought a very professional approach which involved drawing on the expertise of other experts.

It is a great tribute to Morgan, that when Kerry played Cork in the Munster Championship in 2004, Kerry fans were worried not because of any of the Cork players, but because of the admiration they had for Morgan's record against Kerry down the years. Their fears were totally unjustified as Cork had little to offer.

One of the Cork stars, when they regained the All-Ireland in 1990, was John Cleary – a very accurate forward though not the biggest man in the world. Before one of Cork's clashes with Kerry, Jack O'Shea came up to him and in an effort to psyche him out said, 'You're too small and too young for a game like this.' Cleary said nothing until after the game when Cork emerged triumphant and as he walked off the pitch past Jacko he softly said, 'You're too old for a game like this.'

Pat Spillane has a typically different take on this era: 'In Cork, at the very mention of my name, they all burst into song. Mind you the song they sing is 'The Langer!'

'When people think of the great Kerry team of the 1970s and 1980s, they automatically assume that our greatest rivals were Dublin. However, Cork generally pushed us to the pin of our collar. I gave a talk at the Jurys Sportstar of the Year awards – talk about meeting the enemies – and Niall Cahalane was in the audience. He was probably the most difficult player I ever marked. I told the crowd that Niall had such a love of the Kerry jersey that he used to collect bits and pieces of my Kerry jersey by marking me so closely, all through the years.

'In my time, Cork and Kerry players always enjoyed an intense, but generally good-natured, rivalry. To fully understand the rivalry in my playing days, we have to look to Ambrose O'Donovan. His farm in Gneevgullia straddled the Cork–Kerry border. He is a lovely guy, but when we played Cork it was like he was transformed – like Lou Ferrigno into the Incredible Hulk. He had an absolute hatred of losing to Cork. His attitude was that if we beat them in the Munster final that would keep them quiet for twelve months. When Kerry lose to Cork in the Munster Championship, the Cork fans will stay in Kenmare all night. When Cork lose they drive straight through Kenmare at 5.30 that evening as fast as they can.

'Billy Morgan's leadership and motivation is second-to-none, and has two All-Irelands with Cork in 1989 and 1990. He will probably rank as one of the greatest club managers of all time with Nemo Rangers. I have heard it said that he would die for Nemo, but would only get wounded for Cork. He can have a short fuse and you wouldn't want to be around him then. He is a real gentleman though.'

# 32

# THE REVOLUTION YEARS

*Hurling in the 1990s*

Conventional hurling wisdom has the 1990s hailed as 'the revolution years', when Clare, Offaly and Wexford eclipsed the traditional superpowers of Kilkenny, Cork and Tipperary. Mícheál Ó Muircheartaigh is the ideal candidate to offer a balanced perspective on the developments in hurling during this era. He believes that history teaches us that hurling is always in a state of revolution.

'I think that hurling has changed a lot for the better, and many of the players – and this has amazed me because generally a lot of players hang on to the theory that their own generation was the best – that hurled maybe thirty years ago are admitting that the modern generation of hurlers are better than they were. I think that video evidence would swing you around to that view. There is a greater emphasis on skill now. In the past, the man was played more in hurling. Now, it was never as bad as football, but there was a lot of holding in the old days: for example, full-backs penned into the forwards, they held on to their man when the ball came in and kept their man away from the goalie, that would all be deemed a foul nowadays. The emphasis now is on speed and skill, and I think hurling is better for that.

'When you talk about the great teams, it's not nearly as clear-cut in hurling as it is in football. If I were pushed to it, I would say that the best hurling team, with the emphasis on *team*, that I ever saw, was the Kilkenny team of the early 1970s. They won the All-Ireland in '72, '74 and '75, and played the final in 1973 against Limerick. Limerick had a great side in 1973, with the likes of Pat Hartigan and Eamonn Grimes, and they had to have in order to beat that wonderful Kilkenny team. Of course, they pulled off a master-stroke deciding out of the blue to play Eamonn Cregan, possibly the greatest forward Limerick ever had, at centre half-back, to counter Pat Delaney.

'When I think of Kilkenny's wonderful games of the time, usually in Leinster finals and especially against Wexford – who had a great team but who couldn't get the better of Kilkenny – I think they were good in all sectors. Take Eddie Keher in the full-forward line, Pat Delaney at centre-forward, Frank Cummins in midfield, Pat Henderson at centre half-back. They had super men in all parts of the field and played like a team.

'I suppose though I'd have to single out Eddie Keher from that team as one of the all-time greats. I always say that to score a point in an All-Ireland final is something special for a player. I could be wrong now, but I think that he scored seven goals and seventy-seven points in All-Ireland finals alone. What memories must that man have? That tally is a measure of the man's greatness.

'DJ Carey was a star. There was no doubt about it. The crowd got very excited when the ball came towards him. He had speed and tremendous skill. On his day he was unbeatable. Often, on the day of a match when a guy shines, you'll be asked if he is the greatest player you ever saw. I always say that you have to wait a few years after a guy retires to judge him properly. Eddie Keher played senior for Kilkenny for the first time in 1959, having starred in the minor All-Ireland final that year. The senior final ended in a draw and he was drafted on as a sub for the replay. He was still playing for the seniors in 1977, so apart from his superb skill, the fact that he remained at the top for so long was also a factor.

'Then, just as we thought standards could not possibly go any higher, Brian Cody came on the scene, and we all know what happened next. So, for me, it is more about evolution than revolution.'

# 33

# THE DJ FINAL

*Offaly vs Kilkenny 2000*

In the beginning, God and DJ Carey were seen as quite separate individuals. It was only later that confusion crept in.

One story illustrates DJ's status in the game. The 'All-Heaven' hurling final was taking place between Kilkenny and Tipperary. The Tipperary team were powered by some of the giants of deceased hurlers. The Kilkenny team, likewise, had the pick of players from their county who had gone on to their eternal reward, and were captained by Ollie Walsh. With just three minutes to go, Tipperary were leading by three goals and two points. Suddenly, there was a gasp from the crowd as a sub appeared on the Kilkenny team wearing the number 14 jersey. In the final three minutes, four balls were pumped into the square and the super-sub stuck each of them in the net. The Cats won by a point. After the game was over St Peter went over to commiserate with the Tipperary stars. The Tipp players were stunned by the appearance of the sub and asked, 'I never knew DJ Carey died. When did it happen?'

St Peter replied, 'Oh that's not DJ. That's God. He just thinks he's DJ Carey.'

Mind you, a prophet is not always appreciated in his own land. In 1997, before Clare played Kilkenny in the All-Ireland semi-final, Ger Loughnane was asked in an interview what he thought of DJ. He had been absolutely brilliant in the All-Ireland quarter-final in a thrilling game against Galway in Thurles. He practically beat the Westerners all on his own. Loughnane said, 'DJ will prove himself to be an outstanding player when he plays really well against one of the best players in the country in a big match. Next Sunday, he will be playing in a really big match against Brian Lohan, and if he plays really well against Brian, he will prove himself to be a really great player. But I won't regard him as a great player until he does it against somebody like Brian on the big day.'

Nickey Brennan was Kilkenny manager then, and he taped the interview and played it on the bus on the way to the match. According to folklore Nickey said, 'Listen to what that c**t Loughnane said about one of our best players.' Legend has it that Eddie O'Connor is supposed to have piped up, 'He's f**king right!'

A major controversy erupted when DJ was omitted from the official GAA Team of the Millennium. The 2000 All-Ireland final, when Kilkenny beat Offaly comprehensively and DJ was sensational in an undisputed 'man of the match' performance, added fuel to the fire.

Ger Loughnane was pleased for him: 'Everybody knew DJ was a special talent. The perception though was that he had never delivered on the big day, which is the ultimate test of greatness. I have no doubt that perception cost him his place on the Team of the Millennium. In the 2000 All-Ireland final he took control from the start and scored a goal early on which meant Offaly were reeling. He was unmarkable that day, and proved to everybody that on the biggest occasion he was a class apart. That is why that final has special significance for hurling fans and hurling historians alike.'

Nicky English also shares in the plaudits for DJ: 'It is hard to compare players. DJ was one of the best I've ever seen. He had such skill, great hunger, and could get inspirational scores, but above all he had blinding pace and no defender could handle him at his best. In a different way, Henry Shefflin was also an outstanding player and one of the greats. For such a big man he has such skill. I was close to him in the stand when he hit the first ball against Waterford from close to the sideline in the 2008 All-Ireland final. I knew from the sound of the ball hitting the hurley that he had caught it sweetly and I didn't even have to look, I knew it was going over the bar. The only other time I've heard that sound was Tommy Dunne's first ball in the 2001 All-Ireland final. Again I didn't need to look. It was going to take an exceptional player to come out of DJ's shadow and Henry did that.'

# 34

# GALWAY SHOCK MEATH

*The 2001 All-Ireland final*

After trouncing Kerry in the All-Ireland semi-final in 2001, Meath were almost unbackable favourites when they played Galway in the All-Ireland final. Most pundits were left eating humble pie as the Westerners ran out comfortable winners. Pat Spillane believes much of the credit for Galway's victory goes to one man.

'John O'Mahony is a very astute, shrewd manager, who is most meticulous in his preparation. The great managers are often not easy men. They have to be driven by an endless quest to avoid the inevitable, to minimise risks and to maximise potential. Management is a process of replacing one anxiety with another. O'Mahony is noted for his attention to detail. You can never leave anything to chance if you want to be successful. In 2002, the Irish rugby team visited Siberia to play a match in an area renowned for its freezing temperatures. The players can normally get everything they need, but on this trip, incredibly, they found there was one thing they couldn't get – ice cubes! I bet if John O'Mahony was in charge the ice cubes would be there.

'John always has excellent video analysis. After taking Mayo to the All-Ireland final in 1989 the Mayo County Board were almost criminally negligent in the way they treated him. If they had kept faith in him, they would by now have the All-Ireland they craved for so long.

'One of the main reasons why Connacht teams generally struggled so badly in Croke Park in the 1980s and early 1990s was a lack of top-class forwards. Under O'Mahony, Galway had two of the top forwards in the game, Padraic Joyce and Michael Donnellan. Joyce was one of the game's most accurate kickers of the ball. One thing I've always found strange is the way commentators refer to players like him as having a "cultured left foot". Why is it that they never speak of having a cultured right foot?

'Michael Donnellan was one of the great enigmas of Gaelic football, capable of going from hero to zero in the one game. One of the great sights in Gaelic football was seeing Donnellan gathering the ball in defence, soloing up the field, and getting a great point, or, more significantly, one of his trademark goals. To take just one example, people will long recall his great goal against Kerry in the All-Ireland quarter-final in 2002. If he had a problem, it was that there seemed to be a difficult relationship between himself and John O'Mahony, but sometimes you wondered about his temperament. I often think that had Mick O'Dwyer, with his famed man-management skills, been in charge of him, he would have gone on to be one of the greatest players of all time.'

Spillane though believes this was not O'Mahony's greatest achievement: 'I think I got a few brownie points, a very rare occurrence, when after John O'Mahony guided them to only their second Connacht title in 1994, after they beat Mayo in the Connacht final, I said: "Leitrim for Croke Park. Mayo for Croagh Patrick."

'Winning two All-Irelands with Galway was an incredible achievement for O'Mahony, but winning the Connacht title with Leitrim was arguably even greater.'

Between both jobs, after the intercession of Sean Kilbride, he had a stint in Roscommon, and in his one year there he guided St Brigids to their first county title in twenty-eight years. He was then also involved when the club won their first Connacht title, and he created a culture in the club that would eventually see them claim an All-Ireland club title under Kevin McStay. Pat Spillane though sees a flaw.

'The one thing I found frustrating about John O'Mahony was his fence-sitting in interviews. Of course he was not alone in that. I would like all managers to be more forthcoming in the media. GAA managers should learn from Harry Redknapp: when asked about taking the job of Portsmouth manager he replied, "Why did I take the job? Skint."'

# 35

# LAOIS LEAD THE PACK IN LEINSTER

*Laois win the 2003 Leinster final*

In 2003 Laois and Kildare clashed for the first time in the Leinster final since 1946. Laois raced into an early lead, with Ian Fitzgerald in particular playing well in the early stages, and by half-time Laois led by 0-8 to 0-6. Laois struck for two goals on the resumption of play through Beano McDonald and Ross Munnelly, and it looked like Mick O'Dwyer's side were going to cruise to victory. Helped by a well-taken Ronan Sweeney penalty, Kildare managed to get themselves level as they entered the final stages. But Laois dug deep and kicked the final three points of the game through Donal Miller, Ian Fitzgerald and Barry Brennan, to seal a famous 2-13 to 1-13 win. Seamus McCormack's final whistle signalled unprecedented scenes of joy for the Laois fans. After his success in Kerry and Kildare, it was a case of Mick O'Dwyer sprinkling his magic dust again.

Pat Spillane has a very vivid memory of O'Dwyer's involvement with Laois.

'The morning after the 2003 RTÉ Sportstar of the Year

awards ceremony, I woke up with the mother of all hangovers. It could have been worse. The same night Britney Spears got married in haste when under the influence. She regretted it the next morning!

'What galls me to this day is that I was thinking of all the people I had spoken to that night and I can't remember a single thing they said. I spoke at length with John Delaney of the Football Association of Ireland (FAI) – he told me the real story of what happened in Saipan. I spoke for ages with Louis Kilcoyne about what really happened to Shamrock Rovers in Milltown. I talked with Eamon Dunphy, and he explained in great detail to me why his television show had failed – the only thing I remember clearly is that he was very unhappy about a former Kerry footballer and manager who appeared not once but twice on the programme and failed to sparkle on either occasion. I spoke at length with Pat Devlin about his role in Damien Duff's transfer to Chelsea. If I could remember all these conversations I'd have enough for four books.

'That day, through bleary eyes, I scanned the newspapers. All the attention in the sports pages was on Páidí Ó Sé, in his first match in his new role as Westmeath manager. It was the day of his first competitive match in the O'Byrne Cup. I was talking with a friend of mine who had met Páidí the day before when he was out walking. Páidí told him that Westmeath "were playing some match tomorrow" but he didn't know what competition they were playing in.

'As I struggled to eat my breakfast I met Mick O'Dwyer. I marvelled at his enthusiasm. At sixty-six years of age he was about to head off to Dromard in Longford for a Mickey Mouse match in the O'Byrne Cup with Laois. What was bugging him? Martin Delaney couldn't play that day. He had the ebullience of a ten-year-old.'

Spillane was also taken by one more aspect of that Laois season: 'Laois's comprehensive victory over Meath in the Leinster semi-final was a great win for them. Nonetheless, I have to take my hat off yet again to Seán Boylan. He came on television straight after the defeat and said that Laois won because they were the best team. As always he was gracious and magnanimous in defeat. What always impressed me about him in those situations is that he never attempted to spin. Sadly, far too many managers do that today.'

# 36

# AMONGST WOMEN

*Cork Ladies rule the world in the 2000s*

Mirror, mirror on the wall, who is the fairest of them all?

Conventional wisdom is that the Kerry football team of the 1970s and 1980s is the greatest football team of all time. But, in recent years, the phenomenal success of the Dublin team under Jim Gavin has caused some to ask if *they* are the greatest team of all time. However, the statistics tell us very loudly that the Cork Ladies team of the 2000s and beyond are, in fact, the greatest team of all time.

From having never won a senior title, to winning ten All-Irelands in eleven years, nine league titles and ten Munster titles, their record is simply breathtaking. They made house-hold names of players like Valerie Mulcahy, and were led magnificently by the peerless Juliet Murphy, who ranks with Cora Staunton as one of the GAA immortals. Famously, in 2013, Murphy came out of retirement to lead Cork to another All-Ireland victory.

The legendary Neville Cardus was writing of his beloved cricket when he observed that 'a great game is part of the nation's life and environment; it is indeed an organism in an environment . . . as our great game is inevitably an expression in part of our spiritual and material condition as a nation and a people, it must go through metamorphoses; it must shed skins and grow new ones . . .' Cardus could easily have been writing about Gaelic games in the early years of the third millennium.

The GAA should not be arrogant enough to shut themselves off from learning lessons from other sports. If we take rugby, for example, the marketing of the All Blacks rugby team has been incredible. Sales of the famous black jersey have soared by the use of imaginative slogans like 'All jerseys keep you warm but only one makes you shiver.' Of course, there are lessons the GAA can learn from the mistakes of rugby, such as where the arrival of professionalism in one fell swoop, rather than as part of a carefully planned evolution, propelled the sport into a tailspin of administrative egos and red tape. But in some respects the GAA continues to be held back by administrators clinging to the rowing boats of the old ways and the mantra of amateurism. If it was good enough in the old days, it is not good enough now.

There is not a single boy in New Zealand who, because of all the glamour attached to them, doesn't dream of playing for the All Blacks. There was a time that used to be true in Ireland about the GAA, but not any more. But an increasing amount of girls are dreaming of playing in an All-Ireland final, in either camogie or ladies football. No team has done more to achieve this than the Cork Ladies team.

The manager of the Cork team, Eamonn Ryan, was not prepared to accept the old ways. His message was, 'As a team we were feared by everyone out there, but we don't believe in ourselves. The dream can become a reality if they want it bad enough, but they need to believe.'

He told the players to realise the sacrifices needed to get to the top. They had to be more committed, loyal to their teammates and play with pride in the jersey. There were to be no cliques, no gossip, and what was said in the dressing room, stayed in the dressing room.

Ryan invited Cork hurling icon Donal Óg Cusack to speak to the players, to give them a bit of advice and inspire them if he could. Cusack's stirring speech concluded with the exhortation: 'You can never be satisfied with just one All-Ireland, girls. This has to be the start of a much longer journey, remember that.'

They never forgot.

# 37

# FERMANAGH'S FUN FACTORY

*Fermanagh excel in the 2015 qualifiers*

Ulster Championship matches are renowned for their toughness. In 2002, former Monaghan manager Seán McCague, in his role as president of the GAA, expressed his unhappiness at the violence in the first International Rules test between Ireland and Australia. Reporting on McCague's disaffection on *Morning Ireland*, Des Cahill observed, 'He said he wasn't going to support the series' continuance.' Quick as a flash, Cathal Mac Coille quipped, 'Do you think the Ulster Championship is in danger?'

Pat Spillane is the best-known critic of Ulster football, but he wants to sing a hymn of praise to Fermanagh: 'I got a great insight into the Northern mentality at my first function in the North. It was a question and answer session in Coalisland in the early 1990s. You have to try and realise that they are coming at things from a totally different angle. I realised that when a fella put up his hand and asked me: "Do you know why Jack O'Shea never catches the ball at the throw-in?"

'I was puzzled and said I did not. He continued: "I'll tell

you why. It is because Jacko has a contract with Adidas, a foreign company, and that's why he never catches the ball in case he'd be photographed with it."

'In the circumstances, after I got over my initial shock at the suggestion, I thought the politic thing to say was, "You could be right."

'A personal experience of my own threw new light on this peculiar mentality for me. The Tyrone-based company Powerscreen sponsored the All-Star awards for a few years. In an effort to try and avoid some of the selection controversies they decided to get the players to nominate the All-Stars. In the middle of November that year I was stuck for something to write in my column, so I wrote an article on why I thought it was wrong for the players to make the selection. My argument was that they wouldn't have been in a position to see every player in the championship and, above all, some players are popular and some aren't. This meant that nice guys had a better chance of winning it than hard men, or guys who were unpopular with their peers. I thought that was not fair. At that time of the year, when things are slow, the All-Star selection is a hardy perennial for hard-pressed journalists stuck for something to write about, whether it's the selection process, the nominations or the final selection. I didn't think it would have any repercussions because it was such an innocuous article. Not for the first time, I was wrong.

'I had formed a very good relationship with one of the "head honchos" in Powerscreen. After the article he rang me to tell me that he wasn't very impressed. At first I thought it was a wind-up. I had the article in front of me and read it, and asked him if he was serious. He emphatically assured me that he was. I said, "I hope this is not going to affect our friendship."

'He replied, "It has."

'He's never spoken to me since and he's taken it on himself to become my bitter enemy.

'Another reason why Ulster football frustrates me so much in recent years, is that a win-at-all-costs mentality seems to dominate. It wasn't always like this. Tyrone really gave us a scare in the All-Ireland final in 1986. With a great display of positive football they had us on the ropes. Early in the second half we trailed them by seven points. And it could have been worse, had the Tyrone right half-back, Kevin McCabe, not blasted a penalty over the bar.'

In fairness to Spillane he also is keen to acknowledge the positive side.

'When I want to think very positively of Ulster football I do so by recalling the great town team managed by Pete McGrath, that won All-Irelands in 1991 and 1994 at a time when Ulster football ruled the roost. Tony O'Reilly tells a great story about Brendan Behan. Behan turned up on a chat show on Canadian television totally drunk. The presenter was very unimpressed and asked him why he was so drunk. Behan replied, "Well, a few weeks ago I was sitting in a pub in Dublin and I saw a sign on a beer mat which said: 'Drink Canada Dry.' So when I came over here I said I'd give it a go!" O'Reilly deftly uses that incident to speak of the need to have the kind of positive attitude that says, "I'll give it a go." That's the kind of upbeat mentality I would like to see Ulster teams coming in to Croke Park with, and Pete's team had that. Gaelic football at its best is the beautiful game – played with strength and speed, with courage and skill, with honesty and humour. It has the capacity to stop your heart and leave the indelible memory of a magic moment. Think back to that Down team of Pete's in the early 1990s, with a forward line of footballing artists like James MacCartan, Ross Carr, Mickey Linden and Greg Blaney. In full flight they were something unbelievable on the pitch: a miracle of speed, balance and intense athleticism; thoroughbreds leaving in their slipstream a trail of mesmerised defenders who had been as transfixed in wonder as the crowd were by their silken skills. This is why I wanted to play the beautiful game. Pete won two All-Irelands in 1991 and 1994 playing football the way it should be played, and I take my hat off to him.

'The icing on the cake came in 2015 with the great joy he brought to the championship when he brought Fermanagh back to Croke Park with a team who seemed to have discovered that Gaelic football is supposed to be fun. Fermanagh, I salute you.'

# PART IV

# The First Cut is the Deepest

The Saw Doctors sing of the glory when a team 'win just once'. The first All-Ireland, or provincial title, is always the sweetest. Memory rescues experience from total disappearance, and the lamp of memory holds traces and vestiges of everything that has ever happened to us. Nothing is ever lost or forgotten. It is important that the great virgin victories be stored in the popular imagination.

They symbolise all that is great in our games, have captivated the nation with feats of sublime skill and style, and have made a magnificent contribution to Irish life. The GAA can never repay the debt they owe to moments such as these, as is evident in this section, they have inspired subsequent generations to carry the torch that still burns so brightly today.

# 38

# THE MAN WITH THE MAGIC HANDS

*Mayo win the 1936 All-Ireland*

Former Taoiseach Enda Kenny has the inside story of how Mayo won their first All-Ireland in 1936, when over fifty thousand fans came to Croke Park expecting to see a thriller.

'In 1935, Kerry had refused to play in the championship as a gesture of solidarity with interned prisoners in the Curragh. In 1936 they were back, but Mayo ended their interest in the championship in the All-Ireland semi-final, and my father (Henry) was seen as the star, especially since he was in the glamour position of midfield. It was only when I got involved in politics that I came to realise just how revered he was, by older people in particular. A mythology developed in the county about the 1936 team, not least because they went fifty-three games without defeat. People thought they could jump over telegraph poles.

'My father went to teacher training college in De La Salle, Waterford. One of his fellow students was Seán Brosnan, who became a Fianna Fáil TD for Cork. Times were very tough, and food was so scarce there that my father said you needed to have the plates nailed to the tables! After he qualified, he went to teach in Connemara and cycled sixteen miles to train for the club team, and sixty miles to Castlebar to play for Mayo. One of his teammates was Paddy Moclair, who was the first bank official to play county football, and he cycled from Clare. I've seen telegrams from the Mayo County Board at the time telling players, "Train yourself, you've been selected to play."

'Football training included a standing-jump practice. A football was tied on a piece of string and raised on a pulley. The higher you jumped, the higher the pulley was raised. Another form of training included running long distances on roads in heavy boots.

'In 1936 the Mayo team were invited down to play Kerry in the opening match in Fitzgerald Stadium. There were seven or eight of them in the car on the way home. They left for Mayo on the Sunday night and, whether it was the signs or the driver that was at fault, they found themselves in Carlow the next morning. They were all starving and went to a café for breakfast only to discover that nobody had any money to pay for it. Moclair told the rest of them that he would cause a diversion and the rest of them were to make a run for it!

'Another time they were driving home from a match, and were dropping my father off in Connemara very late in the night, when the car plunged into a stream. There must have been a few drinks taken because nobody was too worried and they all fell asleep in the car. When they woke up there were forty or fifty people with shovels round the car. They thought that all the players were dead!

'My father was particularly famous for his fielding of the ball. He grew up on the same street with Patsy Flannelly, another of the stars of the 1936 team. They had no football as kids so they went to the butcher's shop and got pigs' bladders from him to use instead of footballs. Dad always said, "If you could catch those you could catch anything."

'The other thing he was noted for was his ability after he caught the ball in the air to turn before his feet touched the ground. When my brothers and I started playing, his advice to us was always, "Be moving before the ball comes." He found a big change in the way the game was played, especially when they started wearing lighter boots like the soccer players. When he saw a pair of them he said, "These boots are like slippers." He didn't have much time for the solo runs and that's why he called it "the tippy toe". He said he would "beat the solo runner with his cap".'

I spoke with Tom McNicholas, last survivor of the 1936 Mayo team, about his memories. Bureaucracy deprived him of the chance to play in the All-Ireland: 'I played in every match except the final. I was a teacher and neither the school nor the Department of Education would release me to go on collective training with the Mayo team. As a result of that I was only a sub, and as we beat Laois by 4-11 to 0-5 my services were not needed. The great perk of winning the final was that we got a trip for six weeks, courtesy of a building firm in New York, to America. Again, I was not given leave so I resigned my job to travel. We played in Madison Square Garden in New York, in Philadelphia and Boston. It was an incredible adventure.'

Tom retained vivid memories of that team.

'It was a very different time then, on and off the field. We used a leather ball then rather than the pigskin they use now. It was as heavy as lead when it was wet, which means that today you can kick the ball 50 per cent further. Our trainer was Dick Hearns, who was the European cruiserweight champion. He had a very different approach to trainers of today. For instance, once we were driving to a match and I had a sore throat, and was losing my voice. When I told him the problem he just handed me a small bottle of vodka!

'There was none of the hype you have today. We had some great players, like Patsy Flannelly who died tragically in a shooting accident, and Purty Kelly who was a rock in defence. He had a jaw like granite. There wasn't the same cult of personality back then, but there was no question that the star of our team was Henry Kenny. He was wonderful at catching balls in the air. He had great duels with the mighty Kerry midfielder Paddy Kennedy and was probably one of the very few players, if not the *only*, who could hold his own with Kennedy. This was particularly the case in the All-Ireland semi-final in Roscommon, when we beat Kerry 1-5 to 0-6 in 1936 and when Kennedy was the new star in the game. Henry had big hands and he could hold the ball in one of them. He was known as "the man with the magic hands".'

# 39

## SAM CROSSES THE BORDER FOR THE FIRST TIME

*Down win the 1960 and 1961 All-Irelands*

Down made history when in 1960 they became the first team from the 'six counties' to win the Sam Maguire Cup. Within the county there was unrestrained joy, but how was their success seen outside it?

In his role as an analyst on RTÉ, Joe Brolly defers to nobody, especially to Colm O'Rourke. Away from the cameras, the only man who Brolly defers to is his father, Francie.

'I played half-forward for Derry in the 1960s. Anyone who saw both of us play would agree that I was always a much better player than Joe ever was! The 1958 team had crumbled at that stage, despite Jim McKeever, who was both a wonderful man and coach, being in charge of us. Although we had a star player in Seán O'Connell, we would never emulate the '58 side. I think that although Derry lost the final in 1958, it was important for the county to know that we could legitimately dream of eventually winning that elusive

All-Ireland. At the time though we didn't think we'd have to wait so long to have that dream realised.

'In the 1960s it was the Down team that stood out in Ulster, winning three All-Irelands (1960, '61 and '68). They had great individuals and a great team. They raised the bar for GAA teams in Ulster and beyond.'

Kildare's Pat Mangan endorses that view: 'We played Down in a league final in 1968 when I was centre half-back on that team, and I played on Paddy Doherty who was a great footballer. Seán O'Neill though was one of the greatest players I ever saw, and I had the pleasure of playing with him on the All-Star trip to San Francisco. He was a tremendous two-footed player with a great kick of the ball, a very intelligent competitor, his running off the ball was second to none, his vision and his accuracy was outstanding.'

Jimmy Magee saw that Down team as pioneers: 'Like the great Kerry team of the 1970s and 1980s, that Down team were full of stars and had some of the greatest players ever. They were one of the great innovators of Gaelic football. They were one of the first inter-county teams to wear tracksuits, which aroused great curiosity at the time. One young boy captured the bewilderment of the fans when he turned to his father and asked, "Why did they not take off their pyjamas?"'

It was a case of so-near-yet-so-far for Willie Nolan when he captained Offaly to a place in the 1961 All-Ireland final. In front of a record crowd that exceeded ninety thousand, his team lost by a solitary point to the reigning champions Down.

In the Leinster final, Offaly scraped a one point victory over Laois. It was an historic occasion as it was the county's first Leinster senior title in either football or hurling. Their opponents in the All-Ireland semi-final were Down, who had the advantage in terms of experience having contested the All-Ireland semi-final the previous year. The match turned on a controversial incident, as Nolan recalls with a face that is a map of concentration: 'We were leading by two points, with a couple of minutes to go. Jim McCartan got the ball and charged with it towards the goal. Some of our fellas went towards him and the referee gave them a penalty which Paddy Doherty scored. We got a point to equalise. Mick Dunne was writing for the *Irish Press* at the time and in his report the next day he wrote that it shouldn't have been a penalty. It should have been a free out for charging.'

The final score was Down 1-10, Offaly 2-7. Down won the replay by two points, and comfortably beat Kerry in the All-Ireland final.

# 40

# THE LONGFORD LEADERS

*Longford march to glory in the 1960s*

Jimmy Flynn was literally at the centre of the most successful period of Longford's history. His towering performances at midfield helped Offaly to beat the mighty Galway in the National League final in 1966. Longford's only previous successes at national level had been the All-Ireland junior championship of 1937. In 1968, Flynn helped Longford to take their only Leinster senior title.

Flynn made his senior debut for Offaly in 1963, as a nineteen-year-old marking Larry Coughlan. A turning point in Longford's fortunes came when three times All-Ireland winner Mick Higgins, of Cavan, agreed to become county trainer in 1965.

Longford had earlier reached their first Leinster final in 1965, losing out to Dublin by 3-6 to 0-9 after missing a penalty at a crucial stage. That September they won their first senior tournament of note when they defeated Kildare to take the O'Byrne Cup.

As Flynn recalls: 'To win the league was a great achievement for a small county like Longford, and although there was a lot of dedication on the part of the players I think Mick Higgins has to take a lot of the credit for it. He was never a hard taskmaster in training or anything, but he grew into the job with us. There was always great local rivalry between ourselves and Cavan, but up until then Longford people had never had much to shout about in comparison with our northern neighbours, but we changed that. He gave us the confidence to do it.

'We should have won the Leinster final in 1965. We were a far better team than Dublin on the day, but we had neither the experience nor the confidence. We didn't drive home our advantage. I was marking Des Foley that day, and I remember talking to him about it later when he pointed out that they had got two very soft goals from speculative balls that went into the square.'

Flynn though points out that Higgins was not the only one responsible for the upturn in Longford's fortunes.

'We had a great county chairman in Jimmy Flynn (no relation). He had a very cool head and was a very astute man. Another key figure was our manager, Fr Phil McGee (brother of Eugene). He had a great love for the game. It was much more a passion than an interest for him and you need people like that behind you. In 1966 we were invited to go to America. I remember well Fr Phil making a statement that I think he regretted afterwards. He said, "We'll go to America when we're All-Ireland champions." We never got there! There was no such thing as foreign holidays then – you were lucky if you got to stay in a good hotel before a big match.'

In the build-up to the league final, Galway looked invincible, but an indication that they did not regard Longford as pushovers came when they flew in their outstanding half-back, Martin Newell, from Frankfurt, where he was attending university. Longford though won by 0-9 to 0-8. Eight of Longford's points came from Bobby Burns, while Seán Murray got the remaining score. Jimmy Flynn's high fielding and work rate earned him the man of the match accolade.

'There were hardly five thousand people left in the county the day of the final. When we got home on the Monday evening we hopped on a truck. I'll always remember Larry Cunningham, who was at the height of his fame, got up with us and sang a song. As it was the first time we won a national title, there were ecstatic celebrations in the county. Although we didn't become Longford's answer to the Beatles, at least after that match when any of us went to a dance in Rooskey we were recognised!

'The final was one of those days when you are up for it, and the game went well for me. The one incident I remember most from the match was Martin Newell coming up the field with the ball and hitting a diagonal pass to Cyril Dunne. I intercepted it, and there was nobody between me and the goal – which was about seventy yards away. We were two points up at the time, there were about ten minutes to go and I was very tired. I soloed through and had nobody to beat but the goalie; instead, I shaved the post and put it wide. I fell on the ground with exhaustion and I can still hear Jackie Devine saying to me, "Why didn't you f**king pass the ball to me?" It made for an agonising finish because despite Galway throwing everything at us, our backs had held out well.

'The memory though that stays with me to this day is of the joy on the faces of the Longford crowd. We had a hell of a night in Power's Hotel afterwards, and a hell of a day the following. The party finished on Tuesday – but I'm not saying which Tuesday! We came down to earth with a bang though when we lost in the first round of the Leinster Championship against Louth. I thought though it was unfair to us to have to play a championship match just two weeks after winning the league final.'

Having reached the dizzy heights of success, Longford football soon found itself shrouded in controversy: 'After we won the league we had to play a two-header with New York: one in Croke Park and the second game a week later in Longford. The Croke Park match was a fiasco, and ended in an absolute shambles. The Longford fans were livid with the referee because they felt that he let the New York lads away with murder. Murder is too strong to describe what they were up to, but they were very, very physical. I talked to journalists after the match and they told me we should refuse to play them in the second game. A lot of the Longford crowd came on to the pitch to try and get at the New York fellas afterwards. When we played them in Longford it was the first time they had to put barbed wire around the pitch.'

Success though helped to tighten the bonds within the team.

'We would be training in Longford once a week. There were a number of us based in Dublin at the time, and sometimes we would have two carloads of us travelling down to training. There were stories told about fellas coming out of various towns at night with maybe too many on board. I remember a situation one night where a few of the lads, who shall remain nameless, headed off to the *Fleadh Ceoil* in Clones but made a detour into a bog!'

Happy days returned to Longford in 1968, particularly after they beat the reigning All-Ireland champions in the Leinster semi-final in Mullingar.

'Winning the Leinster title against Laois was a big thrill, although I got a knee injury and missed out on the All-Ireland semi-final against Kerry. It was a big disappointment but what really killed me was losing out on the opportunity to mark Mick O'Connell. I was on the sideline, and we lost by two points. One of the problems of Longford, and weaker counties generally, is that we didn't have strength in depth, and that told against us in the Kerry game. We had good players when we were all free from injury, but we couldn't afford to be short of anyone.'

# 41

## DONEGAL'S DAY

*Donegal win their first All-Ireland in 1992*

In 1982, Donegal got a massive boost when they won the All-Ireland under-21 football title. They picked up a lot of new players, like Anthony Molloy, Martin McHugh and Joyce McMullan. The senior team had a nice mixture of young blood and experience. To add to the factors in their favour, in 1989 Brian McEniff took charge of training Donegal again. He invited Seamus Bonner to be a selector. The offer was readily accepted despite the fact that it committed him to extensive travelling up and down to Donegal from his Dublin base. McEniff's Midas touch was soon in evidence again, as Donegal won the Ulster title the following year. What did Bonner believe was the secret of McEniff's success, and what was he like as a player?

'As a forward, he's the sort of guy I would really hate to have marking me. He was very tough and tenacious. He'd be standing on your toes almost and wouldn't give you much time on the ball.

'His dedication is total. Although he's got his own business, if he heard a Donegal man was playing football in Cork he'd drop everything, and travel down to see him play, and it wouldn't cost him a thought. He never missed a single training session in the 1992 campaign, and this encouraged the players to do the same. His willpower rubbed off on the players. He's also got incredible enthusiasm and that's infectious.'

The Bonner–McEniff double act had their finest hour in 1992, when they masterminded Donegal's All-Ireland 0-18 to 0-14 triumph over red-hot favourites Dublin. Before they had even reached that stage, controversy had erupted about Padraig Brogan's appearance in the All-Ireland semi-final, as Seamus Bonner told me: 'Padraig had made his name with Mayo, but had declared for us a couple of years previously and played for us. Then he switched back to Mayo and a year or so later they brought him on against us in an All-Ireland semi-final. Mayo would consider themselves unlucky not to have won the match, but when they brought on Padraig, instead of lifting Mayo it lifted our lads. The feeling among us was that Padraig had left Donegal because he had a better chance of winning an All-Ireland medal with Mayo. Although we were playing poorly, when our boys saw him coming on it made them more determined than ever not to lose the game. The sight of Padraig coming on the pitch caused them to up a gear.'

In conversation with this writer, Padraig Brogan candidly admitted that his arrival on the pitch had the opposite effect to the one intended; in fact, it inspired Donegal players and fans alike, and was a serious tactical blunder. His reason though for transferring back to Mayo was that, 'blood is thicker than water'.

Seamus Bonner had twin ambitions for winning the final: 'Having played club football for so long in Dublin, I knew the

Dublin players better than McEniff did. One of the highlights of my career had been captaining Civil Service to the Dublin Championship in 1980.

'Basically, I was keen that we would do two things in the All-Ireland. Firstly, that we would keep very tight on Vinnie Murphy. I knew he was their target man and if we kept him quiet the other Dublin forwards would struggle. It was also vital that we curbed the Dublin half-back line because we didn't want the likes of Keith Barr running at our defence with the ball. We took steps to do both, and after we got over their penalty chance, which Charlie Redmond didn't take, we were always holding our own.

'We had been so unimpressive in the All-Ireland semi-final against Mayo, that nobody gave us a chance against Dublin. I think that gave the Dublin players a false sense of security. The media really built them up and I think the Dubs started to believe their own publicity. That's a dangerous game. I think something similar happened to Kildare in 1998. In contrast, there was no hype about us because we hadn't done anything to deserve it. None of our fellas were going on radio shows blowing our own trumpet.'

Although the excitement was unprecedented, Donegal's marvellous victory came with a price tag attached for Bonner. 'The hardest part of my time as a selector came in the run-up to the final. Tommy Ryan had played for us in the All-Ireland semi-final, but we felt that Manus Boyle could do a job for us on the day. He scored nine points in the final, so our judgement was vindicated, but nobody wants to miss out on the chance to play in an All-Ireland final so it was incredibly tough to have to tell Tommy that he was going to miss out.'

McEniff and Bonner gave leadership from the sideline, but who were the Donegal leaders on the pitch?

'You can't win an All-Ireland without leaders on the pitch, and we had four of them in 1992, all in different ways: Anthony Molloy, Martin McHugh at centre-forward, Tony Boyle at full-forward and Martin Gavigan at centre-back. Molloy was a superb leader; he could catch a ball in the clouds and that would lift the team. If you could get past Martin Gavigan, you were doing well. Tony and Martin could get you a score from nowhere.'

# 42

# ONE-IN-A-ROW JOE

*Derry win their first All-Ireland final in 1993*

When Derry succeeded Donegal as All-Ireland champions in 1993, Joe Brolly was fast becoming a star name in Gaelic football; 'I always wanted to play for Derry because of the great team of the 1970s that won back-to-back Ulster titles,' he said. 'It was very clear from an early stage that the team was going somewhere. We had a lot of very strong characters on the team. An important catalyst for our success was Lavey winning the All-Ireland club title in 1991. Our captain was Henry Downey, from Lavey, and he was driving us on. He would tell us we were not training enough, so, when Lavey won the All-Ireland club title, we all bought into the belief that the Downey way is the right way. We were training five nights a week after that.

'Our manager, Eamonn Coleman, was also crucial. Eamonn was a rogue, but his heart was in the right place. He wasn't a great tactician but he was a real leader – the boys loved him very dearly because he was a man's man. He once told me I needed to do weight training saying, "Brolly, y-you're a wimp." This was before advanced training methods or anything, and we often started a session with ten 400-metre runs. It was masochistic stuff.

'Then Mickey Moran came in. He is a quiet man, a terrific coach and a football fanatic. He worked very well with Eamonn – the broad brush-stroke man who had the philosophy behind everything was Eamonn, while Mickey was the nuts-and-bolts man. I know in hindsight that Eamonn was not a good trainer, but when Mickey came in, all of a sudden everything was right.

'The other thing that was important to us was Down winning the All-Ireland in 1991. We had nearly beaten them that year in a titanic game at the Athletic Grounds, but when we were a point up at the end they got a free sixty yards out. I was close to the ball at the time and I heard Ross Carr saying to Enda Gormley, "I'm going to drive this over the bar." Enda told him, "Wise up you f**king eejit." But Ross sent it over the bar and they went through instead of us, but when they won the All-Ireland it inspired us because it made us realise how close we were.'

Derry would at last reach the promised land in 1993.

'I've never seen either the 1993 semi-final or All-Ireland final, but anyone who has tells me they never had the slightest worry that we wouldn't win either, despite it being very close against Dublin in the semi-final, and, although Cork got a whirlwind start scoring 1–2 in the first five minutes in the final, we beat them without any problems.

'The strange thing for me was the sense of anti-climax. I thought to myself: is this what it's like? I thought it would open up some promised land. We went to the Cat and Cage, and nobody knew what to do! That was before the time when sponsors looked after everything. The reward was the fulfilment of a lifetime's ambition.

'It was a massive thing for the people. Derry is a huge football county, so when we won the All-Ireland people were delirious. To this day, people speak about time by talking about winning the All-Ireland to fix other dates by. I especially recall people queuing for the Credit Union because nobody worked for two weeks. We had a banquet in the Guild Hall; it was organised by people who wouldn't know if a football was pumped or stuffed. It was like the end of the world. The spiritual side was very important; to Kerry, winning an All-Ireland is just routine, but to Derry it was cathartic. At last, we could take our place among the football counties with self-respect.

'I remember John O'Keeffe wrote in the *Irish Times*, "This Derry team will dominate Gaelic football for the next ten years." We had a lot of advantages, like our midfield – Brian McGilligan was astonishing. There was never a tougher or better athlete than him. He never did weights, but he was like granite. Brian was as tough as they come.

'Anthony Tohill loved playing with him because Brian did all the donkey work, while Anthony played all the football. Tohill was a brilliant finisher. He always wanted to be a professional athlete and he is a huge physical specimen. As a teenager he had gone to Australia to try his luck at Aussie Rules, but came back when Derry started to motor. I think Eamonn Coleman was keen to get him back. When he was twenty-four or twenty-five he went on trial to Manchester United: he was playing in a training match with the United squad and although there was a hundred million pounds worth of talent on display, Anthony was doing sliding tackles and bashing into people. Andrei Kanchelskis went to

Alex Ferguson and said, "Take that f**ker off before he kills someone." Fergie went over to him and said, "Son, I think we've just got to you a bit late in life."

'Anthony was a very popular and respected member of the squad. At one stage, we were all in a bar when Anthony got his results from university. When we heard he got first class honours someone piped up, "The bastard's got no chink in his armour."'

After the high of 1993, Derry made an early exit in the championship in 1994: 'Down beat us in an epic game in Celtic Park. Eamonn Coleman took them for granted because we had beaten them by eighteen or twenty points the year before, and Eamonn positively laughed at the notion that Down could beat Derry in Celtic Park. Mickey Linden kept them in it during the first half, then, in a classic smash and grab, they beat us with a late goal. After one game, we were gone.

'There had been a lot of discomfort in Derry about Eamonn. He was a player's man, not a County Board man. He would have told them to "f**k off", and there was a lot of jealousy. All of a sudden, he was sacked. In his first year he won a National League – Derry's previous league title was in 1947. In his second year he won an All-Ireland. As a player, he had won a minor All-Ireland himself, and had coached Derry to an All-Ireland minor title, with his son Gary as captain, as well as an All-Ireland under-21 team. When he was sacked, it killed the spirit within the team. It had been a very special group, but Eamonn's sacking spread a poison throughout the team. To me it seemed that some of the powers that be were undoing all the good work of 1993. It is also a fact that they weren't the slightest bit interested in winning All-Ireland titles or having success because that put them under the spotlight. They were only interested in running things and getting tickets. That was their mentality. They screwed him. It was impossible to pick up the pieces. Mickey Moran stood on in controversial circumstances, but never had the team with him. We won the National League the following year on autopilot. The interest was gone.'

# 43

## THE FAIR COUNTY

*Armagh win their first All-Ireland in 2002*

The next Ulster team to make a breakthrough was Armagh. One of Ireland's leading sports psychologists, Enda McNulty, was crucial to Armagh's success. He believes Joe Kernan brought Armagh to football's top table when he was appointed Armagh manager: 'The biggest thing that Joe brought to the table was belief. When Joe walked into the Canal Court Hotel in December 2001 for his first team meeting with us he had already won All-Irelands with Crossmaglen. So when he sat down with us, you knew you were in the presence of a winner at Croke Park. Allied to that, he had already played for Armagh in an All-Ireland final. Of course, when Joe walks into the room he brings a great presence because of his physique, and when he said, "Get me to Croke Park and I'll ensure ye'll win," you believed him. We knew we were on the edge of winning an All-Ireland, and believed that Joe was the final piece of the jigsaw – and he was.

'We played Louth in the league in 2002, and they are

always tough to play against. I think we were level at half-time, and remember vividly at the break Joe saying to us, "Do you think that just because I have won an All-Ireland with Crossmaglen that I have a magic wand? Boys, there's no magic wand. You have to make more blocks than you ever made in your life. You have to kick the ball in to the forwards better than you ever have in your life. It's not about anything that I can say or wave. It's about what ye do. It has to do with what ye do in the middle of the game." That struck a chord with me.'

McNulty feels that it was a variety of factors coming together, like converging lines, that paved the way for the team's ultimate success: 'I believe sport is a kaleidoscope of a whole range of small things made perfect. I think that is the road Armagh went down. In 2002, Armagh started to get more of all the small things right than all the other teams. We got some unbelievable guys in, from a psycho-logical point of view. We worked on team cohesion, and did some good bonding sessions. The other thing we did was to bring in Darren Campbell for statistical analysis, which was on a different level because of his basketball background. I remember, before we played Tyrone in the 2002 Ulster Championship, Campbell handed me a sheet of paper with a diagram showing me where exactly on the pitch Peter Canavan had received every ball in the previous five games. From a mental preparation point of view, that was great for me. Not only that, it was also pinpointing when he liked to get the balls in those positions – so, as the game went on, whether he liked to move out or in – that was invaluable. Then we went on a training week in the sun, which, though everybody knows it now, was then very innovative. Apart from the bonding, it was a very serious trip. Not only was there no alcohol or nights out, there wasn't even a discussion about alcohol or nights out. It was very tough training, and the mental resolve that trip gave us was important.

'We were walking up the hill in Clones like an army before the Tyrone game. Everyone knew we had been on the trip in the sun and one of the Tyrone fans shouted at us, "I don't see any suntan lads." When Joe got us in the dressing room he used that incident and said, "We'll show them a f**king suntan before the end of the match." That was the spark we needed.

'There were numerous small things. A nutritionist was brought in, and physical conditioning was brought to a new level, which probably reflected how driven the lads were. Joe brought a good team all around him. Every little detail was sorted out.'

Things came to a happy ending for Armagh in the All-Ireland final against Kerry in 2002. 'We knew we could win if we played to our potential, and most of our team performed, but didn't know we would win. We knew our conditioning was better than Kerry's. We knew we were a tougher team than Kerry, despite what anybody said. There was a bit of a myth about how good that Kerry team were and the press had built them up. We weren't under any illusions though that it was going to be easy. We knew it would probably go down to one kick of a ball, and that's what happened.

'It hadn't gone well in the first half, but what hasn't gone into folklore is that we started off well. Then Kerry had a period of dominance and Oisín [McConville] missed a penalty, and we sort of went off the rails after that. However, we finished well and only went in at half-time trailing by four points. I remember I personally went in at half-time knowing I had to pick my game up, and, having slipped a few times on the pitch, changed to studs rather than blades on my boots. I started marking Gooch Cooper but then was switched to marking Mike Frank Russell. I changed my boots at the break and that made a big difference in the second half. I remember looking around the dressing room and thinking the mood in the team wasn't unbelievably spirited, and the body language wasn't very strong. Joe came in and he started talking, "Listen boys, we aren't playing well. I played in the 1977 All-Ireland final and I remember going home on the bus crying, and with all the boys crying. Do ye want to f**king be like me?" It wasn't really what he said next that made an impact but him physically throwing his loser's medal from that game against the shower, and it rattling all over the wall. The plastic shattered into little pieces and the coin, or whatever it was, rolled all over the floor. Again, I vividly remember looking around and seeing the body language change immediately. Before that, everybody was sitting kind of slumped, and then suddenly everybody was sitting up as if we were all saying, "That's not going to be us." To use a term from sports psychology, we all went up into a "peak state". It was as if we were all saying to each other, "Jesus boys we're going to win this." Then Kieran [McGeeney] brought us into a circle and you knew by looking into the boys' eyes that everybody was ready for a battle. There were other games when you'd look into the boys' eyes and you'd see a bit of uncertainty, but there was none at that stage. It was total euphoria when we won.'

# 44

# TYRONE'S TRIUMPH

*Tyrone win their first All-Ireland in 2003*

At the start of the 2000s few could have predicted that Tyrone would become the team of the decade. Joe Brolly traces their success back to the lessons learned a decade earlier: 'I think it was because of the way Down played that inspired other Ulster teams. They were electrifying. They had six, super classy forwards. Donegal were the same. They all went on attack. Derry were a little different, but still played good football. As a result of those three counties doing so well, there was a serious inquisition in Tyrone, who wondered why they couldn't do the same.

'Then of course you had the advent of Peter Canavan. Any team he had been involved in were champions: Errigal Ciaran were Ulster champions, and he had won minor and under-21 All-Irelands with Tyrone. Suddenly, he found himself in his mid twenties wondering what was going on. In his first four years as a Tyrone senior they didn't win a single match in the Ulster Championship. They set up "club Tyrone" and put in an infrastructure which was state of the art – way beyond anything we had ever seen before. You have no idea of the integration between schools, clubs, parishes and outreach programmes. They set about it like a military campaign because they are a fanatical football county who had never won an All-Ireland before and they were sick, sick, sick about that. In 2003, they had great young players like Eoin Mulligan and Co. arriving on the scene.

'All that was needed was a manager, and then Mickey Harte came along. He had managed the minor team for seven years, so nobody had a better overview of Tyrone football. Of course, that was all part of Tyrone's master plan, to have a minor manager for a long time, who would progress to the under-21 and senior team. He's obviously a genius, a tactical master – which has been recognised. He innovated a new style of football which nobody had seen before, and that's what brought the house down on their heads. I think in 2003 they just wanted to win an All-Ireland. They didn't care whether it was pretty or not, and that's why they used the swarm defence. They played against a great Kerry team and nobody will ever forget the image of Darragh Ó Sé with five Tyrone men around him. Kerry were caught on the hop. Armagh had won the All-Ireland the previous year playing a defensive brand of football, but there was something to admire about it, something heroic about it. Even Armagh couldn't cope that year with Tyrone's play. In Tyrone, the individual was anonymous. Peter Canavan was able to play in that final, kicking on only one leg. People started to ask: is that football at all? But they won their All-Ireland.

'In 2005 Mickey Harte had been working on the team for three years and had a harmonious blend between defence and attack. Although Kerry got off to a great start, Tyrone wiped the floor with them and humiliated them. They played beautiful football and showed they had some great players. At the same time, there was still the stigma of defence attached to Ulster football. I was invited to speak at the presentation ceremony when they got their medals and I said that that particular team could win four or five All-Irelands, but they were cursed by injuries. Finally, they justified my prophecy in 2008.'

Armagh's glory in 2002 was not to be repeated the following year for Enda McNulty: 'There's a lot of regrets about 2003. Probably, on reflection, we played better football in 2003 than we did in 2002, but we made a big mistake. Two weeks before the All-Ireland final we changed a few critical things. We changed the way we had played the whole year, which was a critical mistake. We picked some players in different positions, which was a big mistake in hindsight. Not only the game plan and the positional changes, and I have spoken to Kieran [McGeeney] about this many times, but even more important was the change in our attitude. In all the games leading up to the final we had a "take no sh*t" attitude. We got stuck in, and used our physical capacities, not in any dirty way, but we harnessed the physical strength of the team: Francie Bellew, Kieran, the McEntees, Paul McGrane. In the run-up to the final, there were a lot of articles in the press saying that not only were Armagh a dirty team, but over-the-top dirty. One of the articles stated that somebody was going to be left in a wheelchair because of the way we played. I remember reading that article, which was written by a Fermanagh player, and thinking to myself, "Oh dear", what's going to happen if some of our players are affected by this. We probably subconsciously decided not to be as physical as we were in the previous games, which was an absolute disaster. Armagh's game has been built on our physical nature, and in a lot of games in 2002 we crushed teams just by our physical exertions and, because we were so well conditioned, we could easily deal with anyone else in that respect. Against Tyrone in 2003 we decided we were going to show the whole country that we could win by playing nice football. We tried to play less tough football and more champagne football. We needed to marry the skills with the physical dimension.'

Many in Tyrone took additional joy from the fact that they forced Pat Spillane to eat humble pie after his 'puke football' comments when they beat Kerry in the semi-final earlier that year. The most popular joke in Tyrone afterwards was of Quasimodo sitting in his study, and once again feeling depressed about how ugly he was. Looking for some reassurance, he goes in search of Esmerelda. When he finds her he asks her again if he really is the ugliest man alive.

Esmerelda sighs and says, 'Look, why don't you go upstairs and ask the magic mirror who is the ugliest man alive? The mirror will answer your question once and for all.'

About five minutes later a very pleased looking Quasimodo bounced back down the stairs and gave Esmerelda a great big hug. 'Well, it worked,' Quasimodo beamed. 'But who on earth is Pat Spillane?'

For his part, Spillane is puzzled by one aspect of that game: 'I've now been at five charity auctions where Peter Canavan's boots from that game were auctioned. Who knew he wore so many boots?'

# 45

# WESTMEATH WINNERS

*Westmeath win the 2004 Leinster final*

After a disappointing campaign in 2003, Westmeath parted company with their manager, Luke Dempsey, and turned to their messiah, Páidí Ó Sé. The following year, the Kerry legend led the county to their first Leinster title.

Páidí's triumph with Westmeath came as a surprise to Pat Spillane: 'After an inauspicious league campaign, I was sceptical of Westmeath's chances. On 18 April that year, in my column in the *Sunday World*, I divided counties into various categories. One of my five no-hopers was Westmeath. I wrote:

> *One would not normally expect a team who managed to avoid relegation from Division One to be parked here. But Westmeath's Houdini-like escape from relegation had precious little to do with their own ability and more to do with other counties shooting themselves in the foot, notably Longford, who would have stayed up and put Westmeath down had they managed to beat Fermanagh at home. This*

*is looking like a temporary little management arrangement for Páidí.*

'I had no doubts before the championship that Westmeath were going nowhere. I'm always like that. I may often be wrong, but I never have any doubts!

'Getting predictions wrong does not faze me unduly. I always get my predictions wrong, and a few times a week I will meet people who say something like, "Spillane you're only a chancer. You know nothing about football. You were wrong again last Sunday."

'The great thing is that RTÉ pay me to come and tell the nation what I think will happen. Then, when I make a dog's dinner of it and get it badly wrong, *The Sunday World* pay me the following Sunday to explain why I got it so wrong!

'To add insult to injury Westmeath beat Dublin comfortably in the Leinster quarter-final. I had confidently slotted the Dubs in as number two, behind Laois, on my list of "Glory Hunters".

'Given the desire for success in Westmeath, I wasn't surprised when their County Board pulled out all the stops and, according to popular belief, their chequebook (obviously under GAA rules it can only be for expenses, and we all know how strictly they adhere to that rule), to lure Páidí to the county.

'There were loads of rumours about all the money Páidí was getting from Westmeath for doing the job. I am reminded of the story of the rich GAA manager, the poor GAA manager and the tooth fairy, who are in a room with a €100 note on the table when the lights go out. When the lights come back on, the money is gone. So who took it? It's got to be the rich GAA manager, because the other two are figments of the imagination.

'My view is that whatever Páidí was getting he was worth every penny, because he raised the profile of the game within the county. He really put Westmeath on the football map by taking them to the Leinster final in his first season, created a buzz within the county along with a feeling of togetherness and identity, and now more and more youngsters are wearing the Westmeath jersey.

'The other story is that Páidí was supposed to be getting a helicopter to fly him from Kerry to Westmeath for training sessions. During our days on the Kerry team, Páidí had an amazing fear of flying. Paudie Lynch shared that fear, and when we were travelling on trips abroad the way the two of them coped was to get totally inebriated before the trip.

'I remember one day, when we got to Dublin airport, I said, "Look here Páidí, if it's your day to go, it's your day to go."

'Páidí turned around to me and said, "But if it's the f**king pilot's day to go, he's going to bring me down with him!"'

# PART V
# Special Occasions

The annals of the GAA hold a hallowed place for the special occasions which lit up the Association like a Christmas tree: stories of tremendous teams that entered the nation's hearts; terrifically talented players who shone like the brightest star; and events that transcended sport, sending out ripples of emotion in a country craving drama and spectacle. This section considers some representative samples of these golden greats.

# 46

## LOUTH LEAPFROG TO GREATNESS

*Louth win the 1943 Leinster football final*

In 1990, Eddie Boyle became Louth's first All-Star when receiving the All-time All-Star award. He played for Leinster between 1935 and 1948, and won five Railway Cup medals during that period. In 1932, he made his debut in a Louth jersey with the county minor side. In 1934, he was a member of the Louth junior team that reached the All-Ireland final, but after the semi-final he was promoted to the senior team and was therefore ineligible for junior grade when Louth won the final. However, he was awarded a Junior medal.

The highlight of his inter-county career came in 1943 when he won his first Leinster senior championship medal. Boyle was the spine of the team, along with Jim Thornton at midfield and the classy Peter Corr (a relative of the band The Corrs) in the forwards. In the Leinster semi-final, Louth trailed Offaly by four points, but with his bucket-like hands repelling virtually everything Offaly could throw at him, Boyle and his fellow backs kept them to a solitary point in the second half, while the Louth forwards notched up 1-7

163

to win comfortably. In the actual Leinster final, Laois could only manage two points in the second half, while such was the service to the forwards that the final margin in Louth's favour was fifteen points.

Although Louth were to lose the All-Ireland semi-final to Roscommon, Boyle had the small consolation of keeping Jack McQuillan scoreless for the full sixty minutes. His second Leinster medal came in 1948, when Cavan thwarted their hopes in the semi-final.

When I met him though he told me that neither victories rank as his most memorable match. 'I will always remember a National Football League match against Cavan in the Athletic Grounds in Dundalk. The Grounds were packed, as Cavan were All-Ireland champions and it was their first game after they won the title in New York. Cavan were hot favourites to win, as we were having a bad time, but it was a sizzler of a match and we played some inspired football, and we won by two points. The town was talking about the match for days afterwards.'

How big a disappointment was it for Boyle not to have won an All-Ireland medal?

'I was always playing to get into an All-Ireland final, and if I had succeeded in getting to it, I would certainly have been playing for a medal. But I always enjoyed the game so much – that was what was important. Yet, while saying that, I don't mean that I wasn't always all out to win.'

Mindful of the fact that I was not around to see some of the greatest players of all time, I sought the assistance of one of the most authoritative voices on Irish sport, Jimmy Magee: 'I think the first man on my team of greatest players never to win an All-Ireland would be Louth's Eddie Boyle, especially because of the longevity of his career. He was one of the few men who could have played in any era, with his high catch, great ball-playing skills like John O'Keeffe, and he never fouled. My late father thought the sun shone out of him: he was a full-forward and Eddie was a full-back so they had many a tussle in club football. It was only right and proper that Eddie got a rare Leinster title in 1943, and then was, as always, the heart and soul of the team that won a second Leinster in 1948.'

# 47

# JACK OF ALL TRADES

*Cork vs Cavan 1945*

Jack Lynch won five All-Ireland hurling medals with Cork. He also won an All-Ireland football medal. His football career left him with one enduring memory from the 1945 All-Ireland football final.

'Having completed my law examinations, I was in digs on the southside of Dublin in Rathgar. I met the Cork team at Kingsbridge Station on the Saturday evening and I told the Selection Committee that I would not be at the hotel the next morning as there was a bus route near my digs which passed by Croke Park and that I would go straight to there. I was waiting in a queue about twenty yards long. Bus after bus passed, each taking only a couple of people at a time. At one stage, I barged to the head of the queue but the conductor told me to go back and wait my turn. I pointed to my bag of togs and said I was playing in the All-Ireland football final in Croke Park within the hour. The conductor said sarcastically that this was the best reason for breaking a queue that he'd ever heard, but let me stay on. I alighted from the bus at the junction of Drumcondra and Conyngham roads, and ran around to the back of the Cusack Stand, where the dressing rooms were then located. About fifteen minutes to the throw-in, I knocked at the Cork dressing-room door to be greeted by an ominous silence, except for the sound of footsteps slowly and deliberately pacing the floor. The door opened. It was Jim Hurley, formerly a Cork hurling midfielder, then secretary of UCC and chairman of the Cork Selection Committee. I expected to be bawled out. Instead I got, "Hello Jack Lynch, you were great to come." I had missed the president at the time, Seán T. O'Ceallaigh, coming into the dressing room to wish the team well. I regretted that because he had been in the GPO in the 1916 Rising. I think I escaped any nasty recriminations afterwards because I was involved in the movement that set up the winning goal.'

Lynch also made his mark in a club football match.

'The star-laden Clonakilty side were playing St Nicholas in Bandon. It was during the winter, and the river adjacent to the pitch was flooded. Mick Finn deliberately belted it into the river because Clonakilty were losing and there was only one football, so he hoped the match would have to be abandoned. I jumped into the river and swam out to retrieve the ball. The Clonakilty lads never forgave me for it!'

# 48

## TETCHY MOMENTS

*Cork vs Galway 1953*

Sports journalism almost lost out on the great Mick Dunne when, like so many of his contemporaries at the time, he decided to enter the priesthood. After a year and a half in All Hallows, he decided that the clerical life was not for him. This was a time when there was a considerable stigma attached to being a 'spoiled priest', but his family, unlike many others in that situation, supported his decision fully.

Mick was born into a very political family known as the 'Tailor Dunnes', so called because of the number in the extended family who took up the tailoring profession, as well as distinguishing them from the many other Dunnes in the area. His father, Frank, went to America at an early age but during the War of Independence he was sent back by Liam Mellows with an important message for the 'Big Fella', Michael Collins. He stayed on to fight in the war and became second-in-command of the Fourth Battalion. He spent time in a number of prisons, and took part in a number of daring escapes. He was also very musical and enjoyed a great reputation as a Pipe Major. During the civil war he spent forty-four days on hunger strike in Mountjoy with Seán Lemass, who would go on to succeed Éamon de Valera as Taoiseach, and Sean Coughlan who subsequently became the GAA columnist with the *Irish Press*, writing under the pen name 'Green Flag'. In its long history, the GAA has seen few more astute judges of hurling than Mick Dunne.

'Without question the greatest player I ever saw was Christy Ring. He was probably the greatest player that ever laced a boot. He was the one I admired most, the man I was most happy to report upon and the man I was always pleased to talk with.

'He was involved in a few controversies in his time. In 1953, Galway hurlers, powered by the great Josie Gallagher, had beaten Kilkenny in the semi-final and had qualified to play the Cork side led by Christy Ring in the All-Ireland final. Galway had the game for the winning, but failed to take off Mick Burke despite his obvious concussion. What made their inaction all the more inexplicable was that Burke was marking the great Christy Ring. The controversy ensued from the fact that a large section of the Galway crowd had booed Ring throughout the game, and that Galway appeared to have targeted the Cork legend for "special treatment". The post-match celebration was affected by events on the field. So incensed were five or six of the Galway players by Burke's injury that they had an altercation with Ring that evening at the official reception and returned to the Cork hotel at breakfast the next morning to again vent their displeasure, albeit only using verbal means on that occasion.'

# 49

## SIX OF THE BEST

*Clare vs Limerick 1953*

For twenty years, Jimmy Smyth was never off the Clare team, and during that period he was selected for twelve years on the Munster team, winning eight Railway Cup medals. Having played five years as an inter-county minor, he made his Clare debut in a challenge match in Gort at the age of seventeen with the great Josie Gallagher of Galway: 'I learned a few lessons that day, I can tell you.'

In 1953, he scored an incredible six goals and four points against Limerick in the first round of the Munster Championship. Two years later, his biggest disappointment came against the same opposition.

'We lost the Munster final to them by 2-16 to 2-6. Not only had we defeated Tipperary and Cork in qualifying, but we also beat Wexford in the Oireachtas final the previous October in front of thirty thousand people in Croke Park. Losing to Limerick was a massive blow to Clare, and took us a long time to recover. If Clare had won in 1955, I believe we would have won several All-Irelands.

'We had great teams in the forties and all the way up to the eighties, but it was always the same old story – good management and back-up, commitment in training, but no delivery on the big day. Even on the days when we did deliver, as we did, for instance, against Cork in Killarney in 1986, it was the same old story. You could say it was almost a fear of winning and sheer bad luck. There were so many great players in Clare who would have won several All-Ireland medals if they were with other counties. Our predicament was that we had good hurling teams which were saddled with the sorrows of past years.

'Clare's record was poor, and we had no tradition of winning. When you have a tradition, it seeps into the bones and the psyche. It breeds confidence and even makes a winner out of a loser. A fair team with a good tradition would always be confident of winning against a better Clare side.

'In the past, even the language of the supporters carried the wail and the woe of what was said and unsaid. I hated the question, "Will ye win?" People knew the answer to the question when they asked you. What they were saying was, "We want you to win, we know you can, but you won't."'

Despite the many losses and heartbreaks Smyth endured as a player, he was always acutely aware of the sociological importance of Gaelic games.

'The GAA achieved three very different purposes. It encouraged local patriotism, it inculcated among its members an uncompromising hostility to foreign games, and it revived local and national pride. Its philosophy is that love of country draws its strength and vitality from love of neighbours, fellow parishioners and fellow countrymen and women, and from love of the scenes, traditions, culture and way of life associated with one's home and place of origin: that a club or county provides a sense of importance, belonging and identity, shared goals, a pride and a purpose. All the traditions are equally charged with such values and aspirations.'

# 50

# THE MAN WITH THE GOLDEN VOICE

*The emergence of Mícheál Ó Muircheartaigh*

Des Cahill went to visit his old school. He asked the students if anyone could give him an example of a 'tragedy'. One boy stood up and offered the suggestion that, 'If my best friend who lives next door was playing in the street when a car came along and killed him, that would be a tragedy.'

'No,' Des said, 'that would be an "accident".'

Another boy raised his hand. 'If a school bus carrying fifty children drove off a cliff, killing everybody involved . . . that would be a tragedy.'

'I'm afraid not,' explained Des. 'That is what we would call a "great loss".' The room was silent; none of the other children volunteered. 'What?' asked Des, 'Is there no one here who can give me an example of a tragedy?'

Finally, a boy in the back raised his hand. In a timid voice, he spoke: 'If an airplane carrying you and *The Sunday Game* team were blown up by a bomb, *that* would be a tragedy.'

'Wonderful.' Des beamed. 'Marvellous. And can you tell me why that would be a tragedy?'

'Well,' said the boy, 'because it wouldn't be an accident, and it certainly would be no great loss.'

Nobody would say that about Mícheál Ó Muircheartaigh. He has carved out a unique place in the affections of Irish sport lovers over the last sixty years. The most mundane of matches came alive in his commentary. Everything he said into his microphone was informed by a passion that was as basic to him as breathing. His commentaries were famous for the richness of their texture, abounding with references that delight and surprise.

His story is the broadcasting equivalent of Roy of the Rovers. He was only eighteen, training to be a teacher and still adjusting to life in Dublin, when a friend saw a notice on the college noticeboard for part-time Irish-speaking commentators. The auditions were at Croke Park, a club game was in progress, and each applicant was given a five minute slot – an opportunity to sort out the real thing from the pretenders.

'A group of us went – we went with the idea that it would be great fun. We'd be in Croke Park, a place we revered, and most importantly, we knew we would get in for free. It was an adventure.

'They had to pick somebody and they picked me. It is still a very vivid memory. Naturally none of us knew any of the players, but I knew one who managed to go to school in Dingle, Teddy Hurley, and another player in midfield. I just talked away at random and people I knew featured very prominently, even though they were not on the scene of the action at all! I then moved into the big money league and was offered a massive contract – all of £6! The important thing though is that I still enjoyed it as much at the end as I did then.'

# THE MAN WITH THE GOLDEN VOICE

In his broadcasting career, Mícheál has found evidence that if horse racing is the sport of kings, greyhound racing is the sport of princes. One of his coups was to become the first person to interview a British Royal, Prince Edward, on RTÉ radio. As joint owner of Druid's Johnno, Prince Edward was celebrating his semi-final victory in the English Greyhound Derby at Wimbledon when Mícheál stepped up and asked in his velvety soft tones, as only he can, 'Now, tell me, Prince.'

Few people have done more to promote the whirr of the flying sliotar and the thrilling sound of ash against ash, than the voice from Dingle who makes GAA fans tingle, Mícheál. To shamelessly steal from Patrick Kavanagh, among his earthiest words the angels stray.

Mícheál has left an indelible mark on the GAA landscape with a series of classic comments. This is my top baker's dozen of his gems:

1. I see John O'Donnell dispensing water on the sideline. Tipperary, sponsored by a water company. Cork, sponsored by a tae company. I wonder will they meet later for afternoon tae.

2. He kicks the ball *lán san aer*. Could've been a goal, could've been a point . . . it went wide.

3. Colin Corkery on the forty-five lets go with the right boot. It's over the bar. This man shouldn't be playing football. He's made an almost Lazarus-like recovery. Lazarus was a great man, but he couldn't kick points like Colin Corkery.

4. Stephen Byrne with the puck out for Offaly . . . Stephen, one of twelve . . . all but one are here today. The one that's missing is Mary, she's at home minding the house . . . and the ball is dropping *i lár na bpáirce . . .*

5. Pat Fox has it on his hurl and is motoring well now . . . but here comes Joe Rabbitte hot on his tail . . . I've seen it all now, a Rabbitte chasing a Fox around Croke Park.

6. Pat Fox out to the forty and grabs the sliotar . . . I bought a dog from his father last week, sprints for goal . . . the dog ran a great race last Tuesday in Limerick . . . Fox to the twenty-one, fires a shot, goes wide and left . . . and the dog lost as well.

7. Danny 'the Yank' Culloty. He came down from the mountains and hasn't he done well.

8. Teddy looks at the ball, the ball looks at Teddy.

9. In the first half they played with the wind. In the second half they played with the ball.

10. 1-5 to 0-8, well from Lapland to the Antarctic, that's level scores in any man's language.

11. I saw a few Sligo people at Mass in Gardiner Street this morning and the omens seem to be good for them. The priest was wearing the same colours as the Sligo jersey! Forty yards out on the Hogan Stand side of the field, Ciarán Whelan goes on a rampage, it's a goal. So much for religion.

12. . . . and Brian Dooher is down injured. And while he is down I'll tell ye a little story. I was in Times Square in New York last week, and I was missing the championship back home and I said, 'I suppose ye wouldn't have *The Kerryman* would ye?' To which the Egyptian behind the counter turned to me and said, 'Do you want the North Kerry edition or the South Kerry edition?' . . . he had both . . . so I bought both. Dooher is back on his feet.

13. David Beggy will be able to fly back to Scotland without an airplane he'll be so high after this.

# 51

## WEXFORD'S WONDERLAND

*Wexford vs Galway 1955*

When I asked Mícheál Ó Muircheartaigh to select the first team to lodge in his memory, he recalled Wexford's All-Ireland triumph over Galway in 1955.

'The first hurling team to make a lasting impression on me was the great Wexford team of the 1950s. I had seen John Doyle's great Tipperary three-in-a-row side of 1949 to 1951, but because of Tipperary's tradition you somehow didn't wonder at that. It was different with Wexford because they came from nowhere. Remember, this was a county that had only won one All-Ireland, in 1910, and by the 1950s, they only had added a solitary Leinster title, back in 1918. They showed they had promise when they reached the National League final in 1951, only to lose to Galway. They took another step forward by reaching the All-Ireland the same year, even though they lost heavily to Tipperary. By the next year they were able to run Tipp to a point in the league final, and then they swept all before them in 1955 and '56, winning two All-Irelands and coming from fifteen points down against Tipperary at half-time to win by four points in a pulsating league final. The 1956 All-Ireland final against Cork was an epic, with a late surge ensuring perhaps their greatest ever triumph.

'In the 1990s there was a famous racehorse called Danoli, a Cheltenham winner, who was known as "The People's Champion". It may not have been fully on the scale of the reaction to Clare's triumph in 1995, but when Wexford won in '55 they became the People's Champions.

'The star of that side was Nicky Rackard, but sometimes the invaluable contribution of his brother Bobby is neglected. Bobby was probably the best right full-back I have ever seen. He started off as an elegant centre half-back, but because of an injury to their great full-back Nick O'Donnell he had to move to plug the back there. When Nick recovered, Bobby was slotted into the corner and he produced a string of astounding performances there. He had a marvellous ability to catch the sliotar – high or low – and send it far outfield in sweeping clearances.

'I will never forget one gesture which sums up the true spirit of hurling. After Wexford beat Cork in the 1956 All-Ireland, Bobby and Nick O'Donnell hoisted the defeated warrior Christy Ring on their shoulders. That said it all about the spirit of that Wexford team.'

More than words. It's Coming Home: Galway manager Micheál Donoghue hands the Liam McCarthy Cup to his father, Miko, after the 2017 All-Ireland final.

We did it for Tony: Galway's David Burke and Joe Canning share the Cup with Tony Keady's widow, Margaret, after winning the All-Ireland.

© INPHO / JAMES CROMBIE

© INPHO / CATHAL NOONAN

A shoulder to cry on: Waterford manager Derek McGrath cannot conceal his heartbreak as he seeks comfort from Dan Shanahan after the 2017 All-Ireland.

Catch of the day: Kilkenny's Aisling Dunphy and Alne Connery with Aisling Thompson of Cork.

© INPHO / JAMES CROMBIE

Where we sported and played: Cork manager
Jimmy Barry-Murphy and selector Kieran Kingston.

Jeepers keepers: Tyrone's Tommy McGulgan and Stephen Cluxon of Dublin.

© INPHO / JAMES CROMBIE

Keeper of the flame: the passion still burns brightly in Brian Lohan (far right) as he manages UL.

Peter the Great: Peter Canavan passes on his wisdom to his Holy Trinity team.

Geezer: Kieran McGeeney (centre) is still at the heart of the action in Armagh.

King of the cats: T. J. Reid lands another monster point against Wexford in 2018.

Lilywhite Legend: the terrifically talented Johnny Doyle kicks a wonder point for Kildare.

Simply the best: Carnacon's Cora Staunton and Clara Walsh of Inch Rovers.

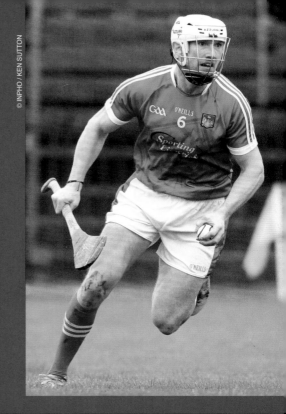

The Limerick Leader:
Seamus Hickey defiantly
resists another attack.

Tipp Top: Nicky English of
Tipperary celebrates victory.

© INPHO / TOMMY DICKSON

Come on the Rossies: although Roscommon struggled in the 2018 Super 8s, Enda Smith still showed his class.

A touch of class: Maurice Fitzgerald glides past the Galway defence in the 2000 All-Ireland final.

© INPHO / ANDREW PATON

# 52

# WHEN DAVID TOOK DOWN GOLIATH

*Kerry vs Derry 1958*

In 1958, the GAA world witnessed a shock of seismic proportions when Derry beat Kerry by 2-6 to 2-5 in the All-Ireland semi-final. The Foylesiders were led to the promised land by a prince of midfielders, Jim McKeever. His ability to jump and catch the ball were the hallmarks of his play. He could jump so tidily that he would be almost like a gymnast in the air, toes extended and fingers outstretched as he grabbed the ball, way above the heads of anybody else, and then he would hit the ground, turn and play. In Ted Walsh parlance, he was 'a great leaper', and one of his most famous feats of fielding was caught on camera and has been immortalised in all the great subsequent coaching manuals under the caption 'the catch'.

The bonus of talking to McKeever is the quiet, self-effacing warmth with which he talks matter-of-factly about a career that must always, in the end, testify to talent so magical that it is too profound to be rationally explained. At the age of seventeen, McKeever made his senior debut for Derry.

'I remember listening to the famous All-Ireland final in the Polo Grounds in 1947. I didn't think then that a year later I'd be playing in a challenge game for the county against Antrim. It wasn't until the following year though that I made my championship debut. When I was in my teens, Derry used to play in the junior championship. We didn't have a senior team then. At that stage there was a tremendous gap between Cavan and Antrim, and the other seven counties in Ulster. We played in the Lagan Cup at the time, which featured the eight counties in Ulster apart from Cavan.'

A major impediment to Derry's advancement was the fact that its footballing base was so narrow, particularly without the foundation stone of a strong colleges scene.

'I believe that success in football or hurling is largely determined by population. In a county where the playing population is small, you are always struggling to fill in the last three or four places.

'You need to be a big school to have a successful colleges side. St Columb's, in Derry, had a great team in the 1960s, but as a boarding school they were mainly powered by players outside the city. I myself went to school in St Malachy's in Belfast and went to train as a teacher in St Mary's, Belfast. After that I went for a year to do postgraduate studies in Physical Education in London. It was difficult to explain the intricacies of the game to some of my classmates! A few times in the year I flew home to play for Derry and Ulster.

'Derry was a soccer stronghold which was a big disadvantage for us. By the law of averages, given the population of the city it should be providing about 40 to 50 per cent of the team, but it has given us nowhere near that. Rule 27 [the GAA ban preventing members from playing non-Gaelic games], worked very badly against us in Derry.'

The high point of McKeever's career came against Kerry in 1958.

'I have no recollection of great excitement when we won the Ulster final. However, when we beat Kerry in the All-Ireland semi-final the response was sensational. I remember the great John Joe Sheehy saying to me, "That's a rattling good team you have there".'

Dublin beat Derry by 2-12 to 1-9 in the All-Ireland final, despite an imperious display from McKeever in midfield.

'I have no great recollection of great disappointment when we lost the final to Dublin. We were happy just to be there. If someone told us a few years before that we would play in an All-Ireland final, we would have been absolutely delighted.'

That year, McKeever was chosen as footballer of the year, much to the chagrin of some Dublin supporters who felt that the honour should have gone to one of their stars, like Kevin Heffernan. There was no precedent for a player to win the award from a county who had not won the All-Ireland final.

'I felt very honoured to win the award, not just for myself but for my county, and I wasn't aware of any begrudgery towards me at the time.'

While he has many happy memories from his career there is a tinge of regret.

'I enjoyed every moment of my playing career. The 1950s, I always think, was the wrong time to be playing football because a number of different counties won an All-Ireland in that decade. Each year there were seven or eight counties who could have won it, which naturally made it difficult for counties like Derry to make the breakthrough. If I had to do it all again, I would take it a lot more seriously. I think we could have won an All-Ireland if we had really given it everything.'

# 53

# CON'S TRACTS

*Con Houlihan charms the GAA nation*

Injury meant that Roscommon star Brendan Lynch's career ended prematurely after another Connacht title victory in 1952. However, his work as a Garda superintendent continued to bring him into contact with some famous GAA figures.

'In my first week I found myself prosecuting a man for a drunk-driving charge. He called a number of character witnesses, the first of which was six foot four and wearing no shirt, but instead Wellingtons and an overcoat. I thought to myself, "What sort of a miscreant is this?" I then checked his name. It was Con Houlihan. In his cross-examination he was asked, "Do you take a drink yourself?"

'"In a social capacity?"

'"How much would you drink?"

'"Not too much . . . Ten or twelve pints at the one sitting."

'The next time I met him was in O'Connell Street. He was wearing running shoes. I wouldn't mind if it was a pair, but he was wearing two odd ones!'

In the print media there has never been a more loved journalist in the world of Gaelic games than Con Houlihan. His columns in the *Evening Press* were must-reads for diehard GAA fans. He had a phrase for every occasion. Here is my fab four of vintage Con:

1. *On bad grammar*: 'A man who will misuse an apostrophe is capable of anything.'

2. *On a fellow journalist*: 'There he is, poor fella, forgotten but not gone.'

3. *On Italia 90*: 'I missed Italia 90, I was in Italy at the time.'

4. *On Paddy Cullen's frantic effort to keep the ball out before Mike Sheehy's famous goal in the 1978 All-Ireland final*: 'He was like a woman who smells a cake burning.'

Dermot Earley won All-Stars in 1974 and 1979, and a National League medal in 1979, but unusually found himself embroiled in controversy in 1977 in the All-Ireland semi-final against Armagh. With the score tied at Armagh 3-9 Roscommon 2-12, as Earley faced up to a long distance free, the last kick of the game, Gerry O'Neill (brother of Irish soccer manager Martin), the Armagh trainer, ran across the field in front of him and shouted something at him. The kick sailed high and wide. There was much press comment on the 'O'Neill–Earley' incident in the following days. In his column in the *Evening Press*, Con Houlihan offered two All-Ireland tickets to the person who could tell him what O'Neill had said to Earley.

# 54

# THE BLACK AND AMBER

*Eddie Keher wins six All-Irelands*

A woman was having her 104th birthday. The intrepid reporter from the local newspaper came and asked, 'What's the best thing about being one hundred and four?'

The woman paused theatrically before replying in a strong voice, 'No peer pressure!'

In the GAA world in the 1970s, one person who had no need to worry about peer pressure was Eddie Keher. In his era, he was simply the best.

When you have won six All-Ireland medals, ten Leinster medals, ten Railway Cup medals, five All-Star awards and a Texaco award, it is more than a little difficult to isolate one great sporting moment, but Eddie Keher only hesitated briefly in making his selection.

'The honour that meant most to me was my first ever All-Ireland senior medal in 1963. Beating Tipperary in the '67 final was also very important because we hadn't beaten them at that level for forty years I think. There was an attitude then that you'll never beat Tipperary in a hard game. Although we always play a certain type of game in Kilkenny, I think we toughened up a bit for that game and it made for a very satisfying victory, particularly as we proved our critics wrong.

'One of the great things about my long career was that I got the chance to meet great characters. In the 1976 league final replay against Clare I got a head injury and the blood was pumping out of me necessitating a long delay while I got attention. Ger Loughnane went up to me and said, "Jaysus Keher, would you ever get up and get on with it. Sure there's nothing wrong with you!"

'From a personal point of view, 1971 was very satisfying. Things went well for me on the day and I made a record score in an All-Ireland final of 2-11 – a record which was broken by Nicholas English in 1989; and I rang him up a few days later to congratulate him on the record. Coincidentally, it was Tipperary who beat us in the 1971 final and we can't have complaints with that because they had so many great players, like Babs Keating who was hurler of the year that year.'

# 55

## FROM VALENTIA WITH LOVE

*Mick O'Connell becomes a national icon*

The most obvious reason for Kerry's football success has been a phenomenal array of fantastic footballers from Dick Fitzgerald, to Paddy Kennedy, to Gooch Cooper.

At the top of the footballing hierarchy in Kerry, for John B. Keane, was Mick O'Connell. In emphasising O'Connell's ability to strike a ball, Keane told a story which showed how ecumenical his appeal was for both the sacred and the profane.

'Mick was rowing from Valentia to the mainland, and decided to practise his striking by taking a free from the boat. He hit it so hard that the ball burst on its journey. The cover of the ball landed outside the presbytery in Lisdoonvarna. The bladder landed outside a hoor house in Buenos Aires.'

Ireland's finest sports writer, Peter Woods, has produced the most elegiac assessments of the man from Valentia.

'I always remember seeing a television programme about the great Kerry footballer, Mick O'Connell. O'Connell used to run the roads of Valentia on his own. It was easy to tell he was well within himself: the camera showing him leaping upward and touching the branches of trees with his fingertips. Those branches were, I was well aware, far beyond the leap of any mortal. It would have been impossible not to have been impressed with the grace of O'Connell. To watch him, as a player, rise upward, field the ball and place a kick in a single fluid motion, like the half-seen dart of a deadly snake, so quickly that it might never have happened.'

Perhaps the best way to offer a measured assessment of O'Connell is to canvas the views of some of the players who played against him.

Ace Kildare midfielder Pat Mangan's view of O'Connell is very positive.

'Mick was a tremendous player. He played football as I liked to play it. He concentrated on the ball and it was never a man-to-man situation when you were playing on him. He went for a ball and he caught it in the clouds; I think one of the great thrills is seeing a high ball floating in the sky and someone grabbing it. He also kicked superbly, and was a tremendous man to lay off the ball. His accuracy was tremendous. He had a very sharp brain and in my opinion he was one of the all-time greats.'

Longford midfielder Jimmy Flynn has no equivocation or qualification when he is asked who was the best player he ever saw?

'Definitely Seán Purcell was the best natural footballer I ever watched playing the game.'

When quizzed about Mick O'Connell he offers a much more nuanced answer.

'I played on Mick O'Connell twice. I especially recall a match down in Killarney. We both caught the ball together and whatever way it happened I kind of dragged him down and landed on his backside. The next time we clashed I was picking up the ball off the ground, and he came in and pulled on me. I said, "Now listen Mick. That's not the way the game is played." But because of the previous incident he said, "Well, it's better than pulling and hauling." I remember that remark well and I kind of laughed. He took football very seriously. I thought he was a purist. He was a complete footballer in that he had all the skills: he could strike the ball off the ground, had a great catch, was a great athlete and could kick with both feet. I don't regard him though as a match-winner in the same way as I would have seen Jack O'Shea or Eoin 'the Bomber' Liston. I had huge time for the Bomber. I would have a question mark about O'Connell's temperament. It wasn't as strong as other parts of his game. It was possible to psyche him out of a match, and the Offaly boys were pretty adept at that.'

# 56

# OFFALY GOOD

*Offaly win back-to-back All-Ireland finals in 1971 and 1972*

Having defeated Galway in 1971, Offaly beat Kerry in a replay in 1972 to claim a second consecutive All-Ireland football final.

For Kildare great Pat Mangan, the Offaly team were a serious obstacle to his county's attempt to drink from the keg of glory.

'The main reason we didn't win any silverware was that we played Offaly a few times in Leinster finals and, although they had great players, it's fair to say they exploited the rules to the fullest, to put it as diplomatically as I can. We were a very skilful team and never resorted to the physical. It's not that we weren't able to, because we had a lot of big fellas, but we weren't that sort of side.

'Offaly's Paddy McCormack was a great character, and had a reputation as the Iron Man from Rhode. Mind you, I saw someone putting it up to him once in a club match and it wasn't so obvious who was the iron man! Another great player on that Offaly team was Willie Bryan. He wouldn't be associated with the type of football I spoke of earlier; a class player who played football as it should be played. He never resorted to dirty play. He didn't need to, but it wasn't his nature to anyway. He always had a great leap when he came in for the ball and had a lovely drop-kick – though he always gave the impression that he wasn't 100 per cent fit.

'Offaly were a very, very tough, physical team, but at the time refereeing wasn't as strict as it is today, and usually they didn't take much notice of what was happening off the ball. The umpires were only there to put up the flags. Offaly were a very, very good team and had a lot of skilful players, but I think everybody knows they had a few hatchet men. Some of those guys prided themselves on being hard men. Today, people speak about winning at all costs, but even back then that Offaly team had that attitude.'

Longford's Jimmy Flynn has strong memories of playing against that team.

'If you're talking about great footballers one of the lads I would have to mention is Willie Bryan. We had some great tussles. I met him a few years after we retired and he said, "I've a great photograph of you and me up in the air catching the ball and we both have of our hands around the ball – but I have mine on the inside!" I thought it was a great remark. He had a great sense of humour and was a lovely footballer.

'Football at the time was very tough. When you played teams like Laois and Offaly you always knew it was going to be a physical battle. There was no quarter given. There was quite a lot of tough stuff and quite a bit off the ball. You nearly had to protect yourself. I remember Jimmy Magee asked me one evening in Power's Hotel to pick my dirtiest team of all time. Any time I mentioned a player for consideration he would come back with three lads that he reckoned were twice as tough. Let's say a few lads on that Offaly team got prominent mention.'

Fitness gurus are all the rage today. According to legend, when the Iron Man from Rhode, Paddy McCormack, was training with Offaly for a year, his style of training was laps, laps and more laps. Eventually the players said to him, 'We're sick to death of all these laps. Tonight we're going to have something different.' Paddy thought for a moment and said, 'OK lads, that's fine. Turn around the other way for a change.'

# 57

## LIMERICK LAUGH LOUDEST

*Limerick win the 1973 All-Ireland*

In 1973, Limerick ended a barren spell by winning their first All-Ireland hurling title since 1940. One of the stars of the Limerick team was Pat Hartigan, ranking with Brian Lohan as one of the great full-backs of the last fifty years. His main memories of the game are surprising even to himself.

'Strangely it's the little things I remember about the game. Firstly, I remember the enthusiasm and spirit of Limerick people going on the train, and the little games we were playing and the jokes we were making. This was only a front for what was facing us the next day. I remember the effect on people we knew, notably a taxi driver, John Lane, a saint in his own right, who had a tremendous occasion.

'The evening before the match the elder statesmen and father figure of the team, Eamon "Ned" Rea, tried to break the ice by talking about "glamour boys" and the way rooms were being allocated in the team hotel. I suppose we were unusual in that we had two brothers in the squad who were both priests – Fr Paudie and Willie Fitzmaurice.

'Ned, Jim O'Donnell, Sean Foley and myself headed into O'Connell Street at about 7.30 p.m. It was a sight to behold. Seeing all the Limerick people there gave us a real lift and made us even more determined to win the title, especially the way they were hooting horns at us. Some of them had been there in 1940 and were looking to see us repeat history, and others were going to attend Croke Park for the first time.

'I recall vividly the pep talk before the final. It was given to us by Jackie Power, Ger's father, who had been part of the Limerick All-Ireland victory in 1940. His voice started to falter and he started to cry. Team captain Eamonn Grimes like a flash stood up and took over.

'I can't remember leaving the dressing room, and I have no memory of going out the tunnel. The next thing I remember, I was outside on Croke Park and in one din of noise.

'The weather was very bad on the day, and we got a little bonus because the wind changed in our favour at half-time. I always feel that the turning point in the game came in the second half. A high ball broke in behind our half-back line and Mick Crotty looked goalbound. Our goalie, Séamus Horgan, made a brilliant save and deflected the ball so it went over the bar. A goal for Kilkenny at this point would have finished us, but the save spurred us on to victory.

'The real highlight of the All-Ireland for me came after the match, and seeing a hundred people crying. It meant so much to them. That was a source of immense satisfaction.

'The post-match celebrations were not all we would have wished for. Such was the throng of people who came to the Crofton Airport hotel that we were locked in – in the interests of safety. I was doing an RTÉ interview and was forced to leave by a back window. There was no dance. The tables were cleared and guards were manning the doors so that people couldn't get in. The result was that there was no team celebration as such. There were pockets of us in different rooms. However, we made up for it the following day when we got back to Limerick to the reception in the Shannon Arms Hotel. Estimates vary at the attendance between fifty and sixty-five thousand people. I will never forget the squad car trying to avoid people as it steered us to our destination, and the joy on the crowds' faces. Let's just say it was very late before we got home!'

Ger Loughnane recalls Limerick's win fondly: 'It was a really brutal, dirty day for hurling. That Limerick team was full of red-blooded warriors who played with such a savage intensity against the aristocrats of hurling that you would almost need a helmet just to watch it! They showed us that while football is a game for great men, hurling is a game for heroes.'

## POSTSCRIPT

Forty-five years later, the county of Limerick rejoiced in August 2018 when John Kiely's men ended nearly a half-century of hurt with a pulsating win over All-Ireland champions Galway to bring the Liam McCarthy cup back to Limerick. And, given the cloud of sadness that had enveloped the county at the start of the year with the death of Delores O'Riordan, it was truly fitting that when the final whistle blew the song that rocked Croke Park was Delores singing the Cranberries anthem, 'Dreams'. For Limerick fans their dreams had indeed come true 'in every possible way'.

The siege of Limerick is lifted.

# 58

# SLIGO'S SHINY HAPPY DAY

*Sligo win the 1975 Connacht title*

The GAA rejoiced when Sligo won only their second Connacht title in 1975 because it was a fitting reward for the supremely gifted Micheál Kearins. The legendary forward put Sligo football on the map. He first played for Sligo minors in 1960, losing out in the Connacht Championship to a Galway side, powered by Noel Tierney and Johnny Geraghty, that went all the way to win the All-Ireland. The following year he made his competitive senior debut, being marked by Gabriel Kelly, against Cavan in a league game in Ballymote, and he played for the county at all three levels that year. He played in seventeen successive championship seasons with Sligo from 1962 to 1978.

His introduction to championship football in 1962, was the story of his career in shorthand: so near and yet so far. Sligo led by a point against the reigning champions but Roscommon stole victory with a goal in the last kick of the game, and went on to contest the All-Ireland final.

Football was in his genes: his father played a lot of club football and lined out a few times for Sligo, beginning something of Kearins' dynasty. Not only did Micheál and his brother James play for Sligo, a generation later Micheál's son, Karl, lined out for the county.

Micheál's place in the lore of Gaelic football is made additionally secure by his phenomenal scoring feats. He was the country's leading marksman in competitive games in four different years: 1996, 1968, 1972 and 1973. In the drawn 1971 Connacht final, he scored a record fourteen points: five from play and nine from placed balls, including two forty-five yards out and one sideline kick. He won two Railway Cup medals, in 1967 and 1969, in a thirteen-year career with Connacht. Two years later, he scored twelve points for Connacht against the Combined Universities in the Railway Cup, all from placed balls. With the Combined Universities leading by 3–9 to 0–17, Connacht got a line ball forty-five yards out in the dying seconds, and Kearins calmly slotted it over the bar to earn Connacht a replay.

He was a natural, rather than a manufactured, talent. Although he ranks with stars like Johnny Sexton as among the greatest place-kickers in the history of Irish sport, he did very little actual practice in that area.

'Especially in the early years I did a lot of physical training on my own', he explained to me. 'I would run a few miles early in the morning, maybe four times a week. I never much bothered practising my free-taking, not even taking a practice one in the kick-about before a match.'

Despite the longevity of his career, Kearins never shed the burden of having the weight of expectations of Sligo fans on his shoulders.

'I was always nervous before a game, knowing Sligo were

depending on me. To slot the first free between the posts was always very important to help me to relax.'

He won an All-Star award in the inaugural year of 1971 at left half-forward. In 1972, Kearins was also a replacement All-Star, though a major controversy ensued when he was omitted from the original selection. He also played in three National League losing semi-finals with Sligo. He played in three Connacht Senior football finals losing to Galway in 1965 and 1971, before finally winning the title in 1975.

With a Cinderella county like Sligo, it was inevitable that Kearins' career would be marked by pain: the anguish of seeing his team lose so often and the horrible inevitability of defeat. But his is also a story of hope and about dreams which sometimes, just sometimes, come true. Like the once-in-a-lifetime ecstasy of winning the Connacht final, the joy is even greater because you have known the pain. It's about being willing to accept a lifetime of frustration in return for one day of utter wonderment. The fact that he scored thirteen points in the Connacht final helped to make the occasion all the more memorable for him.

His reaction was characteristically modest: 'Winning the Connacht Championship in 1975 was a great honour.'

After his retirement from playing he became a referee. His career with the whistle is probably best remembered for the time he sent off Colm O'Rourke.

'It was an incident after half-time and he got a heavy enough shoulder while in possession. It knocked the ball out of his hands but he didn't try to retrieve it, instead he came after me. The play moved down the field and he followed me the whole way down sharing "pleasantries" with me! I had no option but to send him off.'

The two giants of the game had another heated exchange

subsequently, in the 1988 All-Ireland semi-final, when Kearins was a linesman.

'There was a line-ball incident and he felt I gave it the wrong decision. I know myself now that I was wrong and he was right, having seen the replay on telly. I would have to say though he was a great player and actually made the Meath forward line while he was in his prime. He was their play-maker.'

# 59

# THE PURPLE AND GOLD

*Wexford vs Kilkenny 1976*

In 1970, Martin Quigley made his senior debut for Wexford, and he played his last game for the county in 1989. In the course of his career he won four consecutive All-Stars, 1973–6, and was chosen at centre half-forward on the Centenary team of greatest players never to have won an All-Ireland. In 1970, in the first eighty-minute All-Ireland final, he was part of a unique piece of family history when, with his brothers Pat and John, he was part of an all-Quigley half-forward line as Wexford lost to Cork. To add to the family connection, another brother, 'Big Dan', was selected at centre-back. An injury-stricken Wexford amassed a highly creditable 5-10, but Cork ran up a massive 6-21.

Quigley was born into a hurling mixed-marriage. His mother had virtually no interest in the game, while his father was fanatical in his devotion.

'I remember as a kid going to a lot of matches with him. That's where we got our enthusiasm from. Once he invited a referee to the line to have a fight. In his later years, he had to give up going to matches. He used to get totally worked up, which wasn't very good for him.

'My earliest hurling memory goes back to 1960, when I was nine years of age, listening to the great Micheál O'Hehir commentating on the All-Ireland hurling final when Wexford beat Tipperary – although Tipp had been strong favourites. I think he had an unmerciful bearing on my development as a player through his commentaries. After the match was over I went out in the fields to bring in the cows, armed with my hurl and ball as I pretended to be both Billy Rackard and Tim Flood. I was fourteen, in 1965, when I was brought to my first All-Ireland. Nowadays, children are taken to Croke Park at the age of seven or eight. When you are not going to big matches, the media is so important and Micheál was the best evangelist hurling ever had. I'm glad that we have had so much hurling on television in recent years. There were people who said attendances would drop once matches were televised, but the opposite has happened because television has whetted people's appetite for the game.'

Wexford had an assembly line of new talent coming in during the 1950s and 1960s, but the line slowed down considerably in the 1970s. This is a problem that afflicts the most successful counties. Martin Quigley was to be one of the victims of the change in Wexford's fortunes.

Asked about the greatest moment of his career the answer comes with lightning speed.

'Our Leinster final win of 1976. Kilkenny had beaten us in the previous five finals but we beat them by seventeen points that year. I remember looking at the clock with about ten minutes to go and we were leading by fifteen or sixteen points, and I thought to myself there's nothing they can do to us now, though with Kilkenny you can never know. It was such an unusual feeling for me to be so confident against them, that's why I remember the incident so well. The game went reasonably well for me, but nothing exceptional. It was one day though when it was all about the team.'

That year also saw his greatest disappointment.

'We really should have won the All-Ireland that year, having been eight points up against Cork after ten minutes. We had really good teams in Wexford those years and we were very unfortunate not to have won at least one All-Ireland in the seventies.'

# 60

## KILKENNY KINGS AGAIN

*Kilkenny vs Galway 1979*

Hurling is to Kilkenny what films are to Hollywood: a county-wide obsession that sets a pecking order, discussed endlessly and by everyone, complete with its own arcane laws and rituals. Pubs are the churches of this strange sporting religion. Hurling-talk is no idle form of gossip here, but a crucial element in the county's psyche, to which business, love, the land and the weather regularly take second place.

In 1979, the sight of Babs Keating coaching Galway made Kilkenny even more determined to topple the Westerners. Despite the disappointment, Keating looks back on that time with affection.

'I was invited to coach Galway by Fr Jack Solon in the late 1970s. He was a great golfer. I was welcomed by the players, and to this day retain great friendships with them. I was basically a coach and had no role as a selector. One of the key figures though behind the scenes tried to stymie everything I did.

'In training I preached the five S's – speed and stamina,

style and skill, and from these four there should emerge scores. We got to the All-Ireland final in 1979 where we lost to Kilkenny. I remember waking up that day feeling very depressed because it was raining heavily. We had a flashy team with the Connollys, Noel Lane, P. J. Molloy, Bernie Forde – who were dry-ball players. I believe that bad, wet conditions suit an experienced team more than an inexperienced team. Kilkenny were very experienced. We weren't. I believe the wet day cost us two Kilkenny goals.'

Keating is not prepared to go on the record on the internal politics that saw him leaving Galway after that match.

One of the stars on the winning Kilkenny team in 1979 was Nickey Brennan.

'I come from a small country parish, Conahy, with a junior hurling club, Shamrocks, but I got my big break when I went to school in St Kierans, which was a big hurling nursery. To be frank, to survive you had to play hurling morning, noon and night between doing a bit of study. If you get on the teams there it brings you to the notice of the county's underage selectors. I played with Kilkenny from 1973 to 1985 apart from missing out on '76 and '77 because of the small matter of getting married and building a house. I was far from being the greatest hurler ever to play from Kilkenny, but I was a reliable and consistent hurler, and that was probably my greatest strength.

'That Galway team had wonderful players. John Connolly was a hurler I greatly admired because he was such a stylist and had all the skills of the game. He was a complete gentleman, as were all the Connollys. I played through the era of great hurlers of whom one, Ger Loughnane, became even more famous as a manager! I felt very sorry for those great Clare players who never made it to an All-Ireland title.

Certainly their emergence in the 1990s was a major fillip to the game. Tony Doran was an inspiration for Wexford. Offaly's Pat Carroll a great hurler and a very decent guy, though sadly no longer with us.'

In 1979, after Kilkenny beat Galway in the All-Ireland hurling final, Fan Larkin rushed off the field into the dressing room to tog in. A clearly startled Mick Dunne went into the Kilkenny room just minutes after the match to prepare for a live interview only to see Fan already fully clothed. Clearly Fan had missed the presentation. Dunne asked him why he was in the dressing room so quickly.

'I have to go to Mass, Mick,' replied Fan in a matter-of-fact voice.

# 61

## ANTRIM ARRIVE IN THE BIG TIME

*Antrim win the 1989 All-Ireland semi-final*

In 1989, Dessie Donnelly won an All-Star at left full-back for his commanding performances which carried Antrim to the All-Ireland final that year. Dessie's teammates included his brother Brian and cousin Terry, son of the legendary 'Bear' Donnelly, who hurled with distinction for club and county in the 1950s and 1960s.

On a personal level, Dessie's most satisfying moment would come in 1989: 'I was first nominated for the All-Stars in 1986. Although I didn't get selected, I was chosen as a replacement for the trip to America in 1987, which is the nicest consolation prize I ever got for anything. To be selected on the actual team in 1989 was, I'd say, the biggest thrill I ever got in hurling. I can't explain in words just how much it meant.'

That year also presented Donnelly with his sole opportunity to play on the highest stage within the game. Everyone was expecting the day of the All-Ireland hurling semi-finals to produce high drama – mainly because the second semi-final was between old rivals Galway and Tipperary. Eleven days previously, Galway had hammered Antrim in a challenge match, suggesting to neutrals that the Northerners would be like lambs to the slaughter against Offaly.

Antrim's confidence though was high because they had already beaten Offaly twice that year. Although it was an All-Ireland semi-final, the Antrim team did not think of it like that, they were conditioned to think of it just as a match against Offaly. Although Offaly were the form team in Leinster in the 1980s, the men in saffron and white were mentally right for it and would have been more nervous if they had been playing Kilkenny.

It was Offaly who made the better start, and their half-time lead was 1-10 to 1-6.

It was a different story in the second half though as Dessie Donnelly marshalled the Antrim defence superbly and his team ran out 4-15 to 1-15 winners. Ciaran Barr assumed the playmaker role to provide ample scoring opportunities for Olcan 'Cloot' McFetridge (who with Donnelly won an All-Star in 1989), Aidan 'Beaver' McCarry and Donal Armstrong. It was fitting that Armstrong should be part of Antrim's finest hour as his late father, Kevin (dual star, Antrim GAA's most famous son and left half-forward on the Team of the Century of greatest players never to have won an All-Ireland medal), had starred in the last Antrim team to reach the All-Ireland final back in 1943. After beating Galway by 7-0 to 6-2 in the quarter-final they shocked Kilkenny in the semi-final, only to lose to Cork in the final.

In 1989, Antrim kept level with Tipperary for the first quarter of the game. They had chances, but they drove a lot of wides. Then Tipperary got a soft goal which really deflated the Northerners. It took a lot out of their play. The Antrim fans in the crowd were very demoralised by the goal.

Although Dessie Donnelly was clearly disappointed, that defeat was as nothing compared to losing to Kilkenny in the All-Ireland semi-final two years later.

'That was definitely the biggest low of my career because we had a couple of opportunities to put Kilkenny away but we didn't take them. A county like us does not get many opportunities to beat a hurling power like Kilkenny very often, so it was imperative that we took it – but we blew our chance. It was a make or break game for us and, after we lost, the team started to come apart and we never came that close again.'

During the Troubles, Donnelly came to regard the abnormality of that situation as normal.

'Thankfully the Troubles never had a major impact on me. The only time it was an issue for me was when we were travelling for some of the Antrim matches. Of course, you have to be particularly careful when times are especially tense, like the marching season. There are quite a few places in Antrim that you wouldn't walk down the road on your own, or even in company, with a hurley stick in your hand – especially around the twelfth of July.

'Back in the 1970s our changing rooms were bombed', he said. 'The damage was superficial. I'd say that was more a matter of luck than because of careful management on the part of the bombers. There were a lot of theories floating around about who did it as you can imagine, but I can't tell you who was responsible.'

# 62

## EPIC STRUGGLE

*Meath vs Dublin 1991*

After Italia '90, it seemed as if the Irish nation fell in love with soccer. It appeared to some as if the GAA's status in Irish society was under threat. But, in 1991, an epic four-game saga between Meath and Dublin reignited the public love with Gaelic games once more. Meath emerged victorious on the fourth game.

Their star forward, Bernard Flynn, explains why: 'The biggest lesson that Meath team got came in 1985 when Laois beat us by ten points in the Leinster Championship in Tullamore. We were disgusted, and to say it was a back-to-the-drawing-board moment was an understatement. We went to a quiet bar on the outskirts of Tullamore afterwards, and we weren't able to eat. We didn't even sit on seats, we sat on the floor.

'It was time for a new approach, which was not going to be for the faint-hearted.

'It was then than Seán Boylan and the senior players recognised that we were nowhere near the level we needed to be.

From the autumn of 1985 we saw a huge change in terms of physical training, and everyone upped the levels. The raw ambition in that team was relentless.'

The old warriors found talented and willing recruits to take their places in the unique torture chamber that constituted Meath training sessions.

'The change was the way they pushed themselves in training. We used to kill each other. The Laois defeat was the pivotal moment when everything changed. The effort the senior players put in during training, especially for men of their age, was simply incredible. To this day I get goose pimples when I think of those remarkable men.

'Boylan learned as he went. We were lucky to have Noel Keating, and Kepak by his side. We went from being fifteen years behind the times in 1985, to ten years ahead of the times by the late 1980s. I would hear about Kieran McGeeney, and how driven he was with his Armagh team, but I guarantee you they could not match what happened in our training sessions. We were nearly stupid and silly, and it's only when you retire that you realise the belting that went on. It was unreal. I wouldn't go to training sessions in fear, but I wouldn't know if I would come out safe at times. It was that vicious.

'My own experience was that the only time you missed training was on your deathbed. Boylan had instilled that culture into the squad. They were so true to each other, so honest with each other, and so committed to each other. They were committed to the cause to a fault because I believe some of the stuff that went on in training, while it made us, if we had managed it a bit more and released more of the creative spirit within us, we could have won even more. It was madness beyond comprehension the hitting, the thumping and the belting that went on, but it was needed at the time.'

There were times though when it got very personal.

'The day before one of the Leinster finals there was a doubt if David Beggy was fit. I'm not sure what issue some of the lads had with him, but they beat him up and down the field for about fifty minutes. I remember thinking, that man shouldn't be able to play for a week, but they were expecting him to play well in the Leinster final the next day. Nobody asked or said anything because we were afraid to, but it was crazy the torture they put him through.'

Flynn would experience this sensation with blood and sweat, but no tears.

'The only time I thought I was going to be killed, and I really did fear for my life, was in 1988. We got out of jail against Mayo in the All-Ireland semi-final because a number of us were not playing well. Training was not going well. Many of the older players had a lot of miles on the clock at that stage. The intensity and the ferocity wasn't what it should be and Mick Lyons, Joe Cassells and Gerry McEntee were stressing that we needed to up the intensity.

'Mick was an incredible captain; though he never said much, when he did, you listened. During one session the hitting was unreal right across the pitch. When I was on the ball I was trying to watch out for the belts coming, but at one stage Mick hit me a dirty belt. I said, "Mick, if you do that again I'll f**king split you." The next time I was heading into goal he hit me again. So I hit him with everything I had, splitting the bridge of his nose and the blood came pouring out of him. I have incredible regard for Mick, he is one of the most amazing people I have ever met and one of the most inspirational footballers of all time, but there is no point in me saying otherwise, if he caught me again in that match, he would have killed me.'

Would the punishment fit the crime?

'I was apprehensive and a little worried going into the old dressing room in Navan, which was like a scene from *Midnight Express*. It was like a dungeon, and the steam was rising so you couldn't see anything and I was walking into that. Nothing was said, but I was afraid that Mick was going to clock me. I remember showering and as I held the shampoo in one hand I had my other fist clenched ready to respond. My attitude was, if someone was going to give me a box I was going to give one back because otherwise people in the dressing room would lose respect for me. There was no problem if you got sent off for hitting a lad, but if a lad hit you and you didn't hit back there was a problem.

'Finally I saw Mick showering and I could see the shampoo mixing with the blood. I remember thinking he was going to clock me. He came over to me and I saw exactly how much damage I had done to his nose. He put his arm on my shoulder and simply said, "Bernard, that's exactly what we need. We need more of that." There were no hard feelings.'

# 63

## DOWN BUT NOT OUT

*Down win All-Irelands in 1991 and 1994*

Former Irish schoolboy basketball international Joe Brolly believes that Down's All-Ireland victory in 1991, and the three consecutive All-Irelands for Ulster teams that followed it, were fuelled by one man. 'Looking back at the 1970s and 1980s, the reason why the teams from Leinster and Munster always wanted to play an Ulster team in the All-Ireland semi-final, was because Ulster teams were defeated before the match even started because of psychological reasons. Deep down, they didn't believe they could win.

'I'm as sure as I can be about anything that the man who changed the face of Ulster football was James McCartan Jnr. He changed everything. In part it was because his father had played on three All-Ireland winning teams in the 1960s and James had inherited the winning mentality from his dad. The Down team was moribund until he came along. Ross Carr, Greg Blaney, Mickey Linden were all there before. Then McCartan comes in as an eighteen-year-old. He had scored three goals in a McCrory Cup final, and had taken Down to an

All-Ireland minor title. He was a force of nature. I had never seen anything like him. I still haven't. Dermot McNicholl was the closest and, like James, he had that exciting and swashbuckling quality, but he didn't have the fine skills that James had. McCartan changed that entire team. In a way I think he shamed them all because of his bravery, his courage, the way he played and his electrifying confidence and self-assurance.

'In 1991, James was in his second year with Down. He was irresistible. He scored five points in the All-Ireland final against Meath. He changed everything. If Down hadn't won that All-Ireland you could have forgotten about Derry winning an All-Ireland, you could absolutely forget about Donegal winning an All-Ireland, and there wouldn't be Tyrone or Armagh All-Irelands. All of those titles were grafted on the back of Down's '91 win. Donegal realised they could win an All-Ireland, and there was a sense of inevitability that Derry would win the All-Ireland in '93, and then Down came back to win another final in '94. If you had to isolate one reason for all of that, it would be James.

'The strange thing was that he burnt out so quickly. Perhaps it was his size. He wasn't big and took a lot of hits. He was a constant target because of the way he played. He was a phenomenal athlete, and is seminal in the way he changed Ulster football.'

# 64

# A STAR IS BORN

*The year of Jayo, 1995*

In 1995, Jason Sherlock became the GAA's first pin-up boy when, at just nineteen years of age, he helped Dublin to win their first All-Ireland football final in twelve years. His was fame of pop-star proportions after his bootless goal against Laois, his decisive goal against Cork in the All-Ireland semi-final and his pass to Charlie Redmond for the winning goal against Tyrone in the All-Ireland final. Nobody had ever seen anything like it. Hence Marty Morrissey's unique question in the post-match interview: 'Is there a lady in your life?' To his credit, Jason turned defence into attack, 'I know you with the girls, Marty?'

One of the big hits of the time was an Outhere Brothers song featuring the lyric, 'Boom, boom, boom, everybody say wayo'. On Hill 16, this was adapted to 'Boom, boom, boom, everybody say Jayo'.

Jayo's high profile over his fifteen years playing for the Dubs though came with a price, particularly when Dublin's form began to dip. 'I came from Finglas. I had a mother and

I had no father in the household. My father was from Hong Kong, so I looked different, and Dublin or Ireland were in a place where we didn't understand other cultures in our society,' he says.

'Growing up had its challenges. I would have felt sport was a great outlet, because I was invisible. If you were good at sport, people didn't really care what size or shape you were.

'I grew up wanting to be accepted and winning an All-Ireland at that stage probably was the start of being accepted, and when that happened my focus in what I wanted to achieve probably wavered. But as things changed in the Dublin context and we started to lose games, I was singled out and things went back to the old days.'

By his own admission, it took Jason a couple of years for him to come to terms with the situation he was in at the time: 'Looking back now, I was never the biggest, I was never the strongest, but I like to think I had an aptitude and I wanted to commit. After two years I did commit everything I had to play for fifteen years. I probably didn't get the trophies I wanted, but, in saying that, I gave everything to be the best footballer I could be and also to try and encourage and bring my teammates on as well.'

Since his retirement Jason has become involved in talking about racism. When Jason first began speaking about this he talked to his family about what it was like for them when he was growing up. Over the years Jason experienced racism on a verbal and physical level, and did not know how to deal with it. He believes this affected his self-esteem and made him paranoid. In 2013 he was the victim of racial abuse online on the eve of the All-Ireland final between Dublin and Mayo, after his appearance on RTÉ's *Up for the Match* programme.

A message posted on Twitter said: "Sherlock you Na Fianna reject . . . Back to Asia with you, you don't belong here."

'There was a time when I would have been a victim of that, but I retweeted it because I don't want to be a victim any more,' Jason says. 'It was great to get the support that I got. The club he played for contacted me and he was suspended. He and his parents wanted to apologise, which was noble of them, so I met him. One thing I asked him was, when he woke up on Sunday morning and saw the abuse he was getting, how did he feel? He said he felt pretty bad. I said you did something to warrant that. Imagine you didn't do anything, and still you woke up to that every day; can you imagine what effect that has on you as a person?'

# 65

## WRISTY WIZARD

*Máirín McAleenan spreads the camogie gospel*

Before the emergence of Tiger Woods, Jack Nicklaus bestrode the world of golf like a Colossus. During the height of his powers, the *Cork Examiner* sought an interview with Nicklaus, but when their request was put to Jack's PR person he shook his head firmly and said, 'My client would have no interest in being interviewed in a publication that is about nothing but corks.'

There was a time when many 'serious' GAA men looked down their noses on camogie. Thankfully, theirs is a dying breed, and in every county where once there was 'a fierce hurling man' there is now 'fierce camogie women'.

The former president of the Camogie Association, Miriam O'Callaghan, described Máirín McAleenan as 'one of the finest ambassadors that the game has ever had.'

In March 1986, Máirín made her senior debut for Down, in Portglenone against Antrim, as a wing-forward in a game which Down won. She has won a proliferation of honours since, including: Down Senior Championships, Down Senior

League, Ulster Club Championships, Player of Tournament Kilmacud 7's, Ulster Minor Championships, Ulster Minor League, Ulster Junior Championship, All-Ireland Junior Championship, All-Ireland Junior National League, All-Ireland Intermediate Championship, Ulster GAA Writers' Player of the Year and Player of Tournament, Ashbourne Cup and All-Star awards.

She has many happy memories from her playing days: 'My fondest memories are of Sheila McCartan, a highly rated inter-county player, presenting me with my very own Liatroim Fotenoys senior camogie jersey around 1984; winning Féile na nGael Division 3 in Wexford in 1984 and almost bursting with pride at the brilliant Liatriom performance in the Ulster Club Championship final in 1998'.

'My biggest disappointments were losing the Down Championship final in 1990, the poor performance of the Down Team in the All-Ireland Intermediate final against Limerick in 1996, the poor performance of Liatroim Fontenoys in an Ulster Club Championship final against Loughguile in 1997 and not being selected on Liatroim Fontenoys team for the Down final in 1989.'

To what does she attribute her own success as a player? 'Any achievements which I have attained in camogie are as a result of the hard work of all team members, and I think it unfair, in a team game, that scoring forwards always grab the headlines, while tenaciously tackling defenders and midfielders, who always play fairly, are rarely recognised for their contribution. These players I hold in the highest esteem.'

Máirín's career has been enriched by her interaction with a number of characters.

'I was fortunate enough to play for club, county and province, with great players and characters on and off the field. Bonnie McGreevy [Down] talked incessantly throughout a match, frequently using phrases borrowed from other sports, like "Good dee-fence". She instilled great confidence in her teammates with her ability to score or win a free almost every time she got possession, and enjoyed celebrating a score. She scored an unforgettable goal against Tipperary in the All-Ireland Junior final in 1991.

'My clubmate Donna Greeran's performances were all-heart and totally committed. Donna would rather be chased by a Rottweiler than give away a score! She gave lots of encouragement to me during a game', she recalls.

'Another clubmate, the age-defying Bernie Kelly, played every game with the experience of a veteran, and the enthusiasm of an eight-year-old. At forty-three years old, Bernie continued to power Liatroim's efforts from midfield, twenty-two years after helping her club to their first Down Senior title. Bernie possessed and indomitable and unquenchable will to win, as well as a Rolls Royce engine! She scored a goal in each of the All-Ireland Junior finals of 1976 and 1991. On the way to the Ulster Club final in 1998, I was reading a newspaper article on the match. The journalist in question had put Bernie in the "veteran" bracket and questioned the wisdom of playing a forty-two year old in midfield at such a high level of camogie. Fully aware of the effect this would have on Bernie should she hear it, I said to her, "Do you hear that, Bernie – they reckon here that you're past it!"

'"Huh! Past it!" said Bernie, "I'll be hurling for Liatroim when I'm f**king ninety!"'

# 66

# THE LILYWHITES RISE FROM THE DEAD

*Kildare vs Dublin 2000*

When I asked the late Dermot Earley about which of his son's games for the Lilywhites had he most enjoyed, he immediately went for Saturday, 12 August 2000.

'It was the Leinster final replay. The Dubs were on fire in the first half, and led by 0-11 to 0-5. Pat Spillane was writing Kildare's obituary. But ninety seconds into the second half, Dermot got a goal back and then Tadhg Fennin got an equalising goal. The pendulum swung completely in Kildare's direction and Willie McCreery was mighty in midfield. Any Kildare fan who was there that day will never forget it as their team ran out comfortable winners by 2-11 to 0-12. It was a great day for the Lilywhites, and another proud moment for a dad of one of the players. It was like a moment of grace, but a moment of grace that is granted only rarely.'

This was a match that Pat Spillane will never be able to erase from his memory.

'That was the only time I had reservations about Mick

O'Dwyer's methods. I remember meeting him after Kildare's second drawn game in the epic trilogy with Meath in 1997. As usual, the Kildare forwards had generally been kicking the ball everywhere *but* between the posts. He told me he had brought the Kildare team in for extra training that night, and that Pat McCarthy had them down to the Curragh and was going to "run the sh*te out of them". I thought to myself that they should be doing the extra training somewhere with goalposts and loads of footballs, and they should be practising getting the ball between the posts.'

In 1990, Nelson Mandela was freed from his years in captivity. The first thing he allegedly said after he was released was, 'Have Kildare found a decent forward since I was thrown into that bloody place?' Despite their lack of a top forward, O'Dwyer brought the glory days back to Kildare, taking them to a Leinster title after a forty-two-year-gap. The 2000 Leinster final is seared in Pat Spillane's memory.

'One of the games I got into the most serious trouble for as an analyst came in 2000. It was the day of the Leinster senior football replay. Dublin led by 0-11 to 0-5 at half-time and had swept aside the Kildare challenge in the second quarter, scoring seven points without reply and playing some thrilling football. Kildare brought on two subs at half-time, two of their "imports", Karl O'Dwyer and Brian Murphy. I was in a jocose mood and said that Karl couldn't get on to the Kerry team, and Brian wouldn't have got on the Cork Junior team. Within ninety seconds of the re-start the picture had changed dramatically as Kildare got a two goal blitz and Dublin collapsed, only scoring a single point in the second half. Yet again I was left looking silly, and fully expected to eat humble pie, but there was much more in store.

'All hell broke loose. To my mind it was completely over the top. I was making just a few tongue-in-cheek observations, as is my wont, and had not intended to be taken too seriously, but it seemed to be the end of the world to people in Kildare. There was a huge sign outside Monastrevin to the effect that Spillane was a goat. I was driving through Kildare for the next few weeks on wet Monday mornings with sunglasses in case anyone recognised me. It was just ridiculous.

'The most sinister reaction was apparent when I was shown a letter in RTÉ. It was from one of the most influential GAA officials in Kildare, demanding that an apology be issued and that I should be dropped as an analyst by RTÉ, otherwise he would ensure that the GAA would not renew their contract with the channel. As the contract negotiations for the rights to broadcast the GAA games were imminent, the powers that be in RTÉ were genuinely very worried about this threat.

'When all the vitriol had finished, I thought of Brendan Behan's dictum, "All publicity is good, except an obituary notice."'

The most popular joke in Kildare at the time was that when Spillane was a young man his friend, Joe, set him up on a blind date with a young lady friend of his. But Spillane was a little worried about going out with someone he had never seen before. 'What do I do if she's really unattractive? I'll be stuck with her all night.'

'Don't worry,' Joe said, 'just go up to her and meet her first. If you like what you see, then everything goes as planned. If you don't just shout "Aaaaaauuuuuugggghhhh!" and fake an asthma attack.'

So that night, Spillane knocked at the girl's door and when she came out he was awestruck at how attractive and sexy she was. He was about to speak when the girl suddenly shouts, 'Aaaaaauuuuuugggghhhh!'

# 67

# ENGLISH LESSONS

*Tipperary win the 2001 All-Ireland*

In the late 1990s, Nicky English would take on the job of managing Tipperary. At the time, the omens did not seem favourable: 'When I was approached to take on the job as manager, I got lots of advice not to take it. The belief was that the county didn't have the players at the time to match Clare, or whomever. To be honest, everybody told me not to take it, but I couldn't stop myself.

'I think we were unlucky in 1999. I feel that the referee made a bad decision to give a penalty to Clare at the end of the match, which Davy Fitzgerald scored. We had a young team, and our lads thought it was easy after that game because although Clare were still a great team, we had more than matched them. That Clare team had some of the greatest players in the history of the game like Seánie McMahon, Brian Lohan and Jamesie O'Connor, and in the replay they really upped their performance and blew us away. I've heard Loughnane and some of the Clare lads saying since that that was their best-ever performance. I learned from my own

223

mistakes during that game. I had left Declan Ryan on the bench with a view to getting the Tipp crowd going when we brought him on. We sprung him after twenty minutes, but the match was already lost at that stage. I was talking with Seán Boylan shortly after the game and he said he had made the same mistake once by leaving Gerry McEntee on the bench. That day I learnt that you play your best players from the start. We made it to the Munster final the next year, but a lot of our lads got distracted by sideshows like the crowd and getting tickets for the game, and we lost to Cork. I knew that in 2001 we had a great chance of winning the All-Ireland if we could get over Clare in the Munster Championship. By then we were a battle-hardened team and were ready to make the big breakthrough, especially with Eoin Kelly arriving on the scene.

'People talk a lot of nonsense about motivation. I think motivation is a really simple concept. It's about getting a player to give his best but also to do what is best for the team. Before the final I told the players to go out there and make as many mistakes as they could. I wanted to free them up. The last thing you want is players closing in on themselves. People talk about the importance of having a great leader but the best leaders are not always the best players. We had great leaders on that team, like Tommy Dunne, Eddie Enright, Paul Ormond and Declan Ryan.

'My abiding memory of that All-Ireland was that the referee played four minutes of injury time. That was sheer agony because we were just two points up at that stage and if Galway got a goal we were beaten. I couldn't wait for Pat O'Connor to blow the whistle. It wasn't like winning the All-Ireland as a player. What I felt was sheer relief. There is so much pressure on the manager because you are expected to know on the Saturday what everybody then knows on the Monday.

'Kilkenny beat us in the All-Ireland semi-final the next year, and I saw Henry Shefflin saying recently that was one of their greatest ever performances. That was the end of the road for me.'

# 68

# WATERFORD'S WINNING STREAK

*Waterford sparkle in the 2000s*

Cork's supremacy in Munster in the 2000s was threatened with the re-emergence of Waterford as a major power. A Liam McCarthy Cup would ultimately prove elusive, but Babs Keating has a firm view on the reasons for their failure to go all the way: 'I would say the Waterford team of the noughties was very unlucky. Waterford had three massive players: Tony Browne, Ken McGrath and Paul Flynn. On the crucial days they never got the three of them to play well together. For example, in 2004 Paul Flynn got thirteen points in the All-Ireland semi-final against Kilkenny. If he had got any help at all they would have won, but neither Browne nor McGrath backed him up properly. In my opinion, Ken McGrath let them down badly against Cork in 2006. That was their undoing. They were so dependent on those three. They were like the Waterford team of the late 1950s and 1960s. They were just short of two or three players.'

Although best known as a twice world cross-country champion, and for his silver medal in the marathon at the

1984 Olympics, Waterford's John Treacy was inculcated to the culture of the games at an early age.

'Growing up in Villerstown we played football and hurling on the Commons. I went to many a club match where there was skin and hair flying. A number of the games never finished!'

How does he react to the view that Waterford's attempt to physically intimidate Kilkenny before and at the start of the 2008 All-Ireland, belonged to 1995 and not to 2008 as the game had moved on so much?

'One of the greatest lessons I learned in sport is never p**s off your opponents. I remember, when I was in my prime in Providence College, Gerry Deegan and I were running against a guy from Holy Cross College in Massachusetts. We put on a bit of a spurt at one stage but the guy stayed with us and said in a very arrogant way: "You're not going to drop me that easily." We didn't like the way he said that so we dropped him half a mile in the space of a mile!

'Waterford hadn't learned that lesson going in to that final. You never p**s off Kilkenny. The only chance you have is to cosy up to them and tell them that you are delighted to be in their company. It was incredible to watch the game and see how much it has changed from my youth because there is so much speed and skill. I think of Henry Shefflin scoring with consummate ease from an almost impossible angle. Nothing adorns the game like a player of his skill, just like the way players like Brian Mullins and Jack O'Shea lit up Gaelic games in the 1970s and 1980s. In a different way, DJ Carey had lit up the game with his speed and artistry. I marvelled at him because he was fantastic. What really stood out for me attending the 2008 All-Ireland final was their half-back line. They were awesome. Nothing could get past them. I think of Brian Cody as the Alex Ferguson of Irish sport. He is an incredible manager. He sets the bar very high, and demands and gets the highest standards from his players. If you don't reach them, you have no future as a Kilkenny hurler, no matter how much skill you have. He knows everything about every promising player in every corner of the county. He is always looking for ways to improve the team. He leaves nothing to chance and everything about his preparation is always well thought through.'

Treacy had something of an insider's view of the fortunes of the hurling team.

'I really admire many of the players, like Tony Browne, Paul Flynn, Dan Shanahan and John Mullane. Justin McCarthy called me a number of times when he was coach and brought me down to speak to the team. He also got Seán Kelly in as well. Justin did a lot for Waterford hurling, and let's just say the manner in which he was forced to leave the job left a lot to be desired. When I spoke to the team, I tried to instil in them something of the culture of discipline, sacrifice and the desire to win more than anybody else that is essential to success in athletics and, indeed, all sports.'

# 69

# THE BEAUTIFUL GAME

*Remembering Cormac McAnallen*

Tyrone's joy at winning their first All-Ireland was overshadowed, on the first Tuesday morning of March 2004, when the county heard the shocking news that Cormac McAnallen had died. Why would God take such a gifted role model, a superb sportsman, a gentleman to his finger tips and somebody who had contributed so much, both on and off the field, during his twenty-four years of life? Why leave all the bad people and take one of the good guys?

Cormac McAnallen was an icon of modern-day Gaelic football. A tremendous athlete, he was blessed with a great engine. He was an outstanding fielder and a versatile performer, but it was another quality that meant he stood out from all his colleagues. He was blessed with a maturity that stretched way beyond his tender years. It was no surprise when Mickey Harte chose him to captain Tyrone in the 2004 season.

In his tragically short time on earth, Cormac achieved more than most will ever manage in a lifetime. He captained

Tyrone to victory in the All-Ireland minor and under-21 championships; he won an All-Ireland senior medal; was a former Young Player of the Year; an All-Star; and he represented Ireland with distinction in the 2003 International Rules series. And they are just the high points.

There are many compelling arguments for why Tyrone finally reached football's promised land in 2003. There was the deployment of their brilliant two-man full-forward line, their use of the blanket defence and Brian Dooher's role as a link-man. However, Tyrone's trump card was Cormac McAnallen's performances at full-back. The decision of Mickey Harte to switch the star midfielder to the edge of the square after the team leaked four goals in the drawn Ulster final was the final piece of the jigsaw. From that moment on, Tyrone never looked back. While nothing is ever certain in football, it's safe to predict that Cormac would have won more than one Celtic Cross.

Anyone who attended Cormac's funeral will have felt the universal respect that the entire GAA family had for him. More than any medal or award that respect will be his enduring monument.

Cormac is the embodiment of Mícheál Ó Muircheartaigh's assessment of the GAA immortals as, 'The dead who shall live forever and the living who shall never die.'

# 70

# EXPERT COMMENT

*The rise of the GAA pundit*

A man is flying in a hot-air balloon and realises he is lost. He reduces height and spots a man down below. He lowers the balloon further and shouts, 'Excuse me, can you tell me where I am?'

Ciarán Whelan below says: 'Yes, you're in a hot-air balloon, hovering thirty feet above this field.'

'You must be a GAA pundit,' says the balloonist.

'I am,' replies Whelan. 'How did you know?'

'Well,' says the balloonist, 'everything you have told me is technically correct, but it's no use to anyone.'

Whelan says, 'You must be a GAA referee.'

'I am,' replies the balloonist, 'but how did you know?'

'Well,' says Whelan, 'you don't know where you are or where you're going, and you're in the same position you were before we met, but now it's my fault.'

The celebrity GAA pundit has become central to all media outlets in recent decades and the culture of the GAA pundit brings its own specialised language which takes much deciphering – viewers sometimes end up more confused than enlightened watching some of them.

Many GAA fans would compare pundits to Tony Soprano because they would say their mouths are weapons of mass destruction. To those less *au fait* with the nuances of this technical speak, the following samples give an induction into this unique culture.

When a pundit says: This wonderfully historic ground.
*What the pundit really means is: It's a proper dump.*

Pundit: You have to admire his loyalty to the club.
*Meaning: No other club would take him.*

Pundit: Few players have such flair.
*Meaning: He is a complete show-off.*

Pundit: He's a player who relies on instinct.
*Meaning: He hasn't a brain in his head.*

Pundit: This match was not without its moments.
*Meaning: It would be more exciting to watch the TV with the screen turned off.*

Pundit: He has an interesting temperament.
*Meaning: He's a complete nutcase.*

Pundit: He shows great economy around the ball.
*Meaning: He never gets near the thing.*

Pundit: And the long-standing servant.
*Meaning: He must soon be entitled to free bus travel.*

Pundit: This goalkeeper is like Dracula.
*Meaning: He can't cope with crosses.*

## EXPERT COMMENT

Pundit: He's like a big jigsaw.
*Meaning: He falls to pieces under pressure.*

Pundit: You have to admire his competitive spirit.
*Meaning: He is a psychopath.*

Pundit: He's a seasoned veteran.
*Meaning: He's past it.*

Pundit: He showed great promise as a teenager.
*Meaning: He is totally useless now.*

Pundit: The referee had a poor view of the incident.
*Meaning: The ref is as blind as a bat.*

Pundit: He has a distinctive look.
*Meaning: He has a face only his mother could love.*

# PART VI
# Controversies

Where would Ireland be without the GAA? In rural Ireland in particular it dominates all aspects of life. Every Sunday and Monday morning, throughout the summer especially, the topic of conversation is the GAA. It pervades Irish life. Ireland owes the GAA a great debt of gratitude. What really turns the GAA into a national soap opera is when there are major controversies. In its long history, the GAA has produced its fair share. This section marks some of them.

# 71

# THE SPLIT

*Michael Cusack's diplomatic skills*

Like so many Irish organisations before, almost the first thing the GAA did was to have a split. From the beginning the GAA has had a history of abrasive personalities, with the gift of rubbing people up the wrong way. Michael Cusack will always be remembered for his role in founding the GAA in 1884. Yet, having given birth to the Association, Cusack almost strangled it in its infancy because of his abrasive personality. People often miss out on the historical significance of the 'Athletic' in the title of the GAA. In the early years it was envisaged that athletics would play a much greater role in the life of the organisation. One of the people trying to ensure this was John L. Dunbar. He wrote to Cusack in December 1885 suggesting that the GAA and the athletics organisation should meet 'with a view to a possible merger'. Cusack, an enthusiastic hurler, did not mince or waste his words in his response. The letter read as follows:

GAA
4 Gardiners Place
Dublin

Dear Sir,
   I received your letter this morning and burned it.

Yours faithfully,
Michael Cusack

Cusack suffered from 'Irish bad memory' – which forgets everything but the grudge. He also alienated Archbishop Croke, who stated that he could not continue as patron, 'if Mr Michael Cusack is allowed to play the dictator in the GAA's counsels, to run a reckless tilt with impunity and without rebuke'.

# 72

# SHOULDER TO SHOULDER

*The Ban*

In 1887, Maurice Davin had called for a ban on rugby and soccer. The political leanings of the GAA had been clearly manifested in 1902 when Rule 27, 'the Ban', was introduced. It prohibited members of the GAA from playing, attending or promoting 'foreign games' like soccer, rugby, hockey and cricket. In 1938, the GAA controversially expelled its patron, Ireland's first president, Douglas Hyde, for attending an international soccer match.

The ban was clearly shown to be out of step with the times in 1963 when Waterford hurler Tom Cheasty was banned for attending a dance sponsored by his local soccer club. The ban cost him a National League medal.

Willie McGee, that Mayo great of the 1960s, had reason to be worried about being reported on another occasion. 'When I first started playing championship football the ban was still in operation, so you daren't be seen at a soccer or rugby match, or play them either. I vividly remember attending a soccer match in Dalymount Park one day when I heard this chant, "Burrishole, Burrishole!" coming from behind the goal. I'm from Burrishole, and knew it might mean being identified. So, because I was scared stiff of being reported, I lifted my collar up to hide my face, but it was a Roscommon man, and good friend of mine, Noel Carthy. I was glad to know it was him! But the ban did create that kind of climate of fear. It was as if the GAA was saying to the world we are not confident enough to trust our own members. Thankfully that situation has changed.'

In large measure due to an ongoing campaign of Dublin's Tom Woulfe, the GAA ban on members playing, or even watching, non-Gaelic games was revoked in 1971.

# 73

# THE CURSE

*The fallout from Mayo's 1951 All-Ireland win*

Seán Flanagan captained Mayo to All-Ireland titles in both 1950 and 1951.

Even as a teenager in St Jarlaths College, Flanagan was showing his true colours both on and off the field. When he played for Connacht Colleges in 1939, he was involved in an early example of player power. The team suffered a bad beating and the manager, a priest, thought they had disgraced the province and refused to give them their jerseys. The players staged an immediate revolt on the basis that they had tried their best, and held a sit-in at the team hotel until they got their way. When the priest said, 'I give you my word of honour as a priest,' one of the players, showing for the times an untypical lack of reverence for the clergy, replied, 'We need your word of honour as a man.' Victory went to the players, at least in the argument.

Things were also tense when Flanagan began to play for Mayo. Relations with the County Board were less than harmonious and such was Flanagan's frustration with the incompetence of the Board that he resigned from the team in 1947. The county secretary, Finn Mongey, wrote back to say he had placed his letter before the Board, who asked him to reconsider, and make himself available for the 1948 season. The league was beginning in Tralee, but Flanagan said he would not travel. Following intense moral pressure from his friend and teammate Eamonn 'George' Mongey, he was eventually persuaded to go. When the team reached Tralee Flanagan was addressed by a man who asked him what position he played in. When Flanagan told him he was a corner-back the man said in a strong Kerry brogue, 'Aren't you a bit small to play full-back? Kerry always have great backs, big strong men.' Flanagan's blood was boiling and retorted, 'Mayo came here in 1939 and we beat the lard out of you. We propose to do the same tomorrow.'

The incident did not so much light a flame under Flanagan as much as a powder keg. All his hesitancy was vanquished. The Kerry game had become a do-or-die issue for him. Although Mayo had only fifteen players, they drew with the Kerry men, who had contested the historic All-Ireland final the previous year in the Polo Grounds in New York. So desperate were Mayo, that the only subs they could tog out were the county secretary and the rather rotund team driver. The situation could not be left unchallenged. Flanagan, and the established players on the team, drafted a letter which left no room for ambiguity.

> *Year after year we have seen the County Board bring to nought the hours of training which we have put in, but yet, believing it was outside our sphere as players, we have desisted from drawing your attention to the matter. Events in Tralee last Sunday have banished our indecision,*

*however, and we feel the time has come when something must be done before football disappears completely in Mayo – unwept, unhonoured and unsung.*

Two Connacht titles were secured, but Mayo failed to win the All-Ireland. A view emerged within the more progressive elements of the County Board that Sam would not return to Mayo until Flanagan was made captain. The problem was that Flanagan 'only' played for a junior team. This required a change of rule at the convention, giving the captaincy of the senior team to the nominee of the county champions. Flanagan duly repaid the County Board for their benevolence by immediately banning them from any contact with the team until after they had won the All-Ireland! He did make an exception for the chairman of the County Board and the county secretary, Finn Mongey. One other member, a man of the cloth, thought he should be an exception and paid a visit to the team during their collective training. Flanagan was over to him immediately and coolly informed him, 'Get out and I'll see you when I have the Sam Maguire.' While this did nothing for his popularity, winning the next two All-Irelands did surmount any residual problems in that area.

Mayo's full-back on that team was Paddy Prendergast. His conversation draws you to him like a warm fire in a blizzard: 'While we won two All-Irelands, I believe we should have won four in a row from 1948 to 1951. In the 1948 All-Ireland final we trailed Cavan by a point, but were playing with a gale with three and a half minutes to go when the referee blew for full-time. I am certain we would have beaten them if we had played the full match. There was no objection, but it was savage really that this should have happened.

'In 1949, the belief was that we would win the All-Ireland

semi-final by ten points. After twenty-four minutes, Seán Flanagan and I had a chat about how much we were going to win by. Then, inexplicably, the county selectors took off two of our half-backs and replaced them with two forwards. The Meath half-forwards started to waltz through them. The incompetence of the County Board knew no bounds. Their madness cost us an All-Ireland that year. If it was today, we wouldn't have accepted it.'

The ineptitude of the selectors almost cost Mayo the All-Ireland in 1950 as well.

'We had probably the best goalkeeper in the country at the time in Seán Wynne, and he was in excellent form for us all year. Then, for some crazy reason, he was dropped for the All-Ireland final against Louth, and Billy Durkin was brought in for him. Understandably, Billy was very nervous and the first ball he handled, he dropped. Seán Flanagan knew we were in trouble and pulled Billy aside. He signalled to the sideline that Billy was injured and Wynne came on for him. Only for Seán doing that, we would have probably lost that All-Ireland.

'I remember the joy was unconfined after the game. People don't realise how different Ireland was back then. We were on our knees in economic terms. The GAA made an awful difference to people at such a black time. The bonfires that blazed after we won were a sign that people could still have hope.'

Another All-Ireland came in 1951, but legend has it that it was then that the seeds of Mayo's woes were sown for decades to come, as Paddy Prendergast explained: 'People tell it slightly differently, but the core story is that when we returned with the Sam Maguire Cup in 1951, we interrupted either a Mass or a funeral, and the priest was so enraged that he put a curse on the team that we would never win the All-Ireland again while any of that team were on earth.'

# 74

## DARK DAYS

*The shadow of the Troubles*

At half-time during the 1981 Ulster final, the Clones playing field was filled with people carrying black flags, supporting prisoners who were on hunger strike for political status in Long Kesh Prison. Ulster football could not escape the dark shadows cast by the Northern troubles. In July 1972, Frank Corr, one of the most prominent GAA personalities, was shot dead becoming one of the first of more than forty people to die in Northern Ireland because of their involvement with the GAA. In May 1972, during a match between Crossmaglen and Silverbridge, a young British soldier shoved his rifle into the face of Silverbridge player Patrick Tennyson. Indeed, Crossmaglen was to have its ground occupied by the British army for thirty-seven years.

On 21 February 1988, the Troubles also cast a dark shadow when Aidan McAnespie was shot dead by a British soldier as he went to watch his beloved Aghaloo play a football match.

On the playing fields, Aidan's main contribution to his club, was with the junior team. The closest he normally came to the senior team was watching them from the subs bench, and making the occasional appearance in the last few minutes when the result was normally already decided. Yet football, and the club, dominated his life.

Aidan's late sister, Eilish McCabe, subsequently became the best-known opponent of the removal of the GAA's Rule 21, which barred members of the security forces from taking part in Gaelic games.

Eilish told me, 'Aidan was the youngest member of the family, the only one living at home. He had got a job in Monaghan, as a poultry processor in the chicken factory, and he travelled up and down every morning and evening, and we were aware that he was getting a lot of harassment every day at the border checkpoint from British soldiers. He had made complaints to the army, his trade union, parish priest, to anybody who would listen, as well as through his own solicitor. In fact, one national newspaper had featured an article on Aidan a year before his death. The headline asked the question, "Is this the most harassed man in Ireland?" Aidan had gone to the media at the time in the hope of embarrassing the security forces for a while and it would have worked to some extent in the short term.'

What form did this harassment take?

'It took different forms as he drove to work: they might just pull him over to the side of the road and keep him there for five minutes, and on other occasions they might come over and search his car, maybe take out his lunchbox and search it with their bare hands saying, "Enjoy your lunch today, Mac." They sometimes called him Mac. On his return they might keep him back fifteen or twenty minutes at the side of the road, or ask him where he was coming from or going to, or they might pull him into the big shed and take his car apart. But I think the biggest problem was the fear of the unknown – he was never sure what was coming next. The only thing they were certain was that they were going to hassle him. He was never going to be in a car that was waved through.'

Was he physically assaulted?

'On some occasions he was. The most recent one prior to his shooting came one evening as he was coming through the checkpoint on his way home from work. It was raining pretty heavily and the soldiers told him to get out of his car and take off his jacket, which he did. Then they asked him to take off his shoes and socks, and he said, "I can't do that. It's pouring rain." They pounced on him and forcibly threw him down on the road, and removed his shoes and socks. He came up to me that night and there were marks around his face and neck. I said we were going to have to make a formal complaint. He didn't want to go down to the police station on his own so my husband went down with him. About six months later he received a letter which said that no disciplinary action would be taken against any member of the security forces.'

Dealing with death is always difficult but the suddenness of a violent death is almost impossible to accept.

'That weekend we had a death in the family. My mum's sister's husband had died from a long-term illness and we all had been helping my aunt with the wake. He was buried on the Sunday morning and all the family were together. We all went back to my aunt's house for a meal and afterwards Aidan got up from the table and said to me, "I'm away on to see the football match." He had gone back to the family home and lit the solid-fuel cooker so the house would be warm when my mum and dad returned home. He walked

269 yards through the checkpoint when a single shot rang out, and Aidan died instantly.

'We were still at my aunt's house and I was chatting away with cousins I hadn't seen for a long time. Then my husband came inside and said to me, "Eilish, I need to speak to you immediately." I knew from the tone of his voice that it was quite serious but to be honest I thought it was just that our kids had been misbehaving. When I went out he said, "There's been an accident at the checkpoint. I think Aidan's been involved and it's serious."

'We got into the car and drove down. Just as we were driving through, a Garda car arrived and was blocking the road to stop people driving on, but we got through. As we approached the football field I could also see an ambulance in the background and I thought to myself, "I'm on time and I'm going to make it with Aidan to the hospital." I still wasn't sure what had taken place but I could see a body lying on the ground with a blanket over it. I didn't believe it was Aidan because the body looked small, but I went over towards it. I pulled back the blanket and it was Aidan, and he was dead. I immediately held his hand and his hands were very, very warm, and I hugged him and embraced him. The crowd all stood in complete silence and I heard my parents coming through. An anger went through my body but it had gone again as the grief came back. When I saw my parents going to witness Aidan on the roadside that was just unbearable. I couldn't even bear to look at them with Aidan in that situation.

'The ambulance came into where the body was and they said they were going to take him to the morgue. He was put in a body bag and put sitting up in the ambulance, so my dad and I said we were going with him because we couldn't let

Aidan go on his own. We sat in the ambulance in total shock down to the morgue in Craigavon and that's probably one of the longest journeys I'll ever have in my life. As we were travelling in the ambulance we went through Armagh. Children were out playing and people were going on with living, and as it was a sunny day, even though it was February, people were out walking, others kicking a football and you just said to yourself, "This can't be happening."

'My husband drove behind in his car and at the morgue my dad formally identified Aidan, and we had to make arrangements for an undertaker and everything else. When we had everything sorted out we went back to the house which was packed with relatives, and even my poor aunt was there who had just buried her husband, helping my mum who was in a bad way. Then people were coming to me saying that they had heard on the news that there was an accidental discharge. An SDLP councillor told me that he had rung up the Northern Ireland office immediately after the shooting because he was down at the football field and was absolutely furious that they would claim it was an accident without having the opportunity to question the soldier or to involve forensics.

'It was a long night. We were told around 10 o'clock that night that Aidan's body was going to be returned that night. The doctor decided that Mum, who had stayed up all night the previous two nights with my aunt, should be sedated. I tried desperately to get her to wake up when I realised that Aidan's remains were going to be brought back to the house but to no avail. I looked out just before he was being brought in at around 12.30 a.m. I couldn't believe the crowds that were there at the time. There were footballers, old people, very young people and people who had come long distances.

At that point I had never felt so lonely because everyone else in the family, except my mother knocked out in the bed, were in cars after the coffin. In times like that you clasp on to the smallest things. You wouldn't believe this, but it was a comfort to know that Aidan was going to be home in his bedroom and not in the morgue.

'That night we all sat up, and around 6 o'clock I was making tea for all the people who had stayed up with me. Suddenly, I heard terrible crying and howling. I looked out in the hall and it was my mum who had woken up from her sleep in a daze and she was standing in the hall looking in at Aidan's room. Aidan was laid out in his new suit in the coffin, with the candles all lit. My mum had woken up in a nightmare. I suppose she had thought it was a nightmare, but the reality of the situation had hit her. It is hard when you are going through a situation like that, but when you see your parents going through it – it is unbearable.'

The emotional trauma for the family was compounded by further rumours about the circumstances of Aidan's death and the growing realisation that if they were to extract answers to all their questions, drastic measures would be needed.

'On the Monday we heard that the soldier who had shot him had claimed he was cleaning his gun and his finger slipped. That evening we decided we weren't happy with the explanation and nobody from the security forces had come to our door with any comment, so I contacted our solicitor.

'I also contacted our doctor to see if he could carry out an autopsy on Aidan's body. He thought it would be inconclusive if he did that because it was outside his area and that we would be better off getting a pathologist who would be qualified in that field. The Irish government made a statement on the Monday evening that they were going to carry out an investigation. We decided then that we would go ahead with the funeral on the Tuesday morning knowing that there would probably have to be an exhumation of Aidan's body.'

A family funeral is always difficult but how difficult was the burial when there was a strong possibility Aidan would almost certainly be exhumed shortly afterwards?

'It was very tough. It was very tough to see Aidan's body leaving the house on a cold February morning. It was hard to believe the amount of people who were there at the funeral from all parts of Ireland, and I mean all parts. When we walked in we didn't realise that the Cardinal was going to be there saying the Mass, or that Mick Loftus, president of the GAA, was going to be there, and many representatives from the Ulster Council. All the support helped us in a small bit to carry our cross.

'The sensation of it was almost unbearable, knowing that we were going to exhume him. We didn't know when, but we hoped it would be sooner rather than later. When Aidan's coffin was being lowered into the ground, in order to make it easier to take it out again, they also lowered the supports that would normally be raised.

'On the following Saturday we got a phone call from the Irish government saying that we had permission to have the body exhumed the following morning and brought to Monaghan hospital, with the State pathologist, Dr Harbison, in attendance. To me, hearing the news was a relief because I knew an injustice had been done to our family and I had no confidence in British justice so I believed that the autopsy was an opportunity for us to get to the truth.

'For my mother in particular it was unbearable. I remember breaking the news to her that Aidan's body was being exhumed, and I could see in her eyes that it was taking a lot out of her but I knew she too wanted to get to the bottom of it. Indeed, on the Wednesday of that week, there was a soldier who was charged with the unlawful killing of Aidan, but we had no confidence that he was going to be convicted so we knew that the onus was on us to get an investigation.

'On the Sunday night, when the police had finished with all their forensics, the road was re-opened, but then someone came in and told me that the Monaghan road had been closed again. This made us even more suspicious, and someone came to me later that night and told me that they had a light on and there was a red mark on the road where Aidan's body was. I wasn't quite aware of what was going on and we were told that three shots went off where they were re-marking the road. The media covered the story, but the next day the police came back and said they had been shot at and returned fire. That was something that had been denied by everyone in the locality, that shots were fired at them.'

The family's pain was exacerbated by the portrayal of Aidan by the British media.

'In the British media the phrase they consistently used to describe Aidan was a "Sinn Féin activist". That to our family was very hurtful as well. Aidan was a member of the GAA, but had never been involved in any political party or political activity. I myself had stood for Sinn Féin at a local government election in 1985. Aidan had gone out and put up posters for me, as a brother would do for a sister, but neither of us had been involved in any political activity since then. It was like the British media were using this as a stick to beat us. I don't think it's right to treat any person the way Aidan was treated, regardless of their political view, but it hurt more to see him portrayed in this way to justify to people in England what the soldier had done.'

Did the fact that Eilish had stood for Sinn Féin contribute to Aidan's problems with the security forces?

'Aidan had been getting the harassment before I stood for election, and had come in here to me one evening and said, "If you get elected as a councillor, they won't be able to harass me anymore."'

The passing of the years has done little to heal the family's pain, as Eilish told me.

'It's been very difficult. After Aidan's death my husband and I and our two children moved to stay with Mum and Dad for a few weeks. We ended up staying from February until the end of July. They were totally devastated because their lives had revolved around Aidan. When we moved back to our home, I was still expecting Aidan to drop in every evening, the way he always used to. He has been an absent figure from all the happy family events we've had since, like my brother's wedding. You don't ever forget him. You wonder, would he be married now and have children. While everybody else gets older, Aidan will always be twenty-three to us.'

# 75

# FORLORN IN THE USA

*Sam goes missing*

Jimmy Deenihan has the inside story on what threatened to be a huge embarrassment for the GAA.

'In 1980 my club, Feale Rangers, won the Kerry County Championship. To celebrate we decided we would go on an American tour to Pittsburgh and New York. I was organising the trip and didn't want to bring the Sam Maguire Cup but I was persuaded to do so. Pittsburgh Steelers had won the Superbowl the previous year and another Pittsburgh side, the Pirates, won the World Series. Two of the most prestigious trophies in the world would be in the one city. Tom O'Donoghue felt it would be a good idea to have those two trophies photographed with the Sam Maguire Cup.

'We were staying in the Abbey Victoria Hotel next to Rosie O'Grady's pub in Manhattan initially. We had a function on the Saturday night before playing a game the next day in Gaelic Park. Everybody wanted to see the Sam, so I reluctantly brought it along. We left the cup in the safe in Gaelic Park. It was a big strong one.

'The following morning I got a phone call informing me that one of our travelling party had been involved in a serious accident. I went to see him in the hospital. I only just got back to the ground in time for our match against the famous Ardboe club from Tyrone. After the match I had to go back to the hospital. I returned for the cup that night. The watchman told me that someone had come for the cup already, but no one knew who he was.

'We then had to go to Pittsburgh for our match at the Pittsburgh Steelers ground. There were a lot of dignitaries there, all the leading politicians, etc., and former Steelers' stars like Rocky Blair. Everybody was full of expectation. It was a total anti-climax when we arrived without the cup.

'I went back to New York on the Thursday to take up the matter with the local police. Initially they didn't take much notice, but when they saw newspaper reports from Ireland they realised its importance and carried out investigations. I was due home to play a National League semi-final against Galway but stayed on to get the matter sorted out because obviously it would be terribly embarrassing for me to have returned without the cup. It would have been a national scandal. Eventually, I was told that if I turned up in Gaelic Park on Monday I would find it waiting for me. I did, but never bothered to find out who had taken it. The cup was scratched and the words, "Up the IRA. Up Roscommon" were inscribed on it, though I suspect that the person involved was a sympathiser of neither. The irony was that six months later I received the cup when I captained Kerry to the All-Ireland final.'

# 76

## THE DIRTY DOZEN FINAL

*Dublin vs Galway 1983*

In 1983, Galway showed all the signs of a good team when qualifying for the All-Ireland final – they won without playing well, as their midfielder Brian Talty recalls: 'Living and working in Dublin I was trying to keep away from the hype as much as possible, which wasn't easy. I was having a tough year. I had a stomach injury for most of the season and was spending a lot of time on the physio's table. Nowadays there would probably be a name for the condition, like "Gilmore's groin", but back then there wasn't much understanding. My mother said: "It's all in your head."

'Billy Joyce never believed in injuries, and met me one day when I was going to see someone who had a good reputation for dealing with my condition. When I told him where I was going he said, "For Jaysus' sake, if I told you there was an auld wan with a magic cure you'd go to her." Years later I met him in Tuam on crutches and asked him what had happened. He told me that he was getting out of his car and he tore his Achilles tendon. I told him it was all in his head!'

On the day of the final it was a different kind of injury to Talty that would be forever imprinted on the public consciousness.

'I remember waking up on the morning and being very disappointed that it was such a wet and windy day, because I knew it was going to spoil the match a bit. The game ended with us having fourteen players and Dublin only twelve, but it could have been six versus six as there were so many belts flying in. Despite the extra men we still lost, because we missed so many easy chances. The Dubs manager, Kevin Heffernan, got his tactics right. He withdrew everyone else from the full-forward line and left Joe McNally up on his own. With the wet and windy conditions it was the sort of day you could crowd your opponents. We didn't have the tactical variation to respond to the circumstances or even the conditions.'

The boil must be lanced. It is time to hear what really happened with Brian Mullins.

'From a personal point of view, it was a massive disappointment to become embroiled in the worst controversy of my career. That was the hardest part for me, not that Brian nearly took the top of my head off! If you look back at it on TV you will see he really made contact with me. Brian was one of my heroes when I went to Thomond College and played with him. When I got married, in 1980, Brian was at our wedding. I was on my honeymoon when he had that terrible car accident. As he started to rehabilitate I played soccer with him so I knew first-hand how far he had to travel to get back to the level he did. Nobody else would put themselves through what he did to get back to the very top. I'm sorry that his achievement in getting back was tainted a bit by him being sent off in an All-Ireland final, and especially because it was for striking me. I think what Dublin did that day was incredible, but it is such a pity for their own sake that the controversy took away from their achievement. It was heroic stuff.'

Thirty-five years on, the story of what happened in the tunnel continues to be shrouded in mystery. Talty will take the full truth to his grave.

'There was a bit of pushing and shoving, and I was struck. The real damage to me was not that one, nor Brian's one, but after the sending off I was charging through to the Dublin goal when P. J. Buckley caught me in the head. Having said that, after Brian and P. J., I could have done without the one in the tunnel! In the dressing room Billy Joyce asked me if I was OK to continue, and while I said I was, the selectors saw it differently.'

There was unfinished business to be resolved after-wards.

'There was a lot of tension the next day when the two teams met up for the meal which was the tradition at the time. A few words were exchanged! Joe McNally got up to sing "The Fields of Athenry". I remember thinking, "Jesus Christ, wouldn't I love to kill you!"

'Brian and I went outside into the car park to have a conversation. What sticks in my memory is what I was thinking when Brian was coming towards me: "I hope he's not going to strike me again!" He told me, and he was prob-ably right, that I was pulling and dragging out of him, and that is why he reacted. To be honest, I'm not sure if the talk accomplished anything. My other vivid memory is of seeing the way Galway's Stephen Kinneavy and Dublin's Mick Holden, Lord have mercy on him, blocked off the car park, and nobody was going to disturb us.'

Talty is thankful for small mercies.

'Brian was teaching in Kilbarrack at the time. Before I got my teaching job at St David's, Artane, I had done an interview for Brian's school but didn't get the job. Imagine if I had to work with him as well while the controversy was raging!'

# 77

# THE JOHN FINN INCIDENT

*Dublin vs Mayo 1985*

When it comes to disciplinary matters in general, it sometimes seems that the GAA's attitude is see no evil, hear no evil. The 1985 All-Ireland semi-final between Dublin and Mayo is best remembered for the so-called 'John Finn incident', in which the Mayo half-back sustained a broken jaw in an off-the-ball 'challenge'. Despite a protracted investigation no action was ever taken against a Dublin player. Everybody knows the culprit, but he got away as free as a bird. It was heroic for John Finn to play on with a broken jaw – he deserved more from the GAA.

Despite much tut-tutting and wringing of hands, no action was taken against the player in question. What makes many GAA fans' blood boil though is the GAA's penchant for selective justice. No Clare person will need reminding of the striking contrast, and I use the words advisedly, between the GAA's vigorous pursuit of Colin Lynch in 1998 after Clare met Waterford in the Munster final replay, and the way in which the same year the GAA was prepared to turn a blind eye to Michael Duignan striking his hurley across Clare's David Forde. Duignan has since admitted that he was lucky not to be sent off for what he described as a 'desperate' challenge. Everyone saw it live on national television, it was captured in photographs in the national newspapers, but no subsequent action was taken. How can you have faith in consistent standards being applied by the GAA in those circumstances?

The GAA could learn from the way other sports use video evidence. In 2000, twenty-two-year-old Tracy Sergeant streaked at an indoor bowls event. One could not fail to be impressed by the diligence of the officials, and their commitment to the cause of duty, when they later issued a statement: 'Having studied the incident on forty-three occasions, including slow-motion replays, we have decided against implementing a rule that spectators should remain clothed at all times.'

Mind you there are also pitfalls to be avoided when it comes to video evidence. Many years ago, when Jimmy Hill was the chairman of Fulham, his club were due to face an FA inquiry after some of their players were involved in a brawl after a match with Gillingham. Hill set out to prove that Fulham should not be held responsible with a video presentation of the game's flashpoints. He was very pleased with his efforts and boasted to friends before the inquiry that the FA should be selling tickets for his presentation. The only problem was, that when he produced his video as evidence he was shocked to discover that his wife had taped a cookery programme over it!

# 78

## THE TONY KEADY AFFAIR

*Galway legend misses 1989 All-Ireland semi-final*

Inevitably, in a discussion of Galway hurling in the 1980s, the name of Tony Keady features prominently. Tony was immortalised by the 'Keady affair' which saw him receive a twelve-month ban for playing illegally in New York thus ruling him out of the 1989 All-Ireland hurling semi-final against Tipperary.

Sylvie Linnane still mourns the loss of his great friend, whose death at such a young age shocked the nation in the summer of 2017: 'The 1988 final was one of our best games as a unit. It was very close until Noel Lane came on and scored a late goal. *The Sunday Game* had cameras live at our celebratory dinner, and there was a dramatic hush when Ger Canning announced on live television, "And now the moment you have all been waiting for, *The Sunday Game* man of the match is . . . Tony Keady." Suddenly, everybody stared around but there was no sign of Tony. We found out later that he was five miles away in a pub with Brendan Lynskey and their friends.

## THE TONY KEADY AFFAIR

'Tony was Texaco hurler of the year that year. That was why he was such a big loss to us the following year with the infamous "Keady affair". After he was suspended for a year there was an appeal, but he lost that by 20–18. Seán Treacy came in for him and he did well for us, but we weren't the same tight unit of six backs as we had been when he was there. Nothing would have come through the middle with him there, and he would have scored two or three points from long-range frees as he always did. Before the game and the appeal, there was a lot of discussion about whether Tony would play, and that was very distracting for us. Our focus was not as good as it should have been for a team seeking three in a row. In the game itself there were a lot of decisions given against us. Somebody made a comment afterwards about the referee: "He was either biased against us or he was a sh*te referee." Pete Finnerty said he was both.

'I think we all felt angry about the Keady affair because there were hundreds of footballers and hurlers going to play in America at the time, but Tony was the one that was made a scapegoat of.'

Babs Keating has regrets about that year, despite leading Tipperary to the All-Ireland.

'Both All-Ireland semi-finals were played on the same day. Before the match we got the news that Antrim had defeated Offaly in their semi-final. Both teams knew that our match was really the All-Ireland final and that upped the ante. It was a thundery day and there was a black cloud over Croke Park, so there was kind of an eerie atmosphere in the crowd. It was an ill-tempered game, and although we won the fact that Galway had Sylvie and Hopper McGrath sent off took a bit of the gloss off it.

'That year, 1988, was unusual in many ways. We beat

Waterford in a horrible Munster final and the build-up to the semi-final against Galway was dominated by the Keady affair. What really hurt me was that Galway people blamed Tipperary for setting Keady up. Tommy Barrett, the county secretary, was the Tipperary delegate, and he spoke in favour of Tony Keady being allowed to play. He never remembers anyone thanking him for it. I thought it was a very noble thing, and I don't think we could have done any more. We never got involved in the politics of it. At the end of the day, Galway had delegates from their own province who didn't support them.

'Everybody knew the rules. The Galway people in New York knew the rules.

'The atmosphere was very bad before the game. There was a lot of aggression. Hopper McGrath, usually such a gentleman, did the worst thing of all when he really lashed out at Conor O'Donovan. It was a pity. Galway had beat us in the league final that year and it was a superb game.'

# 79

# THE DUNNES STORES CAR PARK

*Player power in Mayo 1992*

The promise of reaching the All-Ireland final in 1989 was not built upon by Mayo, and their All-Star defender Dermot Flanagan looks back on the experience as a lost opportunity.

'The winter of 1989 saw a form of euphoria because we had reached a final after such a long time and had played well, which really took us away from our focus. What should have happened is that we should have cleared off for a week and realised we had lost. People thought we were on the crest of winning an All-Ireland, which created a lot of distractions and left us vulnerable in 1990.'

To this day, Flanagan finds it difficult to assess the way events unfolded after Mayo's defeat to Roscommon in the Connacht final replay in 1991.

'John O'Mahony departed in controversial circumstances. John has never spoken in public about all the details, and I suppose we should let him have his say on that, but it is probably fair to say that part of the reason was that he was not allowed to choose his own selectors. Looking back, the circumstances of Mayo football were not right then.

'Brian McDonald came in as O'Mahony's replacement and a year later would find himself in a huge controversy. Were there any winners? Everybody was a loser to a greater or lesser extent. Brian had been a selector with Liam O'Neill in 1985. To be fair to Brian, he had a lot of good ideas about the game but whether he was the man to get the best out of players was another question. The first thing he asked me when he took over as manager was if I was committed to Mayo football. I was totally committed. I was the first guy to do stretching before and after training. Long before it was fashionable I was doing acupuncture, watching my diet, reading sports injury books and doing power weight lifting – anything that would give me an edge or improve me as a player, so it came as a shock to be asked that.

'The issue that got into the media was about the players pushing cars as part of a training session. That was not the underlying problem. You needed to have a very strong skin to be able to handle Brian's comments in a training session. That was OK for the senior players, but repeated exposure to this for the younger players could have undermined their confidence. We had a lot of younger players in the squad at the time.

'Again in fairness to Brian, we did win a Connacht final in 1992 and could have beaten Donegal in the All-Ireland semi-final. We were simply not in the right frame of mind for an All-Ireland semi-final. There were a lot of problems with organisation. I was a man marker and I was on Tony Boyle for a short time in the game. I did well on him, but I wasn't left on him and he played havoc with us.

'Afterwards, the controversy broke in the media. The team was going nowhere. There were no winners in that situation. The tumultuous saga reflected very badly on the whole scene in Mayo. The County Board had been deaf to any complaints. John O'Mahony had left under a cloud. These situations don't come from nowhere. A lot of mistakes were made.'

The sins of the father were revisited on Flanagan.

'My dad wouldn't have been hugely popular with the County Board in his playing days. One day, he turned around and asked the County chairman if he wouldn't mind leaving the dressing room. For that reason some people believed that I was the most likely instigator of the "revolt" against Brian, but I had nothing to do with it. I never had to push cars because I was training in Dublin and was too busy in my legal career to be "masterminding a coup".'

The 1989 All-Ireland is yet another case of what might have been for Mayo's All-Star midfielder T. J. Kilgannon: 'After Anthony Finnerty got the goal we were in the driving seat because having lost the previous two years they were starting to doubt themselves, but in the last ten minutes we went into disarray and let them off the hook. They finished strongly and got the final three points.

'There were ten thousand people waiting for us when we flew back to Knock. It was awfully moving. There was a real party atmosphere and we went on the beer for three or four days to kill the pain. There was none of the back-stabbing you normally have after a defeat. It was almost a mini celebration, and Mayo people were proud of us for getting there and playing well. There was a feeling that we needed to do a tour of the county as a political move as much as anything else. I went back to work on the Wednesday though because for me it was over and done with – but not achieved.'

Mayo's next attempt at redemption would come in the All-Ireland semi-final in 1992: 'There was kind of a bad vibe all year, and even though we won the Connacht final there was a sense in the camp that things were not going well. Probably the most memorable incident in that game was that Enon Gavin broke the crossbar in Castlebar, and the match had to be delayed.

'Things got ugly after that. It was more personal than it should have been. It was probably an early example of player power. We said that if there wasn't a change of management, a lot of us would walk away. I was asked recently if we really did spend a training session pushing cars. We did! It was the Dunnes Stores car park in Castlebar, and the cars were really big. There was not a great humour in the camp and the manager had to walk the plank. John O'Mahony had stepped down in 1991 because he was not left to choose his own selectors and maybe that's when we should have acted.'

Pat Spillane has a different take on the controversy: 'I often think of what would have happened if Mayo went on to win the All-Ireland in 1992. They came within a whisker of beating the eventual All-Ireland champions, Donegal, in the semi-final. In a highly publicised saga afterwards, the Mayo players signed a petition which called for the removal of their manager, Brian McDonald, and in the process released a list of training methods which they had used during the year which seemed to border on the farcical. Only one side of the story was told in public. Player power saw McDonald bowing out, with Jack O'Shea taking his place, only for Mayo to be absolutely massacred by Cork the following year in the All-Ireland semi-final. With a bit of luck though Mayo could easily have beaten Donegal in 1992 and who knows what would have happened against Dublin in the All-Ireland final. McDonald, being very clever, improvised when there was no field available for training by getting fellas to push cars around the car park. If Mayo had won that All-Ireland, everyone would have said McDonald was a genius and car-pushing would have become a part of training.'

# 80

# THE SUNDAY BLAME GAME

*Pat Spillane gets into trouble – again*

TV pundits can talk themselves into serious trouble. Joe Brolly and Pat Spillane have had plenty of experience in this respect.

Spillane has regularly put his foot in his mouth on *The Sunday Game*. In 2017, Spillane incurred the wrath of Jim Gavin following his comments about Diarmuid Connolly's behaviour against Carlow in the Leinster Championship. It was just one incident among many for the Kerry man.

'I have annoyed counties that people would not expect me to annoy. In the 2004 Carlow versus Longford match in the Leinster Championship, with Luke Dempsey having only been appointed Carlow manager three weeks previously, I confidently stated in my column that it is a bit like re-arranging the deckchairs on the *Titanic*, and they have no chance. What happens? Carlow create the first big shock of the championship and beat Longford. In one of his typical media-shy performances, when Dempsey was interviewed afterwards he said the Carlow players took a few weeks to get used to his "style of football". Carlow fans were not amused at my bemusement.

'Another time, I was reviewing a Carlow match with Joe Brolly sitting beside me. He whispered a comment in my ear as I was seriously analysing the Carlow team. I burst out laughing. The RTÉ switchboard went into meltdown about how much I had disrespected the poor Carlow team. I got the blame, but it was all Brolly's fault! I was afraid to set foot in Carlow for ten years afterwards.'

Sometimes it appears that elements within the GAA think that RTÉ should be an extension of the GAA's PR department, but if you want publicity you have to expect it warts and all. One of the biggest warts is violent play, but speaking out about this has brought Spillane no end of trouble.

On *The Sunday Game*, after Armagh played Derry in the Ulster Championship in 1996, Spillane infamously used the word 'thugs' to describe players whose actions are euphemistically known in the GAA vernacular as 'robust play'. The following Sunday, RTÉ asked him to withdraw the remark but certainly not to apologise.

'I decided to do it off-the-cuff. All was going really well until I said that if they behaved that way off the pitch they would be guilty of "criminal" behaviour.

'To thine own self be true. It was all very well for Shakespeare to write that but he obviously hadn't a GAA analyst in mind when he got that brainwave. Telling it as it is, in my signature style, has got me into no end of trouble.

'The morning after my aborted attempt to diffuse my "thugs" comment I was hauled in front of the Head of Sport at RTÉ, Tim O'Connor. It was one of the scariest moments of my life.

'There are three times in my life I felt intimidated. The

first was when the Dean of St Brendans caught me out of the dormitory late at night and reprimanded me. The second was when a tax inspector gave me a grilling about my taxes. The third time was when Tim O'Connor carpeted me. I was in fear because I thought it was the end of the line; to be perfectly honest it looked like it was curtains for me at RTÉ. Obviously RTÉ Sport were afraid of legal action. They had been taken to the cleaners just before this, following what seemed a harmless enough remark. They were panicking a little that they were going to get stung again. In the end they scripted an apology which I read out from an autocue and I got away with it. I checked it out with a barrister friend of mine afterwards and asked him if calling someone a "thug" is libellous. He said yes. It is only okay to call someone a blackguard.'

# 81

# THE BUST-UP

*Meath vs Mayo 1996*

Billy Keane, son of the much-missed John B., observed, 'The Munster final had more fouls than you would find in a turkey farm the week before Christmas.' Yet when Gaelic football fans think of real aggression, one game looms large in the memory.

Star of the 1950s Mayo team, Paddy Prendergast, winces at the memory of the 1996 All-Ireland final replay. 'Since I retired I look at the failures of Mayo as my personal *via dolorosa*. At the moment I hardly want to see them play. It pains me to see them lose games they should have won, like the All-Ireland against Meath in '96. I am tired of looking at their failures and their lack of determination. You won't win All-Irelands unless you have courage and determination.'

Former Mayo star, and mentor in 1996, Peter Ford was very disappointed by the turn of events which led both teams to get involved in an unedifying mass brawl.

'I am convinced that we were hard done by and I'm not just talking about the sending off of Liam McHale. Pat

McEnaney [the referee] had come down to the team before the final and had talked about what might happen if there was a shemozzle. I found his comments very strange, and was convinced that there could be a very serious incident during the game. People may think this is sour grapes, but I still believe that the referee's decisions influenced the outcome of the game.

'With fifteen minutes to go I could only see one result. Mayo had a comfortable lead but in trying to defend it they pushed back too far and allowed Meath to pick off their points.'

It is very evident that Ford feels a strong grievance about the replay.

'The sending offs were a complete mismatch. Liam McHale was our best player, and while Colm Coyle was a fine player, his loss to Meath in no way compared with the loss of Liam to us. I've heard since from informed sources, shall we say, that the referee had intended to send off one of the Meath midfielders, but that the umpire changed his mind.'

It was a case of so near and yet so far for Mayo's star, Liam McHale: '1996 was my greatest year and my worst year. They say you make your own luck but we were unlucky.'

The old wound must be re-opened and the interview cannot progress without reference to his sending-off in the All-Ireland final replay.

'I will never get over that. I felt I had no choice but to get involved. Fellas on my team were getting hit with haymakers, and I was their leader and had a big bond with those guys. There was no way I could just stand back and watch, and leave them to their own devices. If I had done nothing I would not have been able to live with myself. If I was presented with those circumstances again I would still do the same thing. I have a clear conscience because I didn't shirk my responsibility.'

McHale's regret about the sending off is tied in with his view of the way that game unfolded.

'Well, I believe the outcome would have been different if a Meath midfielder had been sent off. When I went off we had to get another midfielder on which meant that we had to take Ray Dempsey off. Ray had scored 1–2 in the All-Ireland semi-final and was in great form, so losing him was a blow. You have to remember we could only use three subs then. If Meath had lost a midfielder too we wouldn't have had to replace Ray.'

Many people were surprised when McHale stated that getting sent off was akin to hearing that your mother had died.

'Losing an All-Ireland final is far worse than losing any other game. When you get that far and lose, especially to lose by a point in those circumstances, was sickening. We put in an astronomical effort, working very hard but had nothing to show for it.'

The big midfielder tells a tale which he thinks is symptomatic of Mayo's fortunes in Croke Park in recent decades.

'Before the 2004 All-Ireland final, I saw that there were great odds on Alan Dillon scoring the first goal in the match. I called my wife, Sinead, and asked her to place a big bet for me. After five minutes, Alan, on cue, scored the goal and I did a dance for joy. Afterwards, I learned that Sinead had forgotten to place the bet.'

McHale's capacity to tell it as it was during those years did not always endear him to the football constituency in Mayo.

'In 2006 I was on RTÉ's *Up for the Match* programme the night before the All-Ireland final. Mary Kennedy asked me if I was confident. I replied, "I would be confident if we weren't playing Kerry." I got some abuse because of that.'

274

# 82

# BANNER HEADLINES

*Clare vs Tipp 1997*

In 1998, Ger Loughnane's name became a byword for controversy. What is often forgotten though is that the media tide had turned against him the previous year, as he remembers with feeling: 'Following Clare's victory in the epic Munster final in 1997, Anthony Daly made a speech in which he articulated the feelings and motivations of all Clare players and supporters on that day. Daly had that uncanny knack of putting into words exactly what everybody was feeling, and his comment, "We're no longer the whipping boys of Munster" captured perfectly the mood of the day. A massive cheer went up from the Clare supporters when he uttered these words.

'To the utter consternation of everyone in Clare, Liz Howard, the public relations officer of the Tipperary County Board, wrote in a newspaper article that the statement was "conduct unbecoming". Liz, or Libby as she was then known, spent most of her youth living in Feakle, where her father was the local sergeant, so her comments hit a nerve, especially in her former home village.

'However, when she repeated this "conduct unbecoming" theme two weeks later, the whole thing spiralled out of control. Other newspapers picked it up and it became the topic of conversation. Dalo said to me, "This whole thing has gone out of control." So I told Dalo to leave it to me. I wrote an open letter to Liz Howard and that's when the whole controversy really started.

'It finally came to a head when Dalo called me and said that a man came to the door of his shop in Ennis and said, "You shouldn't have said that."

'Dalo replied, "What did I say?"

'The man said, "Well, I don't know. But you shouldn't have said it."

That is the perfect illustration of what people pick up from the papers. That's why I'm glad I always treated the press with the respect they deserved.'

That same year, Loughnane unwittingly found himself in the centre of another media storm.

'The *Irish Examiner*'s Jim O'Sullivan did a lengthy interview with me in shorthand in Buswell's Hotel after we won the semi-final against Kilkenny. At one stage he asked me who did I think would win the second semi-final between Tipperary and Wexford. I answered, "I'm certain that Tipperary are going to win it."

'He replied, "Surely Wexford will be way too tough for them?"

'I responded, "The biggest mistake you could make is think that roughhouse tactics could work against Tipperary." I went on to say that if you look back at the history of Tipperary hurling, you will not beat them by roughing them up. We had played them earlier that year in Cusack Park, and tried that with them but they beat us. The only way you could beat them was by outhurling them.

'The following Thursday or Friday, I was over in London with my wife, Mary. I rang my two sons at home and they told me that a big headline had appeared in the *Examiner* to the effect that I had said Wexford were hatchet men. I didn't know the exact wording at that stage.

'On the Monday morning I was walking down a street off Oxford Street in London and I saw a shop with the *Irish Independent*. I was shocked to discover that Rory Kinsella had been asked in his post-match interview what he was going to do about Ger Loughnane's comment that Wexford were guilty of "roughhouse tactics". What struck me immediately was that if Wexford had qualified for the All-Ireland there would be no denying that I had said it, and it would really have polluted the atmosphere coming up to the final.

'I was debating in my own mind whether I should let it go because Wexford were out, but I decided it was too serious to leave it. When we got home I rang the *Examiner* and asked for Jim O'Sullivan. Most people don't realise that the person who writes the article does not write the headline. The problem was not Jim's article, but the headline that accompanied it, "Loughnane accuses Wexford of roughhouse tactics". The headline writer obviously wanted it to be as sensational as possible. The then editor, Brian Looney, came on the line. I explained how damaging the headline would have been if Wexford had qualified for the All-Ireland. He said, "I admit we made a high tackle. What are you looking for?" I explained that all I was looking for was an apology. They published it down the page but who reads an apology at the bottom of the page?

'The *Sunday Independent* had reproduced the article. I then contacted their then sports editor, Adhamhnan O'Sullivan. They also printed an apology but few people saw it. To this day, most people in Wexford think I said something I never did. Ever since then I've always insisted that if somebody was coming to interview me, they had to have a recorder.'

A new hurling soap opera was about to unfold the following year.

# 83

# AH REF

*The Jimmy Cooney saga 1998*

In 1998, the whole Irish sporting world seemed to be swept up in the myth of Ger Loughnane. Having travelled the stoniest road to stardom, it seemed that the outrageous vicissitudes of his career came to a climax that summer. As the Colin Lynch controversy grew like a monster out of control, Loughnane's role in helping to lift hurling to unprecedented heights was seldom mentioned. Such was the media frenzy that when Clare faced Offaly in the All-Ireland semi-final, the fact that his team were just seventy minutes shy of a third All-Ireland final appearance in four years seemed almost secondary. Hurling's capacity to outreach the wildest imaginings of fiction was shown that year.

'If something wrong happens, you have to speak out about it, whether it costs you an All-Ireland or not. As Anthony Daly said to me afterwards, in October of that year, we wouldn't change a thing about it, and make no apologies for anything we did or said.'

Loughnane's primary purpose, to which he returned again

and again, during his infamous Clare FM interview, was to encourage the Clare fans to lift the team, especially the new players that would have to come on the team on Sunday. The interview achieved its objective.

'There was so much unfavourable comment in the media that the Clare players were starting to wonder when I was going to reply to it. I wanted to leave it as close as possible to the Offaly match to lance the boil. When I came into training that night, all the players were looking at me! Although they said nothing, I knew they were relieved I had taken on the criticism. In all of the controversy, I never spoke to any of them about anything that was going on off the field. I wanted them to concentrate just on the hurling.

'In my experience of Gaelic games I've never seen a team as united with its supporters as that first day against Offaly. When we came on to the pitch there was just an electric feeling and a great ovation. It was an amazing feeling of oneness with the crowd, and considering that at that stage we had already won two All-Irelands, it was just incredible.'

Clare led Offaly by four points with ten minutes to go, but it required a late free from Jamesie O'Connor to tie the match at 1-13, after Offaly scored 1-2 without reply. In the circumstances, Loughnane was delighted: 'I was relieved we had survived and I knew we would play much better in the replay.'

Much of Clare's performance in the replay was a monu-ment to patience, nerve, courage and technical brilliance, the mature masterwork of a great team. As normal, Clare concentrated on setting a dominating, draining pace. This was essential for Loughnane's team in which goals had to be mined like nuggets.

'What I always felt about our team was that in order for us to be effective we had to play the whole game with the pedal to the floor. It had to be constant, constant going, constant closing in on the opposition. When you faced into draws and replays it just sapped your energy. No matter what you did, you didn't have the same zip as if you had a break between games.

'After the three games with Offaly in 1998, everybody felt that the end was nigh. In particular we felt the second Offaly match was like the end of the road. The hurling we produced that day was absolutely out of this world. For the first forty minutes of that game, the Clare hurling was exceptional. The speed of the game, the quality of the scores and then, just as Kilkenny had done against us the previous year, Offaly came back. We let them back in, but were still winning by three points with two minutes to go and Barry Murphy goalbound on the twenty-one-yard line.'

Houdini could not have escaped from the pit the Offaly team were in, and Mr Micawber would have been hard pressed to find any reason for optimism. Clare's calculated challenge was intensifying towards its thrilling crescendo but suddenly . . .

Nobody knows. That's the mystery, the fun, the drama of hurling. Then came a bizarre incident. Jimmy Cooney intervened and blew full-time two minutes prematurely. There was a very thin line between laughter and loss for Loughnane.

'When the game was over there was no sense of elation, just a sense of anger. The question in my mind was: "Why the hell did the ref blow as Barry was going through?" I said to Colm [Flynn], "What's he doing?" Colm said, "It's over." He started jumping up and down. I felt no sense of exhilaration. I was preparing to give the team the most ferocious bollocking in the dressing room for taking the foot off the pedal and allowing Offaly back into the game.

'Jimmy Cooney didn't deprive us of the All-Ireland that year, but he did deprive us of getting there.'

Loughnane had to deal with the fallout. 'When we learned there had to be a second replay after the Jimmy Cooney saga I thought to myself, "Jesus, that's the last thing we want." If ever the mental toughness of Clare was tested, it was against Offaly in that third game.

'Offaly had the hangman's noose around their neck – the next thing they found they were free. They woke up in the next world and they were alive. All of the cards were in their favour. Clare had won and were in the All-Ireland but now not in the All-Ireland.'

Offaly had a massive psychological advantage as Loughnane freely acknowledges: 'We were devastated by injuries. P. J. O'Connell was injured. Ollie Baker was injured. Liam Doyle was injured. Brian Quinn had suffered a blackout the previous Tuesday, which I didn't know about. Barry Murphy was injured.

'I thought we'd be trounced by Offaly. What Clare produced in the second half that day was really out of the top drawer. They did everything you could do when your last ounce of energy is drained and your back is to the wall. They fought like lions, and had it not been for three great saves by the Offaly goalie we'd be in the All-Ireland final. Lucky enough we weren't, because Kilkenny would have beaten us in the final, no question about it.

'It was the day I was most proud of them in every way – with all the odds stacked against them and all the media stacked against them. Their manliness and courage against tiredness and injury was something to be cherished.'

# 84

# THE LYNCH MOB

*The Colin Lynch affair 1998*

Apart from Ger Loughnane, the most talked about person in hurling in 1998 was Colin Lynch, the Clare midfielder. Lynch was controversially suspended for three months following the Clare victory over Waterford in the Munster final replay, despite the absence of any video evidence to convict him. In the immediate aftermath of the Jimmy Cooney 'scandal', a new controversy erupted about whether Lynch's ban would be rescinded. Ger Loughnane was central to the machinations behind the scenes.

'After that match I was sitting down in the Burlington Hotel when someone came in around 7 o'clock and said there was a call for me. It was Marty Morrissey, telling me that RTÉ had been put on standby for 3 p.m. the following Saturday in Thurles. I had just been talking to Phelim Murphy, who was on the Games Administration Committee, about the rumours that had been circulating regarding a replay, and he said it was pure rubbish. There was a massive confusion that night but I said if we were going to have a replay we had to have Colin Lynch back.

'I knew the then president of the GAA Joe McDonagh was supposed to be in the hotel so I asked John Glen, then manager of the Burlington Hotel and who had told me that Joe was staying there, to arrange a meeting with him for me. He later told me that Joe had gone down to Galway to present medals that night, but he would be having breakfast in the Berkeley Court in the morning and I might be able to meet him then. I had the very distinct impression that the president of the GAA did not want to meet me with the controversy about Colin Lynch at its height. So I rang the secretary of the Clare County Board, Pat Fitzgerald. He was halfway home at this stage, so rang me back and told me there was a GAC [Games Administration Committee] meeting set for 10 o'clock the next morning. Then I knew something was definitely up. All the players were in the pub drinking, so I went in and said, "Take it easy lads. There's going to be a replay on Saturday." Anthony Daly summed up the attitude of the players when he said, "Ah, f**k it. We'll take them on again. If they bate us, what about it. If we're going to lose it let's lose it on the field."'

For Hamlet the 'play was the thing', but in 1998 the replay was the thing. The spectre of another replay floated into the consciousness. Loughnane summoned all the officers of the Clare County Board for a council of war meeting at 8 a.m. in his room in the Burlington the next morning. Meanwhile he had instructed Pat Fitzgerald to arrange a meeting with Liam Mulvihill, the GAA's Ard Stiúrthóir, with a view to getting Colin Lynch back into the fold.

'I drove Pat Fitz's car into the back of Croke Park. This man in a black suit and dark glasses opened the gate and waved us through. He told Pat to get out and ordered me to drive over to the Hogan Stand side. Pat went into the labyrinth of the Cusack Stand and we waited and waited for him to come back. About five minutes before the GAC meeting was due to start, Pat returned and said, "There's going to be a management meeting on Wednesday night. We can't say for definite but you can take it for granted that Colin Lynch will be back."

'The Offaly delegation, Christy Todd and Brendan Ward, were waiting in the corridors and looked really uptight. I said to them, "What's to worry about? There's definitely going to be a replay."

'They asked, "How do you know?"

'I replied, "Sure what are we here for? There's going to be another game. It's going to be on next Saturday in Thurles at 3 p.m."

'Both of them were looking at me, "But there's going to be an investigation."

'"There's going to be no investigation. It's already sorted."

'They lightened up then. We went in first and Pat Fitz presented our case as to why there shouldn't be a replay, just as a formality, knowing it was just a whitewash. There was very little argument on either side. Offaly went in and came out as the next step of the charade was played out. Then we were both brought in together and given the verdict.'

To nobody's surprise in the Clare camp, they were told that there would be a replay in Thurles on the following Saturday. Additional features were that the money generated would be given to the Omagh fund, and that there would be a 'big' donation to the holiday fund to both counties. The only shock was the news that Dickie Murphy would be refereeing; it was the practice at the time that the same referee who officiated at the original game also refereed the second game. At this juncture Loughnane intervened to ask why Jimmy Cooney would not be in charge. He was told that the Galway man had asked not to be considered. Loughnane stated, 'I want to make it quite clear that we have no objection to Jimmy Cooney refereeing it.' His comment appeared to fall on deaf ears.

'Then I said, "We have no problem taking on our great friends here from Offaly next Saturday." They were all aghast because they were expecting a massive row over it. My attitude was once you win anything on the field, if there's any question mark over it, what good is winning it? I also believe that no matter what else happens, the All-Ireland is sacrosanct. We would do nothing that would jeopardise or compromise its status in any way.'

The following Wednesday, Colin Lynch's appeal was heard by the Management Committee in Croke Park. Lynch travelled up for the meeting with Pat Fitzgerald but was not asked any questions or afforded the opportunity to speak. The Munster Council produced a witness, a Mr McDonnell from Tipperary, who claimed to have seen Lynch striking Tony Browne.

At the meeting, the chairman and secretary of the Munster Council claimed that they received calls from Joe McDonagh urging them to take action following an incident in the Munster Hurling Final replay. This was one of their strongest arguments in upholding the suspension. This intervention raised questions in the Clare camp. Did any members of the GAC receive similar calls from Joe McDonagh following the All-Ireland semi-final replay?

At the meeting Lynch was told that the GAC could not grant him clemency. As it was the Munster Council who had suspended him, only they could shorten his sentence. Lynch wrote to the Munster Council and delivered the letter personally to the secretary Donie Nealon's house but he didn't recognise him. He asked him who he was and then took the letter from him. The Clare camp were understandably keen to have Lynch's appeal heard before the second replay.

'That night I went to Pat Fitzgerald's house to see if we could get the Munster Council to meet before the game to discuss Colin's case. Pat knew that the chairman of the Munster Council, Seán Kelly, was on holiday in Wexford, so we were told that the only way they could contact him was at a payphone half a mile from where he was staying.

'Months later, after the controversy had died down, Seán Kelly contacted me and asked if he could meet me for dinner. To his great credit he wanted to bury the hatchet between the Munster Council and us. We had a great chat for six hours. At the end I asked him if the only way the Munster Council could have contacted him when he was on holiday in Wexford was at a payphone up the road. He said in this day and age that was nonsense. Enough said!

'The enjoyment of sport is from game to game. People say, "Ye won nothing in '98." We won the Munster Championship. People said in 1999, "Ye won nothing." We had six brilliant days. A year is never wasted once you have matches.

'That year, 1998, was one of the best years we ever had. Even though we didn't win the ultimate prize, we gave it everything to win again. It tested our mettle, mental reserve, hurling, resolve and the unity of the team like never before. There are more fundamental things than winning, like standing up for your principles. You've got to stand up for what you really believe in. If you don't you're nothing.'

# 85

## SHEEP IN A HEAP

*Babs and Offaly end in tears 1998*

After Offaly lost the Leinster final in 1998 to Kilkenny, Babs Keating controversially described the Offaly players as 'sheep in a heap'. Babs met with the County Board and decided to stay, but resigned the next morning when he was 'shocked' by an interview in a newspaper with Offaly's star midfielder, Johnny Pilkington, who had questioned Babs's record with the county, stating that Babs had abandoned Offaly's tradition of ground hurling and questioned the tactics used against Kilkenny.

Pilkington is not someone to hide his feelings: 'It really got to me. Babs was manager of Offaly. We had some very bad wides on the day and we had conceded two soft goals in the last fifteen minutes. It just seemed he was passing the buck. Maybe it was the players' fault, but he was the manager and he could have come down on Tuesday night and said what he had to say in the dressing room. He always referred to Offaly as "them" – never as "us". It was a case of "they" were poor out there and "they" did things wrong.

'Michael Bond came on the scene after about a week. He just said he liked Offaly hurling and off we went training. Nobody knew who he was. Nobody knew his hurling credentials or anything. We knew he was a teacher and someone told us he was a principal. He spoke Irish and some of his instructions were in Irish. The training sessions upped significantly. We were a group of lads who were down at the bottom of the barrel after speaking out against the manager. It wasn't anyone else's responsibility to pick it up – only the thirty lads who were there. After Bond came in there was a great buzz in training and we were thinking we were great lads again. We played Kilkenny in a challenge match though and they gave us an even bigger beating than they had in the Leinster final! So where did that leave us?

'Loughnane took his eye off the ball before we played Clare in the All-Ireland semi-final. If they had been playing Kilkenny or Galway it would have been a different story. He took Offaly for granted.'

Not surprisingly, Babs Keating's reading of the events of 1998 differs sharply from Pilkington's: 'Johnny Pilkington took great exception to my remark, but one of my biggest battles at the time was to get Pilkington to train.'

Broadcaster Peter Woods offers an interesting perspective on Offaly's revived fortunes under Michael Bond, 'You could lead them with a thread, but you can't drive them with an iron bar.'

Hubert Ringey, the Offaly captain, in his victory speech after the team beat Kilkenny in the All-Ireland final said, 'We might have come in the back door, but we're going out the front door.'

Offaly came through the back door, having voted against it, and Offaly, true to form, voted against the back door the following year.

# 86

## THE EXILE OF FITZGERALD

*Páidí vs Maurice 2001*

The late Páidí Ó Sé's managerial record compares favourably with most: he brought to Kerry a National League and under-21 All-Ireland, and two All-Irelands in 1997 and 2000. Those people who doubted Páidí's credentials when he was appointed Kerry manager were proved wrong.

His former teammate Pat Spillane was a keen admirer of his good friend: 'He brought an All-Ireland to Kerry in '97 with what I have publicly stated was the poorest team to ever win an All-Ireland.'

However, the wheels came off the wagon in the 2001 All-Ireland semi-final when Meath beat Kerry by no less than fifteen points. Kerry went through a twenty-nine minute spell in the first half without scoring and then could only muster a single point from substitute Declan Quill in the second half. After the match, Marty Morrissey asked a Kerry fan, 'Where did it all go wrong in Croke Park today?'

The fan replied, 'The green bit in the middle.'

Inevitably, when a Kerry team lost by fifteen points in

Croke Park, serious questions were asked, particularly when Páidí refused to start Maurice Fitzgerald.

Fitzgerald was a forward who could consistently promise to fill the minds of football fans with glittering memories, and delivered on that promise with a series of sublime performances. He is destined to be forever remembered for the All-Ireland quarter-final in 2001 in Thurles when his magical long-range sideline drew the match. Mickey 'Ned' O'Sullivan said of Fitzgerald, 'If he had played in the Kerry team of the 1970s he would probably have gone down in history as one of the greatest forwards of all time.'

Even as a young boy Maurice's exceptional talents were evident to all shrewd observers. His father, Ned, had played for Kerry, and the family were close friends with the legendary Mick O'Connell. Maurice won the first of three All-Star awards in his teenage years in 1988, having scored ten points in the defeat to Cork in the Munster final. It would be nine years later before Fitzgerald won his first All-Ireland medal when Kerry beat Mayo, their first All-Ireland in eleven years.

You can train for all conscious eventualities, but a player's greatest moments are when their instinct takes over, and afterwards they cannot remotely explain why they did what they did. Maurice's career is peppered with moments of genius like that. His finest hour was the 1997 All-Ireland when he regularly broke through with Mayo defenders falling around him like dying wasps, and kicked incredible points from all angles.

Pat Spillane has high praise for him: 'Along with Mike Sheehy, Maurice was the most skilful player I ever played with in the Kerry jersey.'

The later years of Fitzgerald's career were overshadowed

by the controversy created by his relationship with the team manager. Pat Spillane followed the controversy keenly.

'Maurice is very quiet. However, some of the people surrounding him liked publicity as well. The people advising him had Maurice's best interests in mind but not necessarily the best interests of Kerry football, although they purported to have the good of Kerry football at heart. He had two very high profile people backing him in the media, John O'Shea and the then editor of the *Sunday Independent*, Aengus Fanning.

'You can argue that Páidí was right or wrong. At the end of the day, Páidí was proved right. There is a very thin line between success and failure, and on the basis of your decisions you have to be judged on whether you were right or wrong. Páidí was proved right in 2000. Maurice was most effective as an impact sub. It was a big gamble, but it delivered an All-Ireland.'

Quentin Crisp wrote, 'There are three reasons for becoming a writer: the first is that you need the money; the second that you have something to say that you think the whole world should know; the third is that you can't think what to do with the long winter evenings.'

Many GAA fans were looking forward to reading Páidí's autobiography because they thought it would be the perfect opportunity for him to finally reveal what his problem with Maurice was, but on the single issue that most exercised football people he said absolutely nothing.

Ronan Keating was wrong. You do not say it best when you say nothing at all.

# 87

# F**KING ANIMALS

*Páidí loses the plot 2003*

As the late Enoch Powell famously observed of politicians, so one might say of football managers, that every career is bound to end in failure; or, if not failure, at least not complete satisfaction.

Páidí Ó Sé did not savour complete satisfaction as a manager. As a player though he was as tough as teak. When Dublin played Cork in the 1978 Cardinal Cushing Games, the match was the most physically violent in living memory. A lot of old scores had to be settled and markers were put down for the championship later that year. Pat O'Neill broke Jimmy Deenihan's nose. Afterwards O'Neill was very contrite and sent an apology later that night to Deenihan in the Kerry hotel. He told him he was very sorry and never intended to hurt him because he thought he was striking Páidí Ó Sé!

Pat Spillane was a close friend. 'Páidí, like myself, was a rogue and, like myself, was a media animal. He was a good friend of mine and is probably one of the people I was closest to from the great Kerry team. He wore his heart on his sleeve but he was a lot smarter than most people give him credit for. People made him out to be blood, guts, shouting and roaring, and passion, and he was all that, but he was also much more.

'Having said that, I was watching him interviewed on the sideline after Westmeath's victory over Dublin in 2004. He was so passionate – and that's great – but he had a jugular vein that was on the point of bursting. If I had any doubts about whether I should have gone into management they died in that moment.

'No football manager is an island. He needs a good team behind him, on and off the field. It would also have been nice to hear the real story of Páidí's relationship with John O'Keeffe. Johno is a lovely guy and a real gentleman. Páidí initially wouldn't have been given the Kerry job because people thought he was a loose canon but these people underestimated Páidí. At first he was given Seamus McGearailt to "mind" him. There is no doubt that Seamus kept Páidí under control and made a massive contribution to Kerry's success in 1997. What people don't realise though is that if Páidí was unsure about something he was always willing to get advice, but he would do so indirectly and not from anyone close to the Kerry camp. Then, when Seamus moved on, Johno was parachuted in on him because certain people thought Páidí was incapable of training the team on his own. The nature of the imposition put a strain on the relationship straight away. A comparable relationship would have been that of Eddie O'Sullivan and Declan Kidney. At the best of times Johno and Páidí would not have been bosom pals.'

The two big controversies of Páidí's reign, the Maurice and animals controversies, were played out in the full glare of the media. He was unlucky insofar as the animals controversy blew up at a very quiet time of the year when there was nothing else for GAA journalists to write about and, as we all know, paper never refuses ink.

A lot of Páidí's most vocal critics were people with agendas. His interview in South Africa was ill-advised. It was not good for Kerry football to have its dirty linen washed in public, nor to have colleagues and former colleagues on opposite sides. There were no winners in that situation and it left a bitter legacy and a sour taste.

A week after the 2003 All-Ireland semi-final, which saw another spectacular Kerry defeat, a Tyrone and Kerry fella were being executed together. The executioner says to them both, 'I'll grant you one last wish before I hang you.' The Tyrone man says: 'I'm from Tyrone. We beat Kerry in the All-Ireland semi-final a few days ago and I'd like to go to my death after watching those magic moments once again.' The guard said, 'No problem. We'll wheel out a big screen and you can watch the game again.'

Then he turned to the Kerry man and asked him what was his last wish. The Kerry man replied, 'Hang me first.'

After bad defeats against Meath in 2001, Armagh in 2002 and Tyrone in 2003, Páidí Ó Sé's reign as Kerry manager ended badly.

Where did it all go wrong for Kerry in Páidí's last years? As those four great philosophers, Abba, famously suggested when they won the Eurovision in 1974, the history book on the shelf is always repeating itself. When the going got tough for Kerry in Croke Park in successive years against Meath, Armagh and Tyrone respectively, Páidí was unable to come up with a Plan B to reverse the situation.

The wounds from those three losses cut deeply, not because Kerry lost, but because they lost so tamely on each occasion. That is not the Kerry way. To lose abysmally once was bad, for it to happen twice was shocking, but for it to happen to Kerry three years in a row in Croke Park, the ground they think of as their second home, was the end of the world. In some counties success is accidental. In Kerry it is compulsory. After failing so spectacularly three years in a row, Páidí's days were numbered. The only problem was that Páidí himself didn't see it that way.

Páidí's U-turn year was 2003. In January, he gave an interview with the *Sunday Independent* and famously said, 'Being the Kerry manager is probably the hardest job in the world because Kerry people, I'd say, are the roughest type of f\*\*king animals you could deal with. And you can print that.'

A short time later he was forced to meekly apologise: 'I regret very much if I have offended all, or some, of my Kerry supporters, who have been very loyal to me.'

Then, following his reluctant resignation as Kerry manager in October, he said, 'I wouldn't rule anything in or out, but I couldn't see myself at the present time having the bottle to go in and train another team against the green and gold jersey.'

A week later, after taking over as Westmeath manager, he said, 'I now want to transfer all my professional allegiance to Westmeath and will endeavour to coach and improve the team, and achieve success in the future.'

At the height of the animals controversy, one Cork fan suggested immediately that Kerry's nickname should no longer be 'the kingdom' but 'the animal kingdom'. Another suggested that in future Cork should play all their home games against Kerry in Fota Wildlife Park to make the Kerry fans feel at home. Yet a further joke was that they were putting animal grids on the Cork county borders to prevent the animals from crossing over.

# 88

# NO ENTRY

*The Rule 42 controversy 2004*

In March 2004 news broke that there would be no debate on Rule 42, about opening up Croke Park, at Congress. The GAA's Motions Committee, which consists of ex-GAA presidents, decreed that none of the motions pertaining to Rule 42 should be debated as they were 'out of order' on technical grounds. Even by his own standards, Pat Spillane was very agitated by this decision.

'In my long association with the GAA this was the lowest point for me. That was the week that Brazilian World Cup star Gerson was so disgusted at being omitted from Pele's list of the top 125 footballers that he tore it up live on television. I felt like doing the same with my GAA membership card.

'Who were this unelected elite group to defy the wishes of the majority of the GAA members? How dare they deny their fellow members the chance to air their views on this important topic on the floor of Congress? How dare a group who were effectively has-beens, who were handed their P45s long ago, still have such a major say in the running of the organisation?

'Their decision smacked of the worst excesses of dictatorship. They behaved like an ageing politburo, determined to hold on to the strings of the power – and occasionally they managed to do just that. As an organisation, the GAA prides itself on its democracy. The reality couldn't be further from the truth. The GAA's version of democracy is a bit like the one George Orwell wrote about in *Animal Farm*: "All animals are equal, but some animals are more equal than others."

'The decision was yet another nail in the coffin of the GAA's flawed version of democracy. The bottom line is that the motions to amend Rule 42, which I believe would have had the support of a majority of Association members, did not get an airing at Congress in Killarney in April. Why? Because some powerful officials found some technical flaws in the motions and opted not to correct those minor flaws, even though they were well within their rights to do so. The decision wouldn't have been out of place in Ceauşescu's Romania.

'In 2003, Eire Og delegate Pat Daly, at the GAA Convention in Cork, said, "It's about time the GAA woke up. The ban has been gone since 1973 – if Frank Sinatra could play in Croke Park, then why not the Irish international rugby team?" However, Munster Council Treasurer Dan Hoare went for an "out, out, out" approach: "I would not let anybody into the car park, not to mention into Croke Park." That is the kind of no surrender attitude that Ian Paisley would be proud of. The previous year a delegate at the Wicklow GAA County Convention said, "We are being asked to wake up some morning and see the English soccer team playing in Croke Park. Just eighty years ago the English came to Croke Park and shot Gaelic players."

Spillane was taken by some of the contributors to the debate.

'The big hitters in the association had been lining up behind the "No campaign" from early in the year. And boy did they come out firing on all cylinders. Ex-GAA president Jack Boothman was the first to join battle. He sent a letter to selected elected officers pleading with them not to change the rule.

'Then the usual suspects from Ulster came out of the woods. Of course, we should not have been in the least surprised that the Ulster counties were so trenchant in their support of Rule 42. Council secretary Danny Murphy suggested that unless there was a clear case for change, then there were definite reasons not to change. Work out that logic if you can. If you do, you are way smarter than I am.

'The newly elected Ulster Council president weighed in with a real beauty. He said the GAA were not in the business of housing the homeless. So much for the age-old proverb which we teach our children: sharing is caring. I suppose we should not be surprised at the degree of narrow-mindedness emanating from this source. After all, this was the same Council which dug their heels in and insisted that a provincial semi-final between Donegal and Derry be played on the same afternoon as the Republic of Ireland played Spain in a World Cup soccer match in 2002. So long as units of the GAA make those kind of preposterous decisions, opponents of the Association are never short of ammunition to fire at Croke Park.

'To stress the small-mindedness of the Ulster Council on the day of the Ireland–Spain match, a journalist brought a portable television into the press box to keep an eye on the Ireland game. When he was spotted he was promptly, and pompously, told by an official that it was not appropriate to have a TV there for that purpose and that he must turn it off.

'What I found difficult though is that the Ulster Council who espouse such lofty principles, and are such great champions of tradition, could then do a "Jerry Maguire" on it and say, "Show me the money", and have the Ulster final played in Croke Park. Lofty principles are great, but it is one of the hypocrisies of the GAA world that when money comes into it, tradition and ideals go out the window.

'These former GAA bureaucrats had one great weapon which they use with consummate skill, the GAA rule book. They are greatly helped by the fact that the rule book is so badly constructed, and written in such a way that those of us who didn't get a grind in GAA-speak would find it easier to read cave writings from the Stone Age. Of course if, by some miracle, a rule is capable of producing a measure which will drag the organisation kicking and screaming into the twenty-first century, the old guard have yet another weapon in their arsenal – a technicality. What is even more galling for me is that in blocking progress in this way they will say, in all earnestness, that they are acting in "the best interests of the GAA".

'Surely, as the foremost sporting organisation in Ireland, our role is to provide youngsters with as many sporting opportunities as possible, rather than having them messing up their lives with drugs or whatever. Opening up Croke Park would present new possibilities to fund much needed coaching initiatives for the next generation of footballers and hurlers.'

The level of the arguments also distressed Spillane.

'Some of the rhetoric which poured forth from the anti-Rule 42 brigade in March 2004, when the controversy was at its height, made my blood boil. As a GAA member, I felt ashamed when I heard some of the arguments. In particular, the *Prime Time* debate on the subject was cringeworthy. The Cork representative who appeared on the programme was stuck in a time warp of outdated patriotism. He argued that the GAA should keep the ban in place as a result of what happened in Croke Park on Bloody Sunday.

'It is very sad to see people living in the past. If everybody was dwelling on what happened decades ago, we would never have had the Peace Process and we would be still waking up every morning, as we used to in the 1970s and 1980s, to hear headlines like, "A part-time member of the UDR has been murdered by the IRA in County Tyrone." Or we would be hearing about a poor Catholic who had been savagely murdered by a Loyalist organisation. The logic of those still living in the past is that Irish people shouldn't eat Danish bacon or drink Carlsberg because of what the Danes did to poor Brian Boru at Clontarf in 1014!

'What I also found revealing was that at a meeting of Central Council, rather than trying to learn the lessons from the debacle, delegates had expressed annoyance at the manner in which ex-presidents had been "pilloried" for their decision to declare the motions relating to Rule 42 out of order. Down's Dan McCartan said it was disturbing that men who had served the GAA so well were subjected to severe personal attacks: "It is deplorable that they should be treated so badly by our own members. Those who made the attacks brought shame on the Association."

'Yet again, I brought shame on the GAA.'

# PART VII
# Leading from the Front

After Galway beat Waterford in the 2017 All-Ireland hurling final, Conor Whelan, a cousin and teammate of the late Niall Donohue and 2017's Young Hurler of the Year, held a flag with Donohue's name on it minutes after the final whistle sounded in Croke Park. Under it lay the quotation, 'There are three things that we cry about in life; things that are lost, things that are found and things that are magnificent'.

Connotations of pride, resilience and strength make admitting vulnerability difficult. Donohue's clubmates described him as a player that teammates grew taller and brighter around, yet Donohue felt shrinking and dark. Learning from Donohue's parting allows us to use sport to find those who are lost. GAA stars, like Aisling Thompson, discussing their mental-health battles promotes others to appreciate that even the most powerful can feel powerless. The GAA helps the heartbroken find solace, and for Gaelic games to have this ability is truly magnificent. It gives members a sense of purpose, the support of a community, an opportunity to come together and a link with generations past.

Nelson Mandela praised sport's unique power to

bring hope and peace, where before there was only despair. The 2017 All-Ireland gave Galway a chance to honour those like Niall Donohue, provoked by sport to remember times of raw joy and emotion with those no longer with us, but Donohue's life gave these players perspective; a realisation that life's magnificence lies in relationships, health and happiness, and although sport can enable these, it should never surpass them.

In the past the GAA was all about the games, but in recent years players have come to the forefront of national debates surrounding a proliferation of important social issues. They have given great leadership and have ushered in a new chapter in the evolution of the GAA as a national movement. In this way, they honour the Association and energise the nation. This section considers some of them.

# 89

# OUT OF AFRICA

*Alan Kerins leads the way to help the starving*

Ireland's national game is hurling, and few people played it better than Galway star Alan Kerins. Yet it was not his achievements on the field of the play that led to Kerins receiving a prestigious Person of the Year award live on Irish national television.

It began in January 2005 when he took a three-month unpaid leave of absence from his job as a physiotherapist to begin work on an outreach programme with the Presentation Sisters in Mongu, the main township of the Western Province in Zambia, on the edge of the Kalahari desert and the poorest region of the country. Through his work with physically disabled children, he went on to found a charity, the Alan Kerins Zambia project. The experience he had in Zambia completely changed Kerins' life: his initial plan had been to stay working with the disabled, but the extreme deprivation he witnessed compelled him to do more. When he returned to Ireland he set about the task of serious fund-raising, and linked up with the local Cheshire Home in Mongu. The home, run by Sr Cathy Crawford, a native of Laois, is the one facility that caters for disabled children in an area more than two-and-a-half-times the size of Ireland.

She and her sisters dedicate themselves to making a real difference in the fight against poverty by being agents of change in the lives of those communities within which they live and work, engaging in frontline work through the developing world. Sometimes this brought her to dangerous places, but her philosophy was the one who kneels to the Lord, can stand up to anything.

Knowing that the secret of success is consistency of purpose, from the outset Sister Cathy saw the value of collaborating with local people to offer the maximum amount of assistance to the poor. This collaborative process led her to form many fruitful partnerships with Irish volunteers like Alan who work hand-in-hand with local people on the ground to build a new future out of a very troubled past.

Sr Cathy believes that despite the lack of facilities she has a duty to work for justice for those too weak to help themselves. She managed because she had to manage. Historically many missionaries who worked so hard, for so long, on the missions to the developing world shared a wonderful commitment to serve.

After his exposure to Sr Cathy and her work, Alan knew that he could not just come and go. He was challenged to commit himself to helping her, and her flock, in the long term.

He set up funds for a famine-relief project and an irrigation programme to bore holes for water. Other funds were targeted specifically at the disabled, and provided physiotherapy and prosthetic limbs. In 2004, Zambia suffered its worst drought in seventy-seven years and around Mongu the Chesire Home delivered supplies to the elderly and those who had no access to food. Today, it is the money from Kerins' fund-raising that keeps the project alive: seven million, out of a total eleven million, Zambians survive on just 74 cents a day.

A particular focus was helping the disabled. One incident illustrates the scale of the problem: there was a young boy, dressed in torn rags, running a high fever and with a shrapnel wound on the back of his leg that reeked of infection. His eyes were empty, waterless like the rest of his body, and nobody could find a vein to insert the intravenous tube that could save him.

In Zambia, Alan came face-to-face with one of the most compelling challenges to our world. The emergence of any new disease inevitably provokes fear; however, the rapid spread of the disease, the transmissible nature of AIDS and the medical complexity of the disease, have exacerbated the normal problems and tensions associated with a new disease. Kerins got the opportunity to engage with the subject in an emotionally significant and humanising way in Zambia. It would be a decisive moment for him personally: 'It was probably the best thing I've ever done, but no question it was the most difficult thing I had ever done. It had a huge effect on me. The first day I was there I saw people who were in the last stages of AIDS, and were dying. I had very rarely seen anyone dying, let alone dying from AIDS. It's a horrific way to die.'

Since then, Alan has gone to raise millions for the poorest of the poor in Africa. Other GAA stars have followed suit. As an ambassador for Unicef, Joe Canning has gone to see some of the most distressing scenes possible in our time, in war-torn Syria.

# 90

## AGAINST THE ODDS

*Oisín McConville leads the way against addiction*

Sport is an escape for so many people, and Oisín McConville was no different. Submersing ourselves in sport provides escapism, and, growing up in a nationalist Northern Irish village in the 1970s, McConville recollects that football provided an escape from the Troubles. The GAA was radicalised in times of conflict as a key weapon of cultural nationalism, therefore, arguably, the GAA was more of a wing of the conflict than an escape from it. McConville describes himself, as a young boy, being very scared of the violence around him, and in order to remove himself from the fear of day-to-day life, he threw himself into sport.

The Armagh legend shook the GAA public when he first spoke of the escalation of his gambling addiction from recreational to pathological. He used teammates and family for money. He moved bookmakers and concealed his emotions to avoid exposure. He was far from self-fulfilled, despite the honours others bestowed upon him. A prominent feature of a successful athlete is their proud nature, upheld by others for their strength and achievements. The surge and normali-sation of online gambling means it is an addiction that a teenager could pursue in a classroom.

McConville began his gambling addiction at the age of seventeen. At that point he was visiting the local bookies in Crossmaglen three times a week and, by the time he was eighteen, he was gambling every day. McConville describes the bookies in those days as 'a smoke-filled room at the back of a pub'. He aspired to be like the 'high rollers' who gambled there, as he naively believed it was an easy way to make quick money. As years went by, his addiction got worse. He admits that the only place where he felt in control was on the football pitch and in the bookies. In today's society the rise of online gambling apps has led to problems of addiction and users over-spending, particularly among young people. There are numerous reasons for the rapid increase in gambling options: the creation of new technologies has provided a global platform for internet-based gambling, the ease with which gambling can be used as a source of income and the lack of gambling laws in Ireland. There is no doubt that the greater exposure and accessibility ensure young people have access to gambling products and betting apps which significantly increases the prevalence and risk of addiction.

McConville describes himself as a people pleaser, but, because he owed so much money, he became paranoid and suffered from social anxiety. He wanted to portray to the outside world that he was still the 'cock of the walk', that he had everything going well for him. He did not want people to discover how he was truly feeling; that behind closed doors, his life was falling apart. Not only was his addiction losing him money but also friendships, relationships, self-respect, self-esteem and integrity.

During this time his main focus was on how he was going to get money to place his next bet, and how he was going to pay back the loan sharks. McConville acknowledges how he belonged on the football pitch; it was a place where he could express himself and was valued. However, in the outside world he believed he was worthless. Sport gave McConville the framework to become one of the football greats of our time, winning the All-Ireland senior football championship against Kerry in 2002 – and putting in a classy performance – while knowing at the back of his mind that he was drowning in debt.

'I would always stay on the pitch because I knew once I left I would gamble again,' he recalls. A call-up to your county squad is an honour for anyone but he saw it as a mask, that he would be seen as 'Oisín the footballer' and not the gambler. On the pitch he had self-control, discipline, fulfilment and camaraderie, the very virtues he sought off the pitch when he was consumed by a vice-provoking addiction. Although the GAA provided solace and structure, it also provided a mask and a purpose to hide behind, potentially preventing him from addressing his issues sooner.

In 2005, McConville went into treatment for thirteen weeks, and describes it as the best weeks of his life. He recalls how during this time his coaches lacked emotional empathy and support for his mental health issues, and instead questioned him about when he would be back training. His managers had no interest in the underlying cause of his problems.

To compound his problems, he discovered that a betting company, Bar One Racing, were sponsoring his club side, Crossmaglen. McConville declares how difficult this was for him, how his only escape from his addiction, the club team, was now collaborating with the industry which created his demons. This forced him to make a very difficult decision of whether to continue to wear the jersey or to turn away from football completely. Ultimately he decided that, for his own mental health, he should remain playing even if he did not agree with what the club and its sponsor were representing. In 2018, the GAA, at its annual congress, banned betting companies from sponsoring any of its teams.

McConville states that participants in team sports are three times more vulnerable to gambling addictions. Sport's link to gambling is not a recent phenomenon. Even before the birth of Christ, the Romans were betting on chariot races. Immediacy and unpredictability are what make sport captivating, however these features are synonymous with gambling. Sport provides an outlet for adrenaline seekers in a confined area with rules, but does sport give individuals a competitive, invincible and addictive personality that can be destructive in other areas of life? McConville explained how, from a young age, his status as a sporting star in the corridors at St Patrick's Armagh, fuelled this sense of indestructability.

He praises today's more holistic coaches, with 99 per cent of GAA clubs having a health and welfare officer. Welfare officers like McConville himself, and other prominent players like Nicole Owens, are to the forefront of the GAA's new drive to tackle mental health and addiction head on.

# 91

## YOU'VE GOT TO SEARCH FOR THE HERO INSIDE YOURSELF

*Alan O'Mara confronts the voices inside his head*

To outsiders it seemed like Alan O'Mara had a perfect life. The reality was very different; the voices in his head were telling him that he was a mess. He can trace the moment when he was aware things needed to change.

'It was three days after Christmas, in 2011, and I was gazing at the flickering flame in the fireplace at my family home. It was comforting. I could feel the heat rising from the fire and hitting me in the face. I looked at our tree, the gifts I had, the endless food nearby and I was telling myself, I don't want to go to a two-day training camp with my college, Dublin Institute of Technology.

'There was a voice in my head telling me to stay right where I was; it told me I hate football. Despite this internal conversation I forced myself off the couch, packed my bag full of waterproof gear, boots, gloves, towels and got into my car. Football was the Grinch to my Christmas. Despite ongoing injuries and niggling pains, I trained that night.

'My mind was away in the clouds, wondering why football is not enjoyable to me anymore. That little voice was whispering in my ear again; asking me what the hell I am doing here?'

Alan was pining for what he had lost.

'The voice in my head that morning focused on how, since losing the biggest game of my career, every subsequent match I have played has seemed a massive anti-climax to me. It told me football was the reason for my unhappiness. That march to the 2011 All-Ireland under-21 final in Croke Park, the adventure of a lifetime with a special bunch of players, seemed a lifetime ago.

'For some reason, nothing had been able to match the feelings I had playing on that team. Maybe I was too emotionally attached to it; maybe I invested too much energy, physically and mentally. It was the first thing I thought of when I woke up and the last thing that crossed my mind before I went to sleep. My dreams were often about that team.'

It was then that he hit rock bottom.

'Three hours of sleep and a game of football later I was driving home on the motorway. This was a mundane, boring and soulless road. Its markings flashed by in a blur. I was simply staring into space and thinking about how I'd just played the majority of a challenge match with tears in the back of my eyes. I asked myself what the hell was happening to me and why I was feeling like this? I told myself to pull it together and snap out of it, but I couldn't change my train of thought. It was negative.

'The challenge game couldn't have been any further from that innocent and inspiring place I imagined myself to be in my youth. All I remember was looking at the deteriorated surface around me wishing for a hole to open up and swallow me. Anything to get me out of the living hell I found myself in. This was as far from that exhilarating roller coaster I had ever felt.

'That's the conversation I was having in my head as I was driving home. There was nothing to catch my attention on this road, nothing to distract my brain. It was just me in the car, me and the voice that had become more and more prominent lately. It was getting louder. It got to the point where it muffled out the radio but I kept driving. I kept thinking, questioning and wondering. How have I got to this point? The point at which there was even a thought of swerving my car into the concrete wall on the side of the motorway.'

He almost reached the point of no return.

'I felt trapped; it was just me and that voice in the fast lane of a motorway. Deep down, somewhere, I was aware that was not a good mix. The concrete wall to my right looked so appealing. How easy it would have been just to swerve into it and finish it all. The voice whispered in my ear, "Will anybody even care if I do it?" The visualisation of my parents at my funeral rescued me from this horrible train of thought. I wound the window down and let the crisp air hit my face. Eventually, I got home and I wanted to switch off. I'd just had a realisation that I was depressed.'

Alan decided that he needed help.

'A week after a chat with my GP and getting a prescription for sleeping tablets, the experience of playing a game of football with tears in my eyes, and an hour-long conversation with myself in the car, and it had finally sunk in. At least that miserable drive was good for something. Like most mothers, mine has that special talent of immediately sensing when something is wrong, so when I got home she asked what the matter was. I said, "Nothing." She knew I hadn't really been sleeping, I told her that much, but I was not me then. I was a pale shadow of myself and she knew. She asked again. I tried to convince her I was just tired, but she knew I was lying. Mothers always know. Then she asked me if I was feeling depressed?'

It was then that O'Mara began his slow journey to rehabilitation.

'Eerie, creepy silence invaded the room. Should I lie? What excuse could I give? All these thoughts were flying through my brain at a hundred miles an hour. My head had been swirling like that regularly. Sod it, what had I to lose. Look at the state of me. I swallowed the lump in my throat, held back the tears in my eyes and coughed up something that sounded like "yes".

'She asked what was going on with me and what was getting me down, but I didn't open up. I still don't fully understand the whole process myself, and why I felt like that. I headed to my room to try and make sense of how I had reached the miserably low point of suicidal thoughts entering my brain. More thinking, more questioning and wondering, but still no definitive answers.'

But even then there was a hesitation on his part to take the next step.

'I felt like the Smeagol/Gollum creature from *The Lord of the Rings*. Two voices within one person, constantly debating and arguing.

'The waves of emotion kept churning internally so I removed myself from the room, pretending to be shattered, and headed for the sanctuary of my bedroom. I turned off the light and got into bed. I had been warned that this moment

315

was going to arrive. My GPA counsellor, who I had been seeing on a bi-weekly basis since January, told me this was going to happen as part of my healing process. As my depression would lift, my body would need to offload emotions.

'The best thing I ever did was call the GPA counselling service. Twice before I had sat alone with the number typed into my phone, but I just couldn't find the courage to push the green button. Who is on the other end of the line? Will he think I am making a fuss over nothing?

'I was lucky enough that the service was free for me and, ironically, the clinic was based on the road where I was living. On the day I was first due to go to a "session", my body shook with anxiety at the mere thought of opening up to a stranger. Part of me wanted to reach out for help, but the other strand saw the solution as getting back into bed, pulling the pillow over my head and waiting for all my problems to go away. I spent so much time in my bedroom that my friends called it the "Batcave". Day after day I was just lying there, going on Facebook and Twitter and doing nothing, eating crisps and sweets instead of cooking food. I don't remember when or how the negative voice in my head became so prominent, but my brain became poisoned and I needed help.'

The journey forward was not without stumbling.

'When I began my treatment the biggest mistake I made was that I thought I was just trying to beat depression in a one-off fight. Me and Depression. Twelve rounds. When I delivered what I thought was the knockout punch and finally felt good again for the first time in months, I naively thought my fight was concluded.

'When depression stepped back into the ring for a second bout, I was caught with my guard down. I wasn't expecting it, but I'm glad I got taught that lesson.

'The key thing for anyone who is feeling depressed is to always remember there is light at the end of the tunnel. And if you ever get to a point where you are struggling to see it, like I did, then that is the moment to reach out for help. Opening the vault that had become my head was crucial in lifting my depression.'

Given his own experiences, Alan has become a prominent campaigner for mental-health awareness within the GAA and at national level, and has set up the organisation 'Real Talks' to facilitate an informed conversation about mental health.

# 92

## KEEPING PLAYERS SAFE

*Katie Liston leads the battle against concussion*

The GAA is viewed as one of the most traditional communities in Ireland, so when it achieves change it inspires possible and imminent change in other areas of Irish life. Although some may claim that the GAA is reactive, the work of cultural nationalist, and camogie foundress, Cait Ni Dhonnchadha, is an example of the use of sport to move Irish women off the side-lines of society. Her legacy lives on in Katie Liston, who was all too ready to challenge a prominent GAA personality's comment about 'ladies who make tea'. As one of the greatest Kerry footballers of all time, Katie Liston's place in the GAA archive was assured. However, now as a lecturer in the Sociology of Sport at the University of Ulster, her extensive research has helped put the issue of concussion on the agenda in both the GAA and beyond.

The media can assert huge amounts of pressure on sport stars in today's world. With social networks now ingrained in society, it is impossible to hide from the headlines or the taunts of the public. Joe Canning said, 'There is a massive difference between winning and losing.' He went on to explain that even losing by a point can have you portrayed as a villain in the papers and that 'perspective is often lost'.

The fans and journalists can lose sight of the fact that the players tried their best and are hurting the most inside. Defeat is a hard pill to swallow, and even harder when it seems everyone is against you. In order to prevent this from happening, Joe attempts to perform to an exceptional level in every game in order to 'shut them up', and has had to do so from a young age. This can be seen either as motivation, or as a system that forces athletes to try to perform to unachievable standards week in, week out.

Katie Liston talks of how some Olympic athletes were beaten with sticks if their performance was deemed insufficient. Take Jack Wilshere for example. He was thrust into a senior professional scene at Arsenal aged just sixteen, exposing him to all kinds of new challenges, including tougher opponents and mass attention from the media. It is instances like these that prove athletes must be nurtured in a way that aids their well-being and maximises growth in all aspects of life.

In the GAA world, Joe Canning has had to deal with complete strangers chastising him while he's out minding his own business. He gives an amusing, if slightly frightening, anecdote of when he was at a concert and a random man gave out to him for holding pints before a big game. The drinks were for others. He was only drinking coffee! And the game was two weeks away. Do we no longer care about players as individuals and only care about them winning?

Katie Liston points out the existential crises at the heart of the concussion issue: competitive sport involves an active process of socialisation into a culture which normalises pain and injury. Pain is a daily cost of being an athlete, and only once this pain fully inhibits your ability to play does it become an injury.

What Katie incisively exposes in many ways is a social issue of a 'man up' culture which has festered in sports such as NFL, rugby and, increasingly, Gaelic football and hurling. Katie quite rightly points out the fact that the only other field apart from the playing field where such machoism would be celebrated is the field of war. Think of the under-10 coaches telling the star forward to 'play on and see how you go'. The Irish tendency to say 'I'll be grand', combined with the negative stigma surrounding those who discuss their injuries, creates a vulnerable environment for someone who is suffering concussion. We label players as 'soft' when they sit out due to injury, and make heroes of those who play through extreme and risky pain.

Liston promotes changes in the law, education, research and management to help tackle this issue. The necessary change is a change in attitude. Education provokes players and coaches to take a more holistic view.

Liston has documented that concussion is a frequent injury, but many of us do not realise how serious an injury it is. Concussion is 'velocity brain shaking'. She condemns the poor duty of care shown by managers of sports teams who do not take the injury seriously enough. There is a clear relationship between competitive sport and health, but there is also a paradox in competitive sport relating to health, and this is something that must be addressed. Liston states that there is a sense of 'play on', and 'we need you', when it comes to sport. It is second nature to sports people to be told that they must play on after suffering a concussion. Concussion can seriously affect the player, and if not dealt with in a correct manner, the player can suffer life-threatening injuries.

Former Roscommon footballer Karol Mannion is one of the few players who have courageously gone public about his experiences with concussion. He listed the affects: brain function problems, headaches, concentration problems and memory problems, among others. Some of the more serious side-effects include slurred speech, ringing in the ears and fatigue. Concussion is not an injury that is to be taken lightly. It is a serious problem that coaches and managers need to deal with more effectively. It is no longer acceptable to encourage their players to overcome the pain and continue playing. Concussion poses many health risks that managers need to be made more aware of. Ethically, it is wrong to put pressure on our sports stars to perform after having suffered a serious head injury. Liston comments that 'the balance between performance and health is less than even'. Concussion camouflages its location: the brain, one of the most important organs. We must not pressurise our players to accept unnecessary risks to their health; we have already pushed the limits enough when it comes to ethics and duty of care.

In sport, a player is only deemed injured when they can no longer play. If you complain, you are often given the nick-name 'Sick Note', as Spurs' Darren Anderton and Arsenal's Abou Diaby experienced. A lot of the time, it is only when the injury is obvious that people will accept your desire to stop and offer you genuine help.

With concussion it can be more difficult to detect the true extent of the damage. Katie Liston describes brain injuries as 'invisible'. Her case studies highlight the anxiety players face due to concussion damage sustained from sport. She describes it as being 'drunk and hungover at the same time'. However, because they did not need a wheelchair or a cast, people often thought they were fine. Katie Liston leads the way not only in the GAA but in society at large in raising awareness about concussion.

# 93

## SO THIS IS CHRISTMAS AND WHAT HAVE YOU DONE?

*The GAA community responds to homelessness*

Nelson Mandela, John F. Kennedy, Mother Teresa and Mikhail Gorbachev: four remarkable people who have left a distinct imprint on the history of the world. In an Irish context, what unites this famous four is that each of them have received the highest honour the State can confer on anybody – the Freedom of the City of Dublin. Only eighty-two people, the best of the best, from home and abroad, have ever received this honour. It is a small indication of Peter McVerry's contribution to Irish life that he is one of those chosen few. His lifelong commitment to the least, the last and the lost, means that he is a prophetic voice in Irish society today. So what connects him to the GAA?

Just before Christmas 2017, over four hundred current and former inter-county football, hurling and camogie players, joined forces to raise money and awareness for the homeless. The group, Gaelic Voices for Change, held a solidarity sleep-out in thirteen locations around the country from 6 p.m. to 6 a.m. They had hoped to raise €120,000 for charities north and south, as well as draw attention to the homelessness crisis – in the end they raised over €200,000. Those involved believe that the GAA is based on community values and want to use their voices to support the vulnerable members in society.

As well as towns and cities in Ireland, there were sleep-outs in Boston, New York and one former player even did it alone in Quebec, Canada. New Dublin hurling manager Pat Gilroy joined his squad in the capital while the Clare hurling team joined the Limerick event.

The impetus for the response to the homeless crisis was that Gaelic games are built on communities, with a collective sense of belonging and supporting your neighbour. The sleep-out was a wider expression of that ethos by the players involved, extending a helping hand to others in our community.

Prominent former players involved included Valerie Mulcahy, Diarmuid Lyng and Eamonn Fennell. David Brady spoke movingly about why he got involved: in the run-up to the event, he was in the city centre of Dublin when a man shouted across at him and the former Mayo star went over to speak with him. The homeless man was from his home town in Mayo, and in that moment Brady understood the homeless crisis in a real way for the first time.

These players gave Irish society an invaluable moral lesson: We speak when we do not speak.

We act when we do not act.

Gaelic Voices for Change showed us that we do not have to simply curse the darkness. We can light a candle when it comes to the homeless crisis.

# PART VIII
# Comedy Central

A prominent GAA personality was driving home one night, having drunk a glass of lemonade too many, and crashed into another vehicle. He was irate when a member of the Garda told him he was in trouble, and said: 'Do you know who I am? I will have this sorted out within the hour.' He promptly texted the then Taoiseach, Enda Kenny, and wrote: 'Enda, I'm in a bit of bother here and need your help. Ring me as soon as you can.' The only problem was that he mixed up the numbers and texted the Roscommon footballer Enda Kenny!

The late John B. Keane always made the point that the most dangerous animal on the planet was a forty-year-old junior footballer with varicose veins. I especially recall a story he told about a Kerry County junior football final. By the time the final was played, most of the better players had returned to college as it was delayed due to the usual quota of objections. John B. claimed he was drafted in to play at corner-forward, even though he was only about fifteen years old. He gave a vivid description of his increasing trepidation as he went to take up his position and saw a 'seasoned' corner-back advancing to meet him. John B. was getting more intimidated with each step, but was puzzled when the corner-back veered off at the last moment and went back towards his goalkeeper. He took out his false teeth and loudly told his keeper, 'Paddy, mind these in case I forget myself and eat someone.'

A prominent official of the Connacht Council is in Los Angeles, and from the moment he arrives he is struck by the importance of the star system in the city. A major catastrophe ensues when he tries to check into his hotel and discovers that his booking details are wrong. When it looks like he is not going to be checked in to the hotel his exasperated wife digs him in the ribs and whispers, 'Tell them you're from the Connacht Council!'

In its long history, the GAA has created many moments of comedy. This section celebrates a cross-section of them.

# 94

# THE WICKLOW WAY

*The role of the fans*

In its long history, fans have provided the GAA with a motley crew of interesting individuals who have created some moments of mischief, mirth and mayhem. This chapter pays homage to some of their more memorable moments in Wicklow.

Tommy Docherty once remarked, 'After the match, an official asked for two of my players to take a dope test. I offered him a referee.' It sums up the lack of esteem most people have for referees. In Wicklow though, they take things to a whole different level.

Club football in Wicklow is not for the faint-hearted, especially for faint-hearted referees. One of the most famous incidents in its history was when a group of disaffected fans, after losing a club match, locked a referee in the boot of his car. In the return fixture, the nervous referee brought the two teams together and pointing to his whistle said, 'Do ye see this yoke lads? I'm going to blow it now and blow it again at the finish. Whatever happens in between ye can sort out yerselves.'

Wicklow fans often use the analogy of bacon and eggs to describe the difference between involvement and commitment in the GAA – the hen is involved in the process through laying the egg, but the pig is totally committed! It has been said that junior club football in Wicklow has produced so many injuries that it has generated more breaks than KitKat.

A referee's lot in such an environment is not a happy one. Theirs is the only occupation where a man has to be perfect on the first day on the job, and then improve over the years. One spectator at a club match in Wicklow was complaining bitterly all through the game about the referee's poor eyesight. At one stage though the fan was responsible for a Colemanball when he shouted, 'Ah ref, where are your testicles?'

It may have been that knowledge of the GAA scene in Wicklow is what inspired Henry Winter to observe, 'Modern referees need the wisdom of Solomon, the patience of Job, the probity of Caesar's wife, the stamina of Mo Farah and the acceleration of Usain Bolt. Oh, and the thick skin of a rhino.'

One man, concerned about warped priorities, was a gentleman of the cloth at an emergency meeting of a club in Wicklow, which cannot be named for moral reasons, when sixty players went on a weekend tour of Amsterdam for a sevens tournament, at which they were ignominiously dumped out in the first round, one short week after they had failed to drum up fifteen players to face Bray Emmetts, twenty miles down the road. A member of the touring party to Amsterdam responded to the priest's criticism, 'Well father, to the best of my knowledge, there are no ladies of the night in Bray.'

In Blessington, the Wicklow–Kildare rivalry is one of the most keenly contested in football, as was apparent in the

2018 Leinster Championship. An old Wicklow fan was dying and, when it was obvious that he had very little time left, the local priest, a Kildare man, was sent for. After the priest administered the last rites he asked the old man if he had any last wish. He was astounded when the man asked if he could join the Kildare supporters club. The priest duly pulled out a membership card for the man, and helped him to sign his name for the last time. When the priest had left, the man's seven stunned sons crowded around the bed and asked their father why he had made this extraordinary request. With practically his dying breath he said, 'Isn't it better for one of them to die than one of our lads.'

# 95

## NUDIE

*Monaghan dine at the top table*

The GAA needs characters. Monaghan's Eugene 'Nudie' Hughes is certainly one of them. He is also one of its most versatile players. He won an All-Star as a corner-back and two as a corner-forward (in the process becoming the first Ulster player to win three All-Stars); won Railway Cup medals as a right corner-back, right half-back and a right corner-forward; and captained the team in the Ulster final in 1986 as a right half-forward, although his favourite position was centre half-back. He led Monaghan to three Ulster Senior Championships in 1979, 1985 and 1988.

Monaghan made a giant breakthrough in 1979, winning their first Ulster title in forty-one years, only to lose badly to Kerry in the All-Ireland semi-final. Nudie recalls, 'The euphoria of the Ulster title went to our heads. We were completely overawed by our first appearance in Croke Park and up against the greatest team of all time. Although the semi-final went badly wrong for us, everything went right for me that day. I was only twenty-one then and I played well in the Ulster final, but that game gave me a national profile, especially as people remembered my name. At one stage in his commentary Micheál O'Hehir said, "And here comes Nudie Hughes for Nudie reason."

'That year, I became Monaghan's first All-Star, and when I went to the airport for the trip away I was standing back near a pier with my two suitcases, but Tony Hanahoe came over to me and brought me up to the bar, where I found myself having a drink with the biggest names in football.'

In 1985, Monaghan made the breakthrough on to the national stage when they won their first National League title by beating Armagh 1-11 to 0-9.

'For a full week we were treated as kings. Then it was down to serious training and, as everybody knows, we won the Ulster title and qualified for the famous All-Ireland semi-final against Kerry.

'We were flying in the semi-final, leading by five points coming up to half-time, when John Kennedy hit a ball in from the wing very high and it hit the very tip of one of the posts and fell straight into Ger Power's hands: he stuck it in the net from ten yards out. If you were to hit ten thousand balls in that direction, it would never come off the post exactly like that again. We went in at the break only two points ahead, which was a totally unfair reflection of our dominance. Kerry were very lucky to get a draw with us on that day, but they lifted their game to beat us in the replay. We were one of the unluckiest teams not to play in an All-Ireland final.'

Although Meath beat Monaghan in two National League semi-finals, Nudie retains a particular affection for Seán Boylan's side. 'One night, we drew with Meath in the Susan

McCann Cup in Castleblaney, and the whole visiting busload stayed in the pub until half-three in the morning. We agreed to repeat the dose in the event of another draw. Meath beat us, as it turned out, but we had another session all the same.'

# 96

## UP DOWN

*Ireland vs Australia*

As Down manager, James McCartan Jnr steered his county to an All-Ireland final appearance against Cork. His talent was evident at an early age. He scored three goals in a McCrory Cup final and took Down to an All-Ireland minor title with his exciting and swashbuckling quality, and because of his bravery, courage, and electrifying confidence and self-assurance. As a player, he won senior All-Irelands in 1991 and 1994. His father had played on three All-Ireland winning teams in the 1960s, and James had inherited the winning mentality from his dad.

One famous story sums him up. When he was nineteen he played for Ireland against Australia in the International Rules, and was rooming with Jack O'Shea, one of the most iconic names in Gaelic football. An Australian journalist asked him, 'What's it like to room with a legend?'

James shrugged his shoulders and said, 'You'd have to ask Jacko.'

# 97

## SAUSAGE-GATE

*Tipp diet for glory*

When Nicky English became manager of Tipperary, he was determined that he would leave no stone unturned until he got his team to be ready to claim the All-Ireland they won in 2001. Part of this punishing regime was the introduction of a Spartan diet. The results were immediate, and spectacular, throughout the squad, but there was one exception – Eugene O'Neill – whose weight remained unchanged. The Tipp management were baffled, and summoned O'Neill for an interview. If O'Neill was hoping for a friendly chat, he was shocked to discover that it was more in the style of the Spanish Inquisition, before English and his entire management team. After a stubborn initial resistance, O'Neill finally caved in and blurted out the one word that said so little, but so much, 'Sausages.'

English was puzzled. 'What do you mean sausages?'

O'Neill replied, 'Well, as you know Nicky, I'm in college and when I get up in the morning the boys have sausages for me for breakfast. When I'm home during the day, they stick some on the pan and we have some more, and then we have more in the evening. They're f\*\*king killing me!'

# 98

# FRANKIE SAYS

*Roscommon win the 2001 Connacht final*

Two Roscommon players made headlines in 2002 for playing pool in the nude. When a second major breach of discipline occurred that summer, the Roscommon County Board decided to disband the entire county panel. Given the penchant for nude pool among his senior county players, Tom Mullaney, then secretary of the Roscommon County Board, showed a flair for double entendre in his appraisal of the disciplinary measures: 'As a group, all players hang together or hang separately.'

Writing in the *Irish Times*, Keith Duggan's verdict on that Roscommon policy of 'total disclosure' when playing pool made for amusing reading: 'Ah yes, the career of the Gaelic footballer can end in a flash. Just ask any of the Roscommon senior players. It will take many, many years before a Roscommon senior manager can stand before his team in the dressing room and bellow the traditional GAA rallying cry, "Show them yez have the balls for it, lads."'

In 2011, when Fergal O'Donnell stepped down as Roscommon county manager, Joe Brolly referred back to the county's former indignities: 'Fergal O'Donnell's resignation as county manager left the people of Roscommon in shock. The big man did an excellent job. When he began his tenure, Roscommon were a laughing stock – some of their past antics made the English rugby team's dwarf-throwing look like a quiet night in over a hot cup of cocoa.'

Former Roscommon star and St Brigids' manager, Frankie Dolan, is a cult figure. Like his brother, Garvin, Frankie had a turbulent relationship with referees and umpires. When Frankie got married at Christmas 2010, some of the guests were surprised to see so many referees invited. One referee was told in no uncertain terms, 'You were lucky to get an invite.' The official coolly replied, 'I know, especially as I booked Garvin for the way he walked out of the church.'

The father of the bride had been a GAA umpire, and brought the house down at the speeches during the reception when he recalled his first encounter with Frankie when he was umpiring a match, and Dolan had sent a shot inches wide. After signalling the ball wide, his future son-in-law raced in to tell him in the most emphatic terms that he was a 'f**king b***x.' Just as he was regaining his composure he was accosted from behind by Dolan's father, Frankie senior, who also told him that he was a 'f**king b***x'.

Not to be outdone, the best man also had a big hit with the crowd when in his speech he said, 'Frankie has brought unique distinction to his club, his county and his province, whenever he represented them' – dramatic pause – 'in a bar or nightclub.'

In the Connacht final in 2001, Frankie Dolan was perceived by some Mayo fans as engaging in 'theatricals' which 'caused' a Mayo player to be sent off. They gave him a new nickname, 'Frankie goes to Hollywood'.

# 99

## LOST IN TRANSLATION

*Mayo's unorthodox All-Ireland semi-final prequel*

When asked for a funny incident from his career, Liam McHale provides a classic.

'We were staying in Maynooth College for the All-Ireland semi-final the day Princess Diana died. On the Sunday morning I was walking down into the breakfast room with P. J. Loftus, who is a bit of a character, and we were met at the door by the head priest, who is a very holy man.

'He said, "Howya Liam, Howya P. J.. Did you hear the awful news?"

'I immediately went into a panic because I feared that James Nallen or someone might be injured. He told us that Diana died.

'P. J. Loftus replied, "F**k off."

'I asked, "How did she die?"

'The priest, "She was killed in a car crash."

'P. J., "F**k off."

'Me, "What kind of crash was it?"

'The priest, "The paparazzi were chasing her."

'P. J., "What the f**k was Pavarotti chasing her for?"

'At that stage the priest said nothing and walked away in disgust!'

# 100

## THE RINGMASTER

*Christy Ring in America*

Despite his interest in other sports, Gaelic games were Jimmy Magee's first love. It was listening to the wireless commentary of the famous 1947 All-Ireland final between Kerry and Cavan in New York, the only one ever to be played outside Ireland, that that the twelve-year-old boy first dreamed of becoming a commentator. One of his great heroes was Christy Ring, a friendship cemented during their involvement in the Jimmy Magee All-Stars, which raised over €6,000,000 for various charities down through the years.

But Ring was not above putting Jimmy in his place. During one match for the All-Stars, when Magee was not showing much mobility, Ring barked at him from the sideline, 'Did you find it yet Jimmy?'

'What's that Christy?'

'The thing you're looking for. You're running around the same spot, Jimmy. You haven't moved out of it.'

On one occasion the motley crew of Magee All-Stars played a match in New York. Before playing, the team was watching a softball game and when they were asked to try out this strange game, it was decided that Ring should be the team's representative. The Cork legend though feigned ignorance to his hosts: 'Give me that that there what-do-you-call-it. Is that a bat or a stick, or what do you call it?'

After he was told it was a bat he enquired with a puzzled tone, 'Now do you hold it like this or like that?'

After being shown how to hold the bat he asked them to provide their best pitcher. When an athletic young man appeared, he gave a mighty effort but Ring struck it into the stratosphere and out of the stadium. All the softball players looked at him in shock and awe. Ring nonchalantly said, 'That's a home run now, isn't it?'

# ACKNOWLEDGEMENTS

I am very honoured that the great Joe Canning agreed to write the foreword for this book.

I am also deeply grateful to Ciarán Whelan and Bernard Flynn for their generous support of the book.

My profound thanks to the many players and managers, past and present, who generously shared their stories and thoughts with me and who made this book possible.

We sadly lost Christopher Canning as this book was being written. He will be much missed by his brother Rob.

A GAA star in the making, Liam O'Brien was born to light up the playing fields of Dublin in years to come, much to the delight of his parents and grandparents.

Likewise, the birth of Tom Carroll brought unconfined joy in Kildare and Offaly.

Thanks to Simon Hess, Campbell Brown, and all at Black & White for their help.

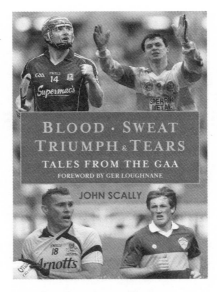

## BLOOD, SWEAT, TRIUMPH & TEARS
*Tales from the GAA*

Full of entertaining anecdotes, inspirational incidents and epic encounters, *Blood, Sweat, Triumph and Tears* captures the magic of the GAA.

'A book to shorten the long winter nights for any GAA fan.'
**Dermot Earley**, Kildare Legend

ISBN: 978 1 78530 073 8

Available from all good bookshops and at
*blackandwhitepublishing.com*

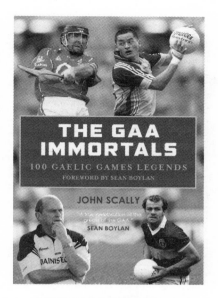

## THE GAA IMMORTALS
*100 Gaelic Games Legends*

With stars from all 32 countries represented, *The GAA Immortals*
is a fascinating account of the greatest heroes and legends of
the games.

'A true celebration of the greats of the GAA.' – **Sean Boylan**

'Celebrates the fantastic players, the unforgettable games, the
great rivalries and the wonderful pride in parish and country
that is part and parcel of the GAA.' – **Eileen Dunne**

ISBN: 978 1 78530 212 1

Available from all good bookshops and at
*blackandwhitepublishing.com*